PLATO

REPUBLIC

PLATO
REPUBLIC

TRANSLATED BY
G.M.A. GRUBE

REVISED BY C.D.C. REEVE

HACKETT PUBLISHING COMPANY, INC.
INDIANAPOLIS/CAMBRIDGE

Plato: 428/7–347 B.C.

It is thought the *Republic* was written ca. 380 B.C.

Copyright © 1992 by Hackett Publishing Company, Inc.

Printed in the United States of America

99 98 97 96 95 94 93   2 3 4 5 6 7 8

Design by Dan Kirklin

For further information, please address

Hackett Publishing Company, Inc.
P.O. Box 44937
Indianapolis, Indiana 46244-0937

Library of Congress Cataloging-in-Publication Data

Plato.
    [Republic. English]
    The Republic/Plato: translated by G.M.A. Grube—2nd ed./
revised by C.D.C. Reeve.
        p.   cm.
    Includes bibliographical references and index.
    ISBN 0-87220-137-6 (alk. paper).
    ISBN 0-87220-136-8 (pbk.: alk. paper)
    1. Political science—Early works to 1800. 2. Utopias.
  I. Grube, G.M.A. (George Maximilian Anthony) II. Reeve, C.D.C.,
1948–   . III. Title.
  JC71.P35   1992b
  321'.07—dc20   92-21578
                                                        CIP

The paper used in this publication meets the minimum requirements of
American National Standard for Information Sciences—Permanence of Paper
for Printed Library Materials. ANSI Z39.48-1984.

∞

CONTENTS

PREFACE

G.M.A. Grube's translation of the *Republic* aimed to combine fidelity to Plato's text with natural readability. It was remarkably successful in achieving these aims, far more successful, in my view, than any other translation. It is a measure of his achievement, indeed, and of its immense popularity that only after twenty years did any revision seem called for. The revision I have produced is nonetheless a thorough one, and a reader familiar with the original will find that quite a lot has been changed. But, though much is new, the foundations remain squarely Grube's, and, without them to build on, I would not have been able to serve Plato nearly so well.

The *Republic* is largely in reported speech. Socrates is relating a conversation he had in the past. Following Grube's lead, but going a little further than he did, I have often omitted the "I said" and "he replied" that signal such indirection. This minimal loss in literalness results in a much more readable and less rebarbative English text.

Every translation, even the most self-consciously and flat-footedly "literal," is an interpretation. The goal is to get the interpretation right. This is hard enough to do with a treatise. It is much more difficult, it has become trite to say, with a great work of art. Nonetheless, it is the task that a translator faces and must not shirk. One cannot avoid it by trying, for example, to translate word for word, always using the same English word for any given word of Greek, for one and the same Greek word may have many different meanings, and different Greek words may have the same meaning. I have not tried vainly to avoid interpretation, therefore, but I have tried—no doubt with mixed success—to get the interpretation right.

The Introduction, Prefaces to the individual Books, and Index are new, as are many of the notes. The Index, as well as enabling the reader to discover where central topics are discussed or key concepts employed, shows in what ways many important Greek terms have been differently handled in different contexts. In most instances the translation follows John Burnet's Oxford edition of the Greek text, but in a few cases (515b, 572a, 607c) I have preferred the text indicated in the notes.

In his original Preface, Grube thanked his wife for her constant assistance and Professors George Edison and Malcolm Brown for their helpful suggestions. It seems fitting to repeat these acknowledgments here and to add some of my own. I am grateful to the Grube family for encouraging this revision, to Hackett Publishing Company for suggesting the project to me and helping in so many different ways to carry it out, and to Walter Englert for his always cheerfully given assistance. I am also immensely grateful to the publisher's readers, John Cooper and Paul Woodruff. I have benefited immeasurably from their wisdom and from the diligence, care, and good humor with which they have suggested revisions, pointed out errors, and urged me to reconsider decisions.

INTRODUCTION

Plato

Plato is traditionally thought to have been born in 428 B.C. and to have died in 348. His father, Ariston, was descended—or so legend has it—from Codrus, the last king of Athens; his mother, Perictione, was related to Solon, the first architect of the Athenian constitution. His family was aristocratic and well off. He had two brothers, Glaucon and Adeimantus, both of whom appear in the *Republic*, and a sister, Potone, whose son, Speusippus, took over as head of the Academy[1] on Plato's death. While Plato was still a boy, his father died and his mother married Pyrilampes, a friend of the great Athenian statesman Pericles. Thus Plato was no stranger to Athenian political life even from childhood. Because he was eighteen in 409, when the Peloponnesian war with Sparta was still in progress, he almost certainly served in the military in that period. He may have served again around 395, when Athens was involved in the so-called Corinthian war.

Given his social class and family connections, it would have been natural for Plato to take a prominent role in Athenian political life. But he did not do this, and, in his *Seventh Letter*, written when he was himself over seventy, he explains why:[2]

> As a young man I went through the same experiences as many others. I thought that as soon as I became my own master, I'd devote myself to public affairs. Now, it happened that the course of political events gave me the chance to do just that. The existing constitution came to be reviled by many people, so that a revolution occurred ... and thirty rulers were set up with supreme powers. Some of these happened to be relatives and friends of mine,[3] and they immediately

1. See p. xii below.

2. I assume that the *Seventh Letter* is genuine. But it may have been written by a disciple soon after Plato's death.

3. Plato's uncle Charmides and his cousin Critias were among these rulers, called "the Thirty" or "the Thirty Tyrants." Their reign lasted only about ninety days.

called on me to join them, on the assumption that theirs was the sort of work appropriate for someone like me. It's no wonder, since I was a young man, that my feeling was that they would govern the city by leading it from an unjust way of life to a just one, and I was intensely interested to see what would happen. But after a short time, I saw that these men made the former constitution seem like a golden age by comparison. Among other things, they sent my aged friend, Socrates, whom I wouldn't hesitate to call the most just man of his time, along with some others to fetch one of their fellow citizens by force, so that he could be executed.[4] Their purpose was to involve Socrates in their activities, whether he wished it or not. He refused, however, and risked the most extreme penalties rather than take part in their unholy deeds. When I saw all this, and other similarly significant things, I withdrew in disgust from the evils then being practiced. Not long after that the Thirty and their entire constitution were overthrown. Then, once more, but this time more hesitantly, I was moved by the desire to take part in public affairs and politics. To be sure, many offenses continued to take place in those troublesome times as well, and it is hardly surprising that during these revolutions some people took excessive revenge on their enemies. But in general the restored democratic exiles exhibited considerable decency. As it chanced, however, some of those in control summoned our companion Socrates before the law courts and brought a most unholy charge against him, one that he least of all deserved, for they charged him with impiety and the people condemned and put to death the very man who, on the earlier occasion, when they themselves had the misfortune to be exiles, had refused to take part in the arrest of one of their friends. . . . The result was that I, who had at first been full of eagerness for public affairs, when I considered all this and saw how things were shifting about every which way, at last became dizzy. I didn't cease to consider ways of improving this particular situation, however, and, indeed, of reforming the whole constitution. But as far as action was concerned, I kept waiting for favorable moments and finally saw clearly that the constitutions of all actual cities are bad and that their laws are almost beyond redemption without extraordinary resources and luck as well. Hence I was compelled to say in praise of the true philosophy that it enables us to discern what is just for a city or an individual in every case and that the human race will have no respite from evils until those who are really and truly philosophers acquire political power or until, through some divine dispensation,

---

4. The citizen in question was Leon of Salamis. See Plato, *Apology* 32c–e.

those who rule and have political authority in cities become real philosophers (324b–326b).

Thus at the heart of Plato's refusal to participate actively in politics, at the heart of his turn from practical politics to political philosophy and education, we find the enigmatic figure of Socrates.

Philosophy for Socrates seems to have consisted almost entirely in examining people about justice, piety, courage, moderation, wisdom, friendship, and the other conventionally recognized virtues. He is always asking *Ti esti?* or What is it? about each of them. And he seems to presuppose that there are definite, unique answers to these questions, that justice, piety, courage, and the rest are each some definite property or universal—some definite *form*—whose nature can be captured in a unique definition or account (see Plato, *Euthyphro* 6d–e).

Socrates' method of examining is the so-called *elenchus*—we see some examples of it in operation in *Republic* I. Polemarchus defines justice as giving to each the things he is owed (331e). Socrates shows him that this is inconsistent with other things he firmly believes. The result is that Polemarchus modifies his original definition, and again Socrates shows him that the new position is inconsistent with other beliefs he has. In the ideal situation, this process continues until a satisfactory definition emerges, one that is not inconsistent with other firmly held beliefs.

Most of the definitions Socrates encounters in the course of his elenctic examinations of others prove unsatisfactory, but a few doctrines do emerge unscathed. Among them is the quintessentially Socratic doctrine that no one ever does what he knows or believes to be other than the best, so that weakness of will, or acting against what one knows or believes to be best, is impossible (*Protagoras* 352b ff.).

The goal of an elenchus is not simply to reach adequate definitions of the virtues or strange doctrines about weakness of will, however; it also has a moral reformatory purpose, for Socrates believes that regular elenctic philosophizing makes people happier and more virtuous than anything else (see Plato, *Apology* 30a, 36c–e, 38a, 41b–c). Indeed, philosophizing is so important for human welfare, on his view, that he is willing to accept execution rather than give it up (29b–d).

It is obvious from the *Republic* that Plato shares Socrates' preoccupation with ethics and with definitions, but it also seems obvious that he soon abandons or significantly modifies Socrates' method of inquiry, as well as some of his specific doctrines. After Book I, for example, the elenchus is conspicuous by its absence. And in Book VII, Plato suggests that its use on or by young people may result in their becoming immoral sensualists

(538c ff.). That seems to be one reason why dialectic—which is a descendant of the Socratic elenchus—must be practiced only by mature people who have mastered the mathematical sciences (531d ff.). In Book IV, a subtle argument for the tripartition of the psyche or soul seems in part designed to allow for the possibility of some kinds of weakness of will (especially 439e ff.). But despite these differences, Plato, like Socrates, is absolutely convinced that philosophy holds the key to human happiness and welfare (see 473c–e, 499a–c).

Socrates was one major influence on Plato, then, perhaps the most important influence of all. But there were others as well. Aristotle tells us, for example, that Plato was acquainted with the Heraclitean philosopher Cratylus "from his youth" (*Metaphysics* 987a32). Now, Cratylus, like his master Heraclitus, believed that "everything flows," that everything is always changing, always in a state of flux. And a similar doctrine is found in *Republic* V, where sensible things and properties—things and properties perceived by the senses—are described as "rolling around as intermediates between what is not and what purely is" (*Republic* 478a–479d). But whether or not this doctrine is a legacy of Cratylus' tutelage, it left Plato with a difficult problem, for if sensible things and properties are always in flux, how can justice and the other virtues be stable forms? How can there be fixed answers to Socrates' questions? And if there are no fixed answers to them, how can there be such a thing as stable ethical knowledge? It was reflection on these questions, Aristotle tells us, that led Plato to "separate" the forms from sensible things and properties (*Metaphysics* 1078b12–32, 1086b7–11). The allegories of the Sun, Line, and Cave, which divide reality into the intelligible and the visible (sensible), seem to embody this separation. But just what it amounts to is a matter of dispute.

After the death of Socrates, Plato and some other Socratics seem to have taken refuge in Megara with the philosopher Eucleides, who was a follower of Parmenides of Elea. Parmenides' doctrines are notoriously difficult to understand, but he seems to have held that it is impossible to say that something *is not*, for if it really *is not*, how can it *be* there to think or talk about? If we cannot talk or think about what is not, however, then we cannot think or talk about a multiplicity of things, A, B, and C, for if A, B, and C are many, then they are *not* one and the same as each other, and we cannot say or think that. It follows that whatever is must be one. By the same token, what is cannot move or change, for something moves if it is *not* now at a place at which it was earlier (yesterday it was in Athens; today it is *not* in Athens), and something changes if it does *not* now have a property that it had earlier (yesterday it was white; today it is *not* white), and we cannot say or think either of these things. Eucleides seems to have tried to combine these puzzling doctrines with Socrates' ethical teaching, arguing that the good, god, reason, justice, and the other virtues are all identical to the one unchanging being defended by Parmenides. The resulting metaphysical views find many echoes in Plato's writings, not the least of which is that Platonic forms seem at times to have some of the traits of Parmenidean being (see Plato, *Symposium* 211a–d).

When Plato was around forty, he may have made another journey away from Athens, this time to Italy and Sicily. It seems likely that he did so in order to visit the Pythagorean philosophers living there, especially the philosopher-statesman Archytas of Tarentum, who is mentioned in friendly terms in the *Seventh Letter*. In any case, the dialogues clearly show the influence of Pythagorean doctrine, with its near-obsessive focus on number and ratio as the key to reality. Archytas himself, for example, among many other significant achievements in mathematics and mechanics, discovered the ratios that underlie the relations between the successive notes in the enharmonic, harmonic, and chromatic scales. One can easily imagine Plato seeing in such achievements the possibility of giving precise definitions in wholly mathematical terms of such apparently vague and evaluative notions as harmony and disharmony, beauty and ugliness, maybe even justice and injustice, good and evil, and the other things of which Socrates sought definitions. In any case, the *Republic* itself provides strong evidence that Plato thought that forms could be satisfactorily defined, not in terms of sensible properties, but only in terms of numbers, ratios, and other precise mathematical notions (see 530d–533e).

Plato may have left Italy somewhat intoxicated with the possibilities of using mathematics to help solve philosophical and political problems, but in another way he was sobered by his Italian journey, for he recoiled in horror at the luxury and sensuality of the life there (*Seventh Letter* 326b–d), and, again, the effects of this recoil are palpable in the *Republic* and in many other of Plato's writings.

From Italy Plato travelled to Sicily, where he made ardent friends with Dion, brother-in-law of the ruling tyrant Dionysius I. Dion became, in effect, Plato's pupil and under his influence came to prefer goodness to the pleasure and luxury with which he was surrounded. Exactly what subsequently transpired in Sicily is unclear, as is the precise length of Plato's stay. There is some reason to believe, however, that Plato was expelled by Dionysius and perhaps even sold into slavery by him, only to be rescued from the slave market by a benevolent stranger.

But whatever exactly happened, Plato returned to Athens, bought some land in the precinct of the hero Academus, and there around 385 founded his famous school, the Academy, which lasted until A.D. 529. With some significant interruptions, to which we shall return, Plato spent the remainder of his life as director of studies in the Academy (see 528b–c). He is thought to have written the *Republic* there in around 380 B.C.

It is not clear that Plato's school was the first European university—a distinction that some would award to schools supposed to predate it on the Ionian coast of Asia Minor (the birthplace of Heraclitus and Herodotus, among others)—but it is the first of which we have any real knowledge, although that knowledge is far from extensive or detailed. Nonetheless, what evidence we do have makes it clear that the Academy was a center of research both in theoretical subjects and also in more practical ones. Metaphysics, epistemology, psychology, ethics, politics, and aesthetics all grew and developed there, as did mathematical science. Eudoxus, who gave a geometrical explanation of the revolutions of the sun, moon, and planets, and developed a general theory of proportion applicable to commensurable and incommensurable magnitudes, studied and taught in the Academy, as did Theaetetus, who developed solid geometry, and Heraclides Ponticus, who discovered the revolution of Venus and Mercury around the sun. But members of the Academy were also invited by a variety of cities—Arcadia, Pyrrha, Cidus, and Stagira are all mentioned—to help them develop new political constitutions. Thus it would be quite wrong to think that Plato and the other academicians perpetually had their heads in the clouds. If this were so, they would hardly have been much use to politicians confronting practical constitutional problems.

One further series of events from Plato's life bears relating. In 368, Dionysius I died, and Dion persuaded his son, Dionysius II, to send for Plato to get his advice on how to run the state. What followed was by all accounts a shambles, for Dionysius II did not want to study mathematics and philosophy in order to become a better ruler. Plato remained in Sicily until 366, when he was allowed to return home. But in 362, to fulfill a promise, he returned to Sicily, where he was kept until 360, at which time he was rescued by ambassadors from Tarentum sent by his friend Archytas.

Plato did not go to Sicily to found a heaven on earth; he was much too hardheaded for that. But he surely thought that he had something to teach Dionysius that would prove of real political significance. Throughout the *Republic*, indeed, he insists that the ideal city he describes is a real possibility that would most easily be realized if a king became a philosopher or a philosopher became a king.[5]

---

5. For further details about Plato's life and writings see W.K.C. Guthrie, *A History of Greek Philosophy*, Vol. 4 (Cambridge: Cambridge University Press, 1986): 8–66, and G. C. Field, *Plato and His Contemporaries* (New York: Dutton, 1930): 1–48.

The Main Argument of the Republic⁶

Thrasymachus is the most interesting of Socrates' interlocutors in Book I of the *Republic*. He defines justice as the advantage of the stronger, it seems, because he thinks something like this: The stronger rule in any city or society and so control the education and socialization of their subjects. But, like everyone else, the rulers are self-interested. Hence they educate and socialize their subjects with their own advantage, not that of their subjects, in view. Consequently, the values—including the ethical values—that subjects acquire are not ones that it is in their own best interests to have, but rather values that serve the interests of their rulers. The actions that subjects value as just, for example, are actions that benefit the rulers, not the subjects who do them.

But these alleged facts about cities or societies and their rulers are not, of course, available to the subjects themselves. *They* see their ethical values as serving their own best interests at least as much as anyone else's. But this, in Thrasymachus' view, is simply because they are unaware of the influence their rulers have had in shaping their whole outlook on the world.

This compelling story about the role of power in shaping our ethical beliefs obviously poses a challenge to any defender of justice, since it entails *that it is not in everyone's best interests to be just.* But the challenge it poses to a theorist like Socrates is particularly sharp, for in searching for definitions of justice and the other virtues by means of the elenchus, Socrates draws on the beliefs of his interlocutors.⁷ But the truth or reliability of these beliefs is put in question by Thrasymachus' account of the role the rulers play in how subjects acquire them. Hence Socrates' method of ethical investigation is flawed because it rests on data whose reliability has been seriously challenged.

It is clear, I think, that this challenge cuts right to the heart of Socratic ethics, as we described it in the previous section. It suggests that the elenchus is useless, that it cannot discover what the virtues are, but only what people think they are, as a result of being victims of a false ideology imposed on them by their stronger rulers. Thus Thrasymachus does not merely give an argument that justice is not in everyone's best interests; he also gives an argument that imposes a severe restriction on the evidence we can use to show that he is wrong.

This two-sided challenge is Plato's major target in the *Republic*. Thus

---

6. First-time readers may want to return to this Introduction after they have read the *Republic* for themselves.

7. See p. x above.

his aim is to show that justice is in everyone's best interests, because it is required for true happiness, and to do so without presupposing that people's beliefs about the virtues (or about happiness, for that matter) are true.

Once we see that this is Plato's aim, many otherwise obscure aspects of his argument become intelligible to us. For example, we can understand why he begins, in Book II, to develop an account of the best kind of city, or kallipolis; for the problem of ideology has to be confronted at the political level, at the level of social or political influence on the formation of people's beliefs. Second, we understand why he might think that the rulers of the kallipolis, the philosopher-kings, must study mathematical science and use it to define justice, courage, moderation, and the other virtues in precisely the way that it was already being used to define harmony in music; for mathematical science is surely less open to ideological influence and contamination than ethical and political beliefs. Hence, by starting with it, the philosopher-kings can develop a theory of ethics that is itself free of the influence of false ideology.

To escape the effects of false ideology, then, a city needs to be governed by rulers whose knowledge of mathematized ethics, politics, psychology, and the rest gives them access to undistorted ethical truth. But how can we be sure that rulers who possess that knowledge won't use it, in the way Thrasymachean rulers do, to feather their own nests at the expense of their subjects? Plato's answer to this question seems to be that only really virtuous people can actually gain genuine knowledge of ethical truth, because they alone can achieve genuine understanding of the good itself (521c–541b).

How does he support this answer? Here are some rather unrefined thoughts. Plato believes that there are three fundamentally different kinds of desires: *appetitive desires* for food, drink, sex, and the money with which to acquire them; *spirited desires* for honor, victory, and good reputation; and *rational desires* for knowledge and truth (437b ff., 580d ff.). These desires, he argues in Book IV, must be located in different parts of the soul. It is these parts of the soul that determine someone's character or fundamental psychological type. He is a money-lover if his soul or psyche is "ruled" by appetite, an honor-lover if it is "ruled" by the spirited part of his soul, and a wisdom-lover, or philosopher, if his soul is "ruled" by its rational part.

Now, what psychic rule—or the rule of a soul by one of its parts—amounts to seems to be this: A part *rules* the soul just in case the whole soul aims primarily at satisfying the desires located in that part, because it believes that a fully good or happy life must be one in which the satisfaction of those desires takes precedence over other things. A money-lover takes the good or happiness to consist in reliably satisfying his appetitive desires; an honor-lover, his spirited desires; a philosopher, his rational desires. Thus money-lovers, honor-lovers, and philosophers have different conceptions of what the good or happiness consists in, and the reason they have these different conceptions is because of a difference in the structure of their desires. To be crude about it: What we think the good is depends on what we want; hence people who want very different things will have very different conceptions of the good.

Now, we know from Book I that the virtues are defined in terms of happiness or the good (352d ff.). Hence, if money-lovers, honor-lovers, and philosophers have different conceptions of the good, they must also have different conceptions of the virtues. And the *Republic* shows us that people do indeed conceive of the virtues quite differently. Compare Polemarchus' account of justice with Thrasymachus', and both of these with the account Socrates defends in Book IV.

One might think that at this point there is little left to be said, that these differences must simply be accepted, but Plato does not agree. He thinks he can show that only one of these conceptions of the good (and hence of the virtues) is correct, that only the philosopher's conception is ultimately credible. His attempt to show this directly is to be found in Book IX (571a–592b). It is underwritten by the argument at the end of Book V, which is intended to show that, without forms, knowledge is impossible and that only philosophers have access to forms (473d–480). Both arguments are extraordinarily deep when properly understood, but both are likely to appear simply bizarre on first reading. Consequently, a charitable reader will want to consider them carefully and to look at what different critics have had to say about them.

Suppose for the moment, however, that we are convinced by these Platonic arguments. We will then believe that the reason philosophers have access to the good and the virtues is that they are ruled by rational desires, or by the rational part of the soul in which those desires reside. But now Plato has a long argument, one of the many triumphs of the *Republic*, that to be virtuous—to be wise, courageous, moderate, and just— is simply to have a soul that is ruled by its rational part. It follows that the philosopher-kings must be virtuous. But if they are virtuous, they will rule the kallipolis as much in the interests of their subjects as in their own (see 590c–e).

It is not surprising, in the light of these arguments and doctrines, that Plato believes that the fundamental goal of education is not to put knowledge into people's souls but to change their desires, thereby turning them around from the pursuit of what they falsely believe to be happiness to the pursuit of true happiness (518b–519d). Since the allegory of the

Cave illustrates the effects of education on us (514a), we ought to be able to see it as illustrating what happens as the internal rule of our soul passes from the desires in one part of our soul to those in another part. Here is a suggestion:

STAGE 1: The prisoners at the bottom of the cave have received no education at all. They are bound by unnecessary appetitive desires (see 558d–559c) and see images of models of "the things themselves" (516a).

STAGE 2: When they have been appropriately educated in a craft or in music, poetry, and physical training, some of these prisoners are released from the bonds of unnecessary appetites and are then ruled only by necessary ones. They then see the models of the things of which they previously saw only images.

STAGE 3: Through education in mathematical science, some of these people are released from the bonds of necessary appetites and are then bound by their spirited desires. They escape the cave and see the things themselves.

STAGE 4: Through education in dialectic and practical city management, some of these people take the final step. They escape the bonds of their spirited desires and are then ruled only by their rational ones. They see "the greatest object of study" (505a), the good itself, and see that it is in some way the cause of all the other things they have seen.

Not everyone is able to take all these steps; there are some at each stage whose desires are too strong for education to break. That is why there are producers (money-lovers), guardians (honor-lovers), and philosopher-kings (wisdom-lovers) in Plato's ideal city. Nonetheless, everyone in the kallipolis travels as far out of the cave as education can take him, given the innate strength of his desires.

One more piece of supposing: Suppose we accept everything that has been said so far. Now let us ask ourselves this question: What sort of city would I most like to have been brought up in? Surely the answer would be something like this: I would like to be brought up in a city that would so educate me that I would come as close as possible to being ruled by the rational part of my soul, by my rational desires, for that way I'd have the best chance of achieving true happiness.

If that is the answer, then two things follow. First, we have a reason to want to be just and virtuous. Plato argues that a soul ruled by reason has to be just—indeed, he argues that justice in a soul simply is rational rule (441c–444e). It follows that Thrasymachus is mistaken: justice and happiness are so intimately bound up with one another that it is not possible to achieve true happiness without being just. Second, we have a reason to want to have been brought up in the city Plato describes in the *Republic*, for it now looks as if he designed that city to be one in which every one of us would receive the kind of education that would bring us as close to being ruled by reason as our nature (or the strength of our various desires) allows. As we read the *Republic*, we are likely to be disturbed by this conclusion. Anyone's initial reaction to Plato's ideal city is likely to be one of repugnance. Almost anyone nowadays will think that it is a repressive, even totalitarian place and that the freedoms we prize would be restricted there. This is a natural reaction, but it is one we ought to submit to the most careful scrutiny, for, if Plato is right, we may value these freedoms simply because of our enslavement to desires that distort our perception of the good and cause us to chase after things that will never make us really happy.[8]

---

8. For a more detailed defense of the views expressed in this section, see C.D.C. Reeve, *Philosopher-Kings* (Princeton: Princeton University Press, 1988).

BIBLIOGRAPHY

Knowledge of the world in which Plato wrote can be acquired most easily by reading *The World of Athens* (Cambridge: Cambridge University Press, 1st ed., 1984) together with the relevant chapters of T. H. Irwin, *Classical Thought* (Oxford: Oxford University Press, 1989). Readers who want to know more about the pre-Socratic philosophers, such as Heraclitus and Parmenides, might begin with Edward Hussey, *The Pre-Socratics* (London: Duckworth, 1972). The sophists are well discussed in W.K.C. Guthrie, *The Sophists* (Cambridge: Cambridge University Press, 1971). Selections from the writings of the lyric poets Plato mentions in the *Republic* are translated in Richmond Lattimore, *Greek Lyrics* (Chicago: Chicago University Press, 1960).

The first things to read on Socrates are, of course, Plato's Socratic dialogues. Each of the following works are guides to them and to their interpretation: T. H. Irwin, *Plato's Moral Theory* (Oxford: Clarendon Press, 1977); Richard Kraut, *Socrates and the State* (Princeton: Princeton University Press, 1984); C.D.C. Reeve, *Socrates in the Apology* (Indianapolis: Hackett, 1989); Gregory Vlastos, *Socrates: Ironist and Moral Philosopher* (Ithaca: Cornell University Press, 1991).

It is useful, when reading the *Republic*, to have some sense of Plato's philosophy as a whole. T. H. Irwin, *Plato's Moral Theory*, is insightful about the dialogues up to and including the *Republic*. I. M. Crombie, *An Examination of Plato's Doctrines* (London: Routledge and Kegan Paul, 1962), though out of date in lots of ways, is still worth reading, as are W.K.C. Guthrie, *A History of Greek Philosophy*, vols. 4–5 (Cambridge: Cambridge University Press, 1975–78), J.C.B. Gosling, *Plato* (London: Routledge and Kegan Paul, 1973), and G.M.A. Grube, *Plato's Thought* (Indianapolis: Hackett, 1980).

On the *Republic* itself, the following works may be recommended: James Adam, *The Republic of Plato* (Cambridge: Cambridge University Press, 1902) is still the best commentary on the Greek text, and much of it is accessible to Greekless readers. Julia Annas, *An Introduction to Plato's Republic* (Oxford: Clarendon Press, 1981) is a lively philosophical discussion, accessible to undergraduates. Karl Popper, *The Open Society and Its*

Enemies, vol. 1 (Princeton: Princeton University Press, 1971) is a challenge to Plato that still deserves to be taken seriously. C.D.C. Reeve, *Philosopher-Kings* (Princeton: Princeton University Press, 1988) is a philosophical reconstruction of the overall argument of the *Republic*, accessible to more advanced undergraduates. Nicholas White, *A Companion to Plato's Republic* (Indianapolis: Hackett, 1979) is a useful commentary on the *Republic*, accessible to beginning students.

The following articles on special topics in the *Republic* will be found particularly helpful:

Myles Burnyeat, "Platonism and Mathematics: A Prelude to Discussion." In A. Graeser, ed., *Mathematics and Metaphysics in Aristotle* (Bern: Paul Haupt, 1987).

John M. Cooper, "The Psychology of Justice in the *Republic*." *American Philosophical Quarterly* (1977) 14: 151–57.

——————, "Plato's Theory of Human Motivation." *History of Philosophy Quarterly* 1 (1984): 3–21.

Gail Fine, "Knowledge and Belief in *Republic* V–VII." In S. Everson, ed., *Companions to Ancient Thought 1: Epistemology* (Cambridge: Cambridge University Press, 1990).

——————, "Separation." *Oxford Studies in Ancient Philosophy* 2 (1984): 31–87.

J.C.B. Gosling, "*Republic* Book V: *ta polla kala* etc." *Phronesis* V (1960): 116–28.

T. H. Irwin, "Plato's Heracleiteanism." *Philosophical Quarterly* 27 (1977): 1–13.

Sabina Lovibond, "Plato's Theory of Mind." In S. Everson, ed., *Companions to Ancient Thought 2: Psychology* (Cambridge: Cambridge University Press, 1991).

Alexander Nehamas, "Plato on Imitation and Poetry in *Republic* 10." In Julius Moravcsik and Philip Temko, edd., *Plato on Beauty, Wisdom and the Arts* (Totowa: Rowman and Littlefield, 1982).

C.D.C. Reeve, "Socrates Meets Thrasymachus." *Archiv für Geschichte der Philosophie* 67 (1985): 246–65.

David Sachs, "A Fallacy in Plato's *Republic*." *Philosophical Review* 72 (1963): 141–58.

Gregory Vlastos, "The Theory of Social Justice in the *Polis* in Plato's *Republic*." In Helen North, ed., *Interpretations of Plato* (Leiden: Brill, 1977).

——————, "Elenchus and Mathematics: A Turning-Point in Plato's Philosophical Development." *American Journal of Philology* 109 (1988): 362–96.

——————, "Was Plato a Feminist?" *Times Literary Supplement* March 17–23 (1989).

BOOK I

On his way back from the Piraeus, where he has been attending a religious festival, Socrates meets Polemarchus and goes with him to the house of his aged father, Cephalus (327a–328b). Socrates and Cephalus discuss the burdens of old age. Cephalus claims that, while these burdens are eased by wealth, it is people's character and habits that really determine whether or not their lives are hard to bear, not their age. Wealth is important mostly because it reduces the likelihood that someone will be tempted into being unjust because he is poor, and so lessens his fear of what will happen to him after he dies (328b–331b). This leads in a natural way into a discussion of what justice is, for Cephalus has suggested in his remarks that it is speaking the truth and paying one's debts.

Cephalus goes off to attend to religious matters, and Polemarchus becomes heir to his argument, as he will later become heir to his estate. There follows a lengthy examination of Polemarchus, in the course of which he is forced to abandon a number of views about justice he has adopted along the way (331c–336b). One of these, suggested not by Polemarchus but by Socrates, is that virtue is a craft or technē *(332d). This is also assumed in the subsequent exchange with Thrasymachus.*

Thrasymachus is irritated by this examination and demands that Socrates give his own positive account of justice, instead of simply refuting other people's. Socrates claims that he cannot give such an account, because he does not know what justice is, and he persuades Thrasymachus to give an account in his place (336b–338a). The account Thrasymachus gives is that justice is the advantage of the stronger (338c). He defends this account in two separate arguments (338d–341a, 343a–344c). Socrates makes a number of attempts to refute these arguments (342c–d, 345b–347d, 348b–350c, 351a–352d, 352d–354a), but, though Thrasymachus cannot defend himself against them, they leave him unconvinced (341a–b, 349a, 350d–e, 352b, 353e, 354a). Since Glaucon, Adeimantus, and indeed Socrates himself (354b) are also dissatisfied with the outcome of Book I (358b, 367b), we must wonder how successful Plato himself thought Socrates' refutations of Thrasymachus actually were.

I went down to the Piraeus yesterday with Glaucon, the son of Ariston. I
327 wanted to say a prayer to the goddess,[1] and I was also curious to see how
they would manage the festival, since they were holding it for the first
time. I thought the procession of the local residents was a fine one and
that the one conducted by the Thracians was no less outstanding. After
we had said our prayer and seen the procession, we started back towards
b   Athens. Polemarchus saw us from a distance as we were setting off for
home and told his slave to run and ask us to wait for him. The slave caught
hold of my cloak from behind: Polemarchus wants you to wait, he said. I
turned around and asked where Polemarchus was. He's coming up behind
you, he said, please wait for him. And Glaucon replied: All right, we will.

Just then Polemarchus caught up with us. Adeimantus, Glaucon's
c   brother,[2] was with him and so were Niceratus, the son of Nicias, and some
others, all of whom were apparently on their way from the procession.

Polemarchus said: It looks to me, Socrates, as if you two are starting
off for Athens.

It looks the way it is, then, I said.

Do you see how many we are? he said.

I do.

Well, you must either prove stronger than we are, or you will have to
stay here.

Isn't there another alternative, namely, that we persuade you to let us
go?

But could you persuade us, if we won't listen?

Certainly not, Glaucon said.

Well, we won't listen; you'd better make up your mind to that.
328 Don't you know, Adeimantus said, that there is to be a torch race on
horseback for the goddess tonight?

On horseback? I said. That's something new. Are they going to race on
horseback and hand the torches on in relays, or what?

In relays, Polemarchus said, and there will be an all-night festival that
will be well worth seeing. After dinner, we'll go out to look at it. We'll be
joined there by many of the young men, and we'll talk. So don't go; stay.
b   It seems, Glaucon said, that we'll have to stay.

If you think so, I said, then we must.

So we went to Polemarchus' house, and there we found Lysias and
Euthydemus, the brothers of Polemarchus, Thrasymachus of Chalcedon,

---

1. The Thracian goddess Bendis, whose cult had recently been introduced in the
Piraeus, the harbor area near Athens.

2. Glaucon and Adeimantus were Plato's brothers. They are Socrates' chief interlocutors after Book I.

Charmantides of Paiania, and Cleitophon the son of Aristonymus.³ Polemarchus' father, Cephalus, was also there, and I thought he looked quite old, as I hadn't seen him for some time. He was sitting on a sort of cush-   *c* ioned chair with a wreath on his head, as he had been offering a sacrifice in the courtyard. There was a circle of chairs, and we sat down by him.

As soon as he saw me, Cephalus welcomed me and said: Socrates, you don't come down to the Piraeus to see us as often as you should. If it were still easy for me to walk to town, you wouldn't have to come here; we'd come to you. But, as it is, you ought to come here more often, for you should know that as the physical pleasures wither away, my desire for con-   *d* versation and its pleasures grows. So do as I say: Stay with these young men now, but come regularly to see us, just as you would to friends or relatives.

Indeed, Cephalus, I replied, I enjoy talking with the very old, for we should ask them, as we might ask those who have travelled a road that we too will probably have to follow, what kind of road it is, whether rough and   *e* difficult or smooth and easy. And I'd gladly find out from you what you think about this, as you have reached the point in life the poets call "the threshold of old age."⁴ Is it a difficult time? What is your report about it?

By god, Socrates, I'll tell you exactly what I think. A number of us, who   *329* are more or less the same age, often get together in accordance with the old saying.⁵ When we meet, the majority complain about the lost pleasures they remember from their youth, those of sex, drinking parties, feasts, and the other things that go along with them, and they get angry as if they had been deprived of important things and had lived well then but are now hardly living at all. Some others moan about the abuse heaped on old people by their relatives, and because of this they repeat over and over   *b* that old age is the cause of many evils. But I don't think they blame the real cause, Socrates, for if old age were really the cause, I should have suffered in the same way and so should everyone else of my age. But as it is, I've met some who don't feel like that in the least. Indeed, I was once present when someone asked the poet Sophocles: "How are you as far as sex goes, Sophocles? Can you still make love with a woman?" "Quiet,   *c*

---

3. Lysias was a well-known writer of speeches for use in legal trials. Socrates discusses a speech attributed to him in the *Phaedrus*. Thrasymachus was a sophist, a paid teacher of oratory and virtue. The few fragments of his writings that survive are translated in Freeman, *Ancilla to the Pre-Socratic Philosophers* (Cambridge: Harvard University Press, 1977). Charmantides is otherwise unknown.

4. Homer, *Iliad* 22.60, 24.487; *Odyssey* 25.246, 348, 23.212.

5. "God ever draws together like to like" (Homer, *Odyssey* 17.218). See Plato, *Lysis* 214a–215c.

man," the poet replied, "I am very glad to have escaped from all that, like a slave who has escaped from a savage and tyrannical master." I thought at the time that he was right, and I still do, for old age brings peace and freedom from all such things. When the appetites relax and cease to importune us, everything Sophocles said comes to pass, and we escape
d from many mad masters. In these matters and in those concerning relatives, the real cause isn't old age, Socrates, but the way people live. If they are moderate and contented, old age, too, is only moderately onerous; if they aren't, both old age and youth are hard to bear.

I admired him for saying that and I wanted him to tell me more, so I urged him on: When you say things like that, Cephalus, I suppose that
e the majority of people don't agree, they think that you bear old age more easily not because of the way you live but because you're wealthy, for the wealthy, they say, have many consolations.

That's true; they don't agree. And there is something in what they say, though not as much as they think. Themistocles' retort is relevant here. When someone from Seriphus insulted him by saying that his high reputa-
330 tion was due to his city and not to himself, he replied that, had he been a Seriphian, he wouldn't be famous, but neither would the other even if he had been an Athenian.[6] The same applies to those who aren't rich and find old age hard to bear: A good person wouldn't easily bear old age if he were poor, but a bad one wouldn't be at peace with himself even if he were wealthy.

Did you inherit most of your wealth, Cephalus, I asked, or did you make it for yourself?

What did I make for myself, Socrates, you ask. As a money-maker I'm
b in a sort of mean between my grandfather and my father. My grandfather and namesake inherited about the same amount of wealth as I possess but multiplied it many times. My father, Lysanias, however, diminished that amount to even less than I have now. As for me, I'm satisfied to leave my sons here not less but a little more than I inherited.

The reason I asked is that you don't seem to love money too much. And those who haven't made their own money are usually like you. But those
c who have made it for themselves are twice as fond of it as those who haven't. Just as poets love their poems and fathers love their children, so those who have made their own money don't just care about it because

---

6. Themistocles, a fifth-century Athenian statesman, was the chief architect of the Greek victory over Persia. By building up the navy, he secured Athens' future as a naval power and also paved the way for the increased political power of the poorer classes, from which sailors were largely drawn. Seriphus is a small island in the Cyclades.

it's useful, as other people do, but because it's something they've made themselves. This makes them poor company, for they haven't a good word to say about anything except money.

That's true.

It certainly is. But tell me something else. What's the greatest good *d* you've received from being very wealthy?

What I have to say probably wouldn't persuade most people. But you know, Socrates, that when someone thinks his end is near, he becomes frightened and concerned about things he didn't fear before. It's then that the stories we're told about Hades, about how people who've been unjust here must pay the penalty there—stories he used to make fun of—twist his soul this way and that for fear they're true. And whether because of *e* the weakness of old age or because he is now closer to what happens in Hades and has a clearer view of it, or whatever it is, he is filled with foreboding and fear, and he examines himself to see whether he has been unjust to anyone. If he finds many injustices in his life, he awakes from sleep in terror, as children do, and lives in anticipation of bad things to come. But someone who knows that he hasn't been unjust has sweet good *331* hope as his constant companion—a nurse to his old age, as Pindar[7] says, for he puts it charmingly, Socrates, when he says that when someone lives a just and pious life

> Sweet hope is in his heart,
> Nurse and companion to his age.
> Hope, captain of the ever-twisting
> Minds of mortal men.

How wonderfully well he puts that. It's in this connection that wealth is most valuable, I'd say, not for every man but for a decent and orderly one. Wealth can do a lot to save us from having to cheat or deceive someone *b* against our will and from having to depart for that other place in fear because we owe sacrifice to a god or money to a person. It has many other uses, but, benefit for benefit, I'd say that this is how it is most useful to a man of any understanding.

A fine sentiment, Cephalus, but, speaking of this very thing itself, namely, justice,[8] are we to say unconditionally that it is speaking the truth and paying *c*

---

7. Pindar (518–438 B.C.), a lyric poet from Boeotia, was most famous for his poems in celebration of the victors in the games, such as the Olympian and Pythian, held in various parts of Greece.

8. Unlike their usual equivalents "just" and "justice," the adjective *dikaios* and the noun *dikaiosunē* are often used in a wider sense, better captured by our words "right" or "correct." The opposite, *adikia*, then has the sense of general wrongdoing.

whatever debts one has incurred? Or is doing these things sometimes just, sometimes unjust? I mean this sort of thing, for example: Everyone would surely agree that if a sane man lends weapons to a friend and then asks for them back when he is out of his mind, the friend shouldn't return them, and wouldn't be acting justly if he did. Nor should anyone be willing to tell the whole truth to someone who is out of his mind.

d   That's true.

Then the definition of justice isn't speaking the truth and repaying what one has borrowed.

It certainly is, Socrates, said Polemarchus, interrupting, if indeed we're to trust Simonides at all.[9]

Well, then, Cephalus said, I'll hand over the argument to you, as I have to look after the sacrifice.

So, Polemarchus said, am I then to be your heir in everything?

You certainly are, Cephalus said, laughing, and off he went to the sacrifice.

Then tell us, heir to the argument, I said, just what Simonides stated
e   about justice that you consider correct.

He stated that it is just to give to each what is owed to him. And it's a fine saying, in my view.

Well, now, it isn't easy to doubt Simonides, for he's a wise and godlike man. But what exactly does he mean? Perhaps you know, Polemarchus, but I don't understand him. Clearly, he doesn't mean what we said a moment ago, that it is just to give back whatever a person has lent to you, even if he's out of his mind when he asks for it. And yet what he has lent
332 to you is surely something that's owed to him, isn't it?

Yes.

But it is absolutely not to be given to him when he's out of his mind?

That's true.

Then it seems that Simonides must have meant something different when he says that to return what is owed is just.

Something different indeed, by god. He means that friends owe it to their friends to do good for them, never harm.

I follow you. Someone doesn't give a lender back what he's owed by giving him gold, if doing so would be harmful, and both he and the lender
b   are friends. Isn't that what you think Simonides meant?

It is.

But what about this? Should one also give one's enemies whatever is owed to them?

---

9. Simonides (c. 548–468 B.C.), a lyric and elegiac poet, was born in the Aegean island of Ceos.

By all means, one should give them what is owed to them. And in my view what enemies owe to each other is appropriately and precisely—something bad.

It seems then that Simonides was speaking in riddles—just like a poet!—when he said what justice is, for he thought it just to give to each what is appropriate to him, and this is what he called giving him what is *c* owed to him.

What else did you think he meant?

Then what do you think he'd answer if someone asked him: "Simonides, which of the things that are owed or that are appropriate for someone or something to have does the craft[10] we call medicine give, and to whom or what does it give them?"

It's clear that it gives medicines, food, and drink to bodies.

And what owed or appropriate things does the craft we call cooking give, and to whom or what does it give them?

It gives seasonings to food.   *d*

Good. Now, what does the craft we call justice give, and to whom or what does it give it?

If we are to follow the previous answers, Socrates, it gives benefits to friends and does harm to enemies.

Simonides means, then, that to treat friends well and enemies badly is justice?

I believe so.

And who is most capable of treating friends well and enemies badly in matters of disease and health?

A doctor.

And who can do so best in a storm at sea?   *e*

A ship's captain.

What about the just person? In what actions and what work is he most capable of benefiting friends and harming enemies?

In wars and alliances, I suppose.

All right. Now, when people aren't sick, Polemarchus, a doctor is useless to them?

True.

And so is a ship's captain to those who aren't sailing?

Yes.

---

10. The Greek word translated as "craft" here is *technē*. It has the sort of connotation for Socrates and Plato that "science" has for us. Thus fifth-century doctors tried to show that medicine is a craft, much as contemporary psychoanalysts try to convince us that psychoanalysis is a science. For further discussion see Reeve, *Socrates in the Apology*, 37–45.

And to people who aren't at war, a just man is useless?

No, I don't think that at all.

Justice is also useful in peacetime, then?

333   It is.

And so is farming, isn't it?

Yes.

For getting produce?

Yes.

And shoemaking as well?

Yes.

For getting shoes, I think you'd say?

Certainly.

Well, then, what is justice useful for getting and using in peacetime?

Contracts, Socrates.

And by contracts do you mean partnerships, or what?

I mean partnerships.

Is someone a good and useful partner in a game of checkers because

b   he's just or because he's a checkers player?

Because he's a checkers player.

And in laying bricks and stones, is a just person a better and more useful partner than a builder?

Not at all.

In what kind of partnership, then, is a just person a better partner than a builder or a lyre-player, in the way that a lyre-player is better than a just person at hitting the right notes?

In money matters, I think.

Except perhaps, Polemarchus, in using money, for whenever one needs to buy a horse jointly, I think a horse breeder is a more useful partner,

c   isn't he?

Apparently.

And when one needs to buy a boat, it's a boatbuilder or a ship's captain?

Probably.

In what joint use of silver or gold, then, is a just person a more useful partner than the others?

When it must be deposited for safekeeping, Socrates.

You mean whenever there is no need to use them but only to keep them?

That's right.

Then it is when money isn't being used that justice is useful for it?

d   I'm afraid so.

And whenever one needs to keep a pruning knife safe, but not to use it, justice is useful both in partnerships and for the individual. When you need to use it, however, it is skill at vine pruning that's useful?

Apparently.

You'll agree, then, that when one needs to keep a shield or a lyre safe and not to use them, justice is a useful thing, but when you need to use them, it is soldiery or musicianship that's useful?

Necessarily.

And so, too, with everything else, justice is useless when they are in use but useful when they aren't?

It looks that way.

In that case, justice isn't worth much, since it is only useful for useless *e* things. But let's look into the following point. Isn't the person most able to land a blow, whether in boxing or any other kind of fight, also most able to guard against it?

Certainly.

And the one who is most able to guard against disease is also most able to produce it unnoticed?

So it seems to me, anyway.

And the one who is the best guardian of an army is the very one who can steal the enemy's plans and dispositions?   *334*

Certainly.

Whenever someone is a clever guardian, then, he is also a clever thief.

Probably so.

If a just person is clever at guarding money, therefore, he must also be clever at stealing it.

According to our argument, at any rate.

A just person has turned out then, it seems, to be a kind of thief. Maybe you learned this from Homer, for he's fond of Autolycus, the maternal grandfather of Odysseus, whom he describes as better than everyone at *b* lying and stealing.[11] According to you, Homer, and Simonides, then, justice seems to be some sort of craft of stealing, one that benefits friends and harms enemies. Isn't that what you meant?

No, by god, it isn't. I don't know any more what I did mean, but I still believe that to benefit one's friends and harm one's enemies is justice.

Speaking of friends, do you mean those a person believes to be good and useful to him or those who actually are good and useful, even if he *c* doesn't think they are, and similarly with enemies?

Probably, one loves those one considers good and useful and hates those one considers bad and harmful.

But surely people often make mistakes about this, believing many people to be good and useful when they aren't, and making the opposite mistake about enemies?

They do indeed.

11. The reference is to *Odyssey* 19.392–8.

And then good people are their enemies and bad ones their friends?

That's right.

d   And so it's just to benefit bad people and harm good ones?

Apparently.

But good people are just and able to do no wrong?

True.

Then, according to your account, it's just to do bad things to those who do no injustice.

No, that's not just at all, Socrates; my account must be a bad one.

It's just, then, is it, to harm unjust people and benefit just ones?

That's obviously a more attractive view than the other one, anyway.

Then, it follows, Polemarchus, that it is just for the many, who are mistaken in their judgment, to harm their friends, who are bad, and benefit

e   their enemies, who are good. And so we arrive at a conclusion opposite to what we said Simonides meant.

That certainly follows. But let's change our definition, for it seems that we didn't define friends and enemies correctly.

How did we define them, Polemarchus?

We said that a friend is someone who is believed to be useful.

And how are we to change that now?

Someone who is both believed to be useful and is useful is a friend; someone who is believed to be useful but isn't, is believed to be a friend

335 but isn't. And the same for the enemy.

According to this account, then, a good person will be a friend and a bad one an enemy.

Yes.

So you want us to add something to what we said before about justice, when we said that it is just to treat friends well and enemies badly. You want us to add to this that it is just to treat well a friend who is good and to harm an enemy who is bad?

b   Right. That seems fine to me.

Is it, then, the role of a just man to harm anyone?

Certainly, he must harm those who are both bad and enemies.

Do horses become better or worse when they are harmed?

Worse.

With respect to the virtue[12] that makes dogs good or the one that makes horses good?

12. If something is a knife (say) or a man, its *aretē* or virtue as a knife or a man is that state or property of it that makes it a good knife or a good man. See *Charmides* 161a8–9; *Euthyphro* 6d9–e1; *Gorgias* 506d2–4; *Protagoras* 332b4–6; *Republic* 353d9–354a2. The *aretē* of a knife might include having a sharp blade; the *aretē* of a man might include being intelligent, well-born, just, or courageous. *Aretē* is thus broader than our notion

The one that makes horses good.

And when dogs are harmed, they become worse in the virtue that makes dogs good, not horses?

Necessarily.

Then won't we say the same about human beings, too, that when they are harmed they become worse in human virtue?   *c*

Indeed.

But isn't justice human virtue?

Yes, certainly.

Then people who are harmed must become more unjust?

So it seems.

Can musicians make people unmusical through music?

They cannot.

Or horsemen make people unhorsemanlike through horsemanship?

No.

Well, then, can those who are just make people unjust through justice?

In a word, can those who are good make people bad through virtue?   *d*

They cannot.

It isn't the function of heat to cool things but of its opposite?

Yes.

Nor the function of dryness to make things wet but of its opposite?

Indeed.

Nor the function of goodness to harm but of its opposite?

Apparently.

And a just person is good?

Indeed.

Then, Polemarchus, it isn't the function of a just person to harm a friend or anyone else, rather it is the function of his opposite, an unjust person?

In my view that's completely true, Socrates.

If anyone tells us, then, that it is just to give to each what he's owed and   *e*
understands by this that a just man should harm his enemies and benefit his friends, he isn't wise to say it, since what he says isn't true, for it has become clear to us that it is never just to harm anyone?

I agree.

You and I shall fight as partners, then, against anyone who tells us that

---

of moral virtue. It applies to things (such as knives) which are not moral agents. And it applies to aspects of moral agents (such as intelligence or family status) which are not normally considered to be moral aspects of them. For these reasons it is sometimes more appropriate to render *aretē* as "excellence." But "virtue" remains the best overall translation, and once these few facts are borne in mind, it should seldom mislead.

Simonides, Bias, Pittacus, or any of our other wise and blessedly happy men said this:[13]

I, at any rate, am willing to be your partner in the battle.

336   Do you know to whom I think the saying belongs that it is just to benefit friends and harm enemies?

Who?

I think it belongs to Periander, or Perdiccas, or Xerxes, or Ismenias of Corinth, or some other wealthy man who believed himself to have great power.[14]

That's absolutely true.

All right, since it has become apparent that justice and the just aren't what such people say they are, what else could they be?

While we were speaking, Thrasymachus had tried many times to take
b   over the discussion but was restrained by those sitting near him, who wanted to hear our argument to the end. When we paused after what I'd just said, however, he couldn't keep quiet any longer. He coiled himself up like a wild beast about to spring, and he hurled himself at us as if to tear us to pieces.

Polemarchus and I were frightened and flustered as he roared into our midst: What nonsense have you two been talking, Socrates? Why do you
c   act like idiots by giving way to one another? If you truly want to know what justice is, don't just ask questions and then refute the answers simply to satisfy your competitiveness or love of honor. You know very well that it is easier to ask questions than answer them. Give an answer yourself, and tell us what you say the just is. And don't tell me that it's the right, the
d   beneficial, the profitable, the gainful, or the advantageous, but tell me clearly and exactly what you mean; for I won't accept such nonsense from you.

His words startled me, and, looking at him, I was afraid. And I think that if I hadn't seen him before he stared at me, I'd have been dumbstruck. But as it was, I happened to look at him just as our discussion began to
e   exasperate him, so I was able to answer, and, trembling a little, I said: Don't be too hard on us, Thrasymachus, for if Polemarchus and I made an error in our investigation, you should know that we did so unwillingly.

13. Bias of Priene in Ionia (now the region of Turkey bordering on the eastern shore of the Aegean) and Pittacus of Mytilene (on the island of Lesbos in the eastern Aegean), both sixth century B.C., were two of the legendary seven sages of Greece.

14. Periander was tyrant of the city of Corinth (650–570 B.C.). Perdiccas is probably Perdiccas II, King of Macedon (c. 450–413 B.C.), who is also mentioned in the *Gorgias* 471a–e. Xerxes was the king of Persia who invaded Greece in the second Persian war (begun in 480 B.C.). Ismenias is mentioned in the *Meno* 90a. All four are either notorious tyrants or men famous for their wealth.

If we were searching for gold, we'd never willingly give way to each other, if by doing so we'd destroy our chance of finding it. So don't think that in searching for justice, a thing more valuable than even a large quantity of gold, we'd mindlessly give way to one another or be less than completely serious about finding it. You surely mustn't think that, but rather—as I do—that we're incapable of finding it. Hence it's surely far more appropriate for us to be pitied by you clever people than to be given rough treatment.   *337*

When he heard that, he gave a loud, sarcastic laugh. By Heracles, he said, that's just Socrates' usual irony.[15] I knew, and I said so to these people earlier, that you'd be unwilling to answer and that, if someone questioned *you*, you'd be ironical and do anything rather than give an answer.

That's because you're a clever fellow, Thrasymachus. You knew very well that if you ask someone how much twelve is, and, as you ask, you warn him by saying "Don't tell me, man, that twelve is twice six, or three   *b* times four, or six times two, or four times three, for I won't accept such nonsense," then you'll see clearly, I think, that no one could answer a question framed like that. And if he said to you: "What are you saying, Thrasymachus, am I not to give any of the answers you mention, not even if twelve happens to be one of those things? I'm amazed. Do you want me to say something other than the truth? Or do you mean something else?" What answer would you give him?   *c*

Well, so you think the two cases are alike?

Why shouldn't they be alike? But even if they aren't alike, yet seem so to the person you asked, do you think him any less likely to give the answer that seems right to him, whether we forbid him to or not?

Is that what you're going to do, give one of the forbidden answers?

I wouldn't be surprised—provided that it's the one that seems right to me after I've investigated the matter.

What if I show you a different answer about justice than all these—and a better one? What would you deserve then?   *d*

What else than the appropriate penalty for one who doesn't know, namely, to learn from the one who does know? Therefore, that's what I deserve.

You amuse me, but in addition to learning, you must pay a fine.

---

15. The Greek word *eirōneia*, unlike its usual translation "irony," is correctly applied only to someone who intends to deceive. Thus Thrasymachus is not simply accusing Socrates of saying one thing while meaning another; he is accusing him of trying to deceive those present. See G. Vlastos, "Socratic Irony," *Classical Quarterly* 37 (1987): 79–96.

I will as soon as I have some money.

He has some already, said Glaucon. If it's a matter of money, speak, Thrasymachus, for we'll all contribute for Socrates.

I know, he said, so that Socrates can carry on as usual. He gives no
e answer himself, and then, when someone else does give one, he takes up the argument and refutes it.

How can someone give an answer, I said, when he doesn't know it and doesn't claim to know it, and when an eminent man forbids him to express the opinion he has? It's much more appropriate for you to answer, since
338 you say you know and can tell us. So do it as a favor to me, and don't begrudge your teaching to Glaucon and the others.

While I was saying this, Glaucon and the others begged him to speak. It was obvious that Thrasymachus thought he had a fine answer and that he wanted to earn their admiration by giving it, but he pretended that he wanted to indulge his love of victory by forcing me to answer. However,
b he agreed in the end, and then said: There you have Socrates' wisdom; he himself isn't willing to teach, but he goes around learning from others and isn't even grateful to them.

When you say that I learn from others you are right, Thrasymachus, but when you say that I'm not grateful, that isn't true. I show what gratitude I can, but since I have no money, I can give only praise. But just how enthusiastically I give it when someone seems to me to speak well, you'll know as soon as you've answered, for I think that you will speak well.

c Listen, then. I say that justice is nothing other than the advantage of the stronger. Well, why don't you praise me? But then you'd do anything to avoid having to do that.

I must first understand you, for I don't yet know what you mean. The advantage of the stronger, you say, is just. What do you mean, Thrasymachus? Surely you don't mean something like this: Polydamas, the pancratist,[16] is stronger than we are; it is to his advantage to eat beef to build up his physical strength; therefore, this food is also advantageous
d and just for us who are weaker than he is?

You disgust me, Socrates. Your trick is to take hold of the argument at the point where you can do it the most harm.

Not at all, but tell us more clearly what you mean.

Don't you know that some cities are ruled by a tyranny, some by a democracy, and some by an aristocracy?

Of course.

16. *Pancration* was a mixture of boxing and wrestling combined with kicking and strangling. Biting and gouging were forbidden, but pretty well everything else, including breaking and dislocating limbs, was permitted.

And in each city this element is stronger, namely, the ruler?

Certainly.

And each makes laws to its own advantage. Democracy makes democratic laws, tyranny makes tyrannical laws, and so on with the others. And *e* they declare what they have made—what is to their own advantage—to be just for their subjects, and they punish anyone who goes against this as lawless and unjust. This, then, is what I say justice is, the same in all cities, the advantage of the established rule. Since the established rule is *339* surely stronger, anyone who reasons correctly will conclude that the just is the same everywhere, namely, the advantage of the stronger.

Now I see what you mean. Whether it's true or not, I'll try to find out. But you yourself have answered that the just is the advantageous, Thrasymachus, whereas you forbade that answer to me. True, you've added "of the stronger" to it.

And I suppose you think that's an insignificant addition. *b*

It isn't clear yet whether it's significant. But it is clear that we must investigate to see whether or not it's true. I agree that the just is some kind of advantage. But you add that it's *of the stronger*. I don't know about that. We'll have to look into it.

Go ahead and look.

We will. Tell me, don't you also say that it is just to obey the rulers?

I do.

And are the rulers in all cities infallible, or are they liable to error? *c*

No doubt they are liable to error.

When they undertake to make laws, therefore, they make some correctly, others incorrectly?

I suppose so.

And a law is correct if it prescribes what is to the rulers' own advantage and incorrect if it prescribes what is to their disadvantage? Is that what you mean?

It is.

And whatever laws they make must be obeyed by their subjects, and this is justice?

Of course.

Then, according to your account, it is just to do not only what is to the *d* advantage of the stronger, but also the opposite, what is not to their advantage.

What are you saying?

The same as you. But let's examine it more fully. Haven't we agreed that, in giving orders to their subjects, the rulers are sometimes in error as to what is best for themselves, and yet that it is just for their subjects to do whatever their rulers order? Haven't we agreed to that much?

I think so.

e   Then you must also think that you have agreed that it is just to do what is disadvantageous to the rulers and those who are stronger, whenever they unintentionally order what is bad for themselves. But you also say that it is just for the others to obey the orders they give. You're terribly clever, Thrasymachus, but doesn't it necessarily follow that it is just to do the opposite of what you said, since the weaker are then ordered to do what is disadvantageous to the stronger?

340   By god, Socrates, said Polemarchus, that's quite clear.

If you are to be his witness anyway, said Cleitophon, interrupting.

Who needs a witness? Polemarchus replied. Thrasymachus himself agrees that the rulers sometimes order what is bad for themselves and that it is just for the others to do it.

That, Polemarchus, is because Thrasymachus maintained that it is just to obey the orders of the rulers.

He also maintained, Cleitophon, that the advantage of the stronger is
b   just. And having maintained both principles he went on to agree that the stronger sometimes gives orders to those who are weaker than he is—in other words, to his subjects—that are disadvantageous to the stronger himself. From these agreements it follows that what is to the advantage of the stronger is no more just than what is not to his advantage.

But, Cleitophon responded, he said that the advantage of the stronger is what the stronger believes to be his advantage. This is what the weaker must do, and this is what he maintained the just to be.

That isn't what he said, Polemarchus replied.

It makes no difference, Polemarchus, I said. If Thrasymachus wants to
c   put it that way now, let's accept it. Tell me, Thrasymachus, is this what you wanted to say the just is, namely, what the stronger believes to be to his advantage, whether it is in fact to his advantage or not? Is that what we are to say you mean?

Not at all. Do you think I'd call someone who is in error stronger at the very moment he errs?

I did think that was what you meant when you agreed that the rulers aren't infallible but are liable to error.

d   That's because you are a false witness in arguments, Socrates. When someone makes an error in the treatment of patients, do you call him a doctor in regard to that very error? Or when someone makes an error in accounting, do you call him an accountant in regard to that very error in calculation? I think that we express ourselves in words that, taken literally, do say that a doctor is in error, or an accountant, or a grammarian. But
e   each of these, insofar as he is what we call him, never errs, so that, according to the precise account (and you are a stickler for precise ac-

counts), no craftsman ever errs. It's when his knowledge fails him that he makes an error, and in regard to that error he is no craftsman. No craftsman, expert, or ruler makes an error at the moment when he is ruling, even though everyone will say that a physician or a ruler makes errors. It's in this loose way that you must also take the answer I gave earlier. But the most precise answer is this. A ruler, insofar as he is a *341* ruler, never makes errors and unerringly decrees what is best for himself, and this his subject must do. Thus, as I said from the first, it is just to do what is to the advantage of the stronger.

All right, Thrasymachus, so you think I'm a false witness?

You certainly are.

And you think that I asked the questions I did in order to harm you in the argument?

I know it very well, but it won't do you any good. You'll never be able *b* to trick me, so you can't harm me that way, and without trickery you'll never be able to overpower me in argument.

I wouldn't so much as try, Thrasymachus. But in order to prevent this sort of thing from happening again, define clearly whether it is the ruler and stronger in the ordinary sense or in the precise sense whose advantage you said it is just for the weaker to promote as the advantage of the stronger.

I mean the ruler in the most precise sense. Now practice your harm-doing and false witnessing on that if you can—I ask no concessions from you—but you certainly won't be able to.

Do you think that I'm crazy enough to try to shave a lion or to bear false *c* witness against Thrasymachus?

You certainly tried just now, though you were a loser at that too.

Enough of this. Tell me: Is a doctor in the precise sense, whom you mentioned before, a money-maker or someone who treats the sick? Tell me about the one who is really a doctor.

He's the one who treats the sick.

What about a ship's captain? Is a captain in the precise sense a ruler of sailors or a sailor?

A ruler of sailors.

We shouldn't, I think, take into account the fact that he sails in a ship, and he shouldn't be called a sailor for that reason, for it isn't because of *d* his sailing that he is called a ship's captain, but because of his craft and his rule over sailors?

That's true.

And is there something advantageous to each of these, that is, to bodies and to sailors?

Certainly.

And aren't the respective crafts by nature set over them to seek and provide what is to their advantage?

They are.

And is there any advantage for each of the crafts themselves except to be as complete or perfect as possible?

e   What are you asking?

This: If you asked me whether our bodies are sufficient in themselves, or whether they need something else, I'd answer: "They certainly have needs. And because of this, because our bodies are deficient rather than self-sufficient, the craft of medicine has now been discovered. The craft of medicine was developed to provide what is advantageous for a body." Do you think that I'm right in saying this or not?

You are right.

342   Now, is medicine deficient? Does a craft need some further virtue, as the eyes are in need of sight, and the ears of hearing, so that another craft is needed to seek and provide what is advantageous to them?[17] Does a craft itself have some similar deficiency, so that each craft needs another, to seek out what is to its advantage? And does the craft that does the seeking need still another, and so on without end? Or does each seek out *b*   what is to its own advantage by itself? Or does it need neither itself nor another craft to seek out what is advantageous to it, because of its own deficiencies? Or is it that there is no deficiency or error in any craft? That it isn't appropriate for any craft to seek what is to the advantage of anything except that of which it is the craft? And that, since it is itself correct, it is without either fault or impurity, as long as it is wholly and precisely the craft that it is?

Apparently so.

c   Medicine doesn't seek its own advantage, then, but that of the body?

Yes.

And horse-breeding doesn't seek its own advantage, but that of horses? Indeed, no other craft seeks its own advantage—for it has no further needs—but the advantage of that of which it is the craft?

Apparently so.

Now, surely, Thrasymachus, the crafts rule over and are stronger than the things of which they are the crafts?

Very reluctantly, he conceded this as well.

---

17. Sight is the virtue or excellence of the eyes (see 335b n. 12). Without it, the eyes cannot achieve what is advantageous to them, namely, sight. So eyes need some further virtue to seek and provide what is advantageous to them. But Socrates assumes throughout Book I that virtues are crafts (see 332d). Hence he can conclude that the eyes need a further craft to achieve what is advantageous to them.

No kind of knowledge seeks or orders what is advantageous to itself, then, but what is advantageous to the weaker, which is subject to it.   *d*

He tried to fight this conclusion, but he conceded it in the end. And after he had, I said: Surely, then, no doctor, insofar as he is a doctor, seeks or orders what is advantageous to himself, but what is advantageous to his patient? We agreed that a doctor in the precise sense is a ruler of bodies, not a money-maker. Wasn't that agreed?

Yes.

So a ship's captain in the precise sense is a ruler of sailors, not a sailor?

That's what we agreed.   *e*

Doesn't it follow that a ship's captain or ruler won't seek and order what is advantageous to himself, but what is advantageous to a sailor?

He reluctantly agreed.

So, then, Thrasymachus, no one in any position of rule, insofar as he is a ruler, seeks or orders what is advantageous to himself, but what is advantageous to his subjects; the ones of whom he is himself the craftsman. It is to his subjects and what is advantageous and proper to them that he looks, and everything he says and does he says and does for them.

When we reached this point in the argument, and it was clear to all that his account of justice had turned into its opposite, instead of answering,   *343* Thrasymachus said: Tell me, Socrates, do you still have a wet nurse?

What's this? Hadn't you better answer *my* questions rather than asking *me* such things?

Because she's letting you run around with a snotty nose, and doesn't wipe it when she needs to! Why, for all she cares, you don't even know about sheep and shepherds.

Just what is it I don't know?

You think that shepherds and cowherds seek the good of their sheep   *b* and cattle, and fatten them and take care of them, looking to something other than their master's good and their own. Moreover, you believe that rulers in cities—true rulers, that is—think about their subjects differently than one does about sheep, and that night and day they think of something besides their own advantage. You are so far from understanding about   *c* justice and what's just, about injustice and what's unjust, that you don't realize that justice is really the good of another, the advantage of the stronger and the ruler, and harmful to the one who obeys and serves. Injustice is the opposite, it rules the truly simple and just, and those it rules do what is to the advantage of the other and stronger, and they make the one they serve happy, but themselves not at all. You must look at it as follows, my most simple Socrates: A just man always gets less than an   *d* unjust one. First, in their contracts with one another, you'll never find, when the partnership ends, that a just partner has got more than an unjust

one, but less. Second, in matters relating to the city, when taxes are to be paid, a just man pays more on the same property, an unjust one less, but when the city is giving out refunds, a just man gets nothing, while an
e   unjust one makes a large profit. Finally, when each of them holds a ruling position in some public office, a just person, even if he isn't penalized in other ways, finds that his private affairs deteriorate because he has to neglect them, that he gains no advantage from the public purse because of his justice, and that he's hated by his relatives and acquaintances when he's unwilling to do them an unjust favor. The opposite is true of an unjust man in every respect. Therefore, I repeat what I said before: A person of
344 great power outdoes everyone else.[18] Consider him if you want to figure out how much more advantageous it is for the individual to be just rather than unjust. You'll understand this most easily if you turn your thoughts to the most complete injustice, the one that makes the doer of injustice happiest and the sufferers of it, who are unwilling to do injustice, most wretched. This is tyranny, which through stealth or force appropriates the property of others, whether sacred or profane, public or private, not little by little, but all at once. If someone commits only one part of injustice
b   and is caught, he's punished and greatly reproached—such partly unjust people are called temple-robbers,[19] kidnappers, housebreakers, robbers, and thieves when they commit these crimes. But when someone, in addition to appropriating their possessions, kidnaps and enslaves the citizens as well, instead of these shameful names he is called happy and blessed,
c   not only by the citizens themselves, but by all who learn that he has done the whole of injustice. Those who reproach injustice do so because they are afraid not of doing it but of suffering it. So, Socrates, injustice, if it is on a large enough scale, is stronger, freer, and more masterly than justice. And, as I said from the first, justice is what is advantageous to the stronger, while injustice is to one's own profit and advantage.
d   Having emptied this great flood of words into our ears all at once like a bath attendant, Thrasymachus intended to leave. But those present didn't let him and made him stay to give an account of what he had said. I too begged him to stay, and I said to him: After hurling such a speech at us, Thrasymachus, do you intend to leave before adequately instructing

18. Outdoing (*pleonektein*) is an important notion in the remainder of the *Republic*. It is connected to *pleonexia*, which is what one succumbs to when one always wants to outdo everyone else by getting and having more and more. *Pleonexia* is, or is the cause of, injustice (359c), since always wanting to outdo others leads one to try to get what belongs to them, what isn't *one's own*. It is contrasted with *doing or having one's own*, which is, or is the cause of, justice (434a, 441e).

19. The temples acted as public treasuries, so that a temple robber is the equivalent of a present-day bank robber.

us or finding out whether you are right or not? Or do you think it a small   *e*
matter to determine which whole way of life would make living most
worthwhile for each of us?

Is *that* what I seem to you to think? Thrasymachus said.

Either that, or else you care nothing for us and aren't worried about
whether we'll live better or worse lives because of our ignorance of what
you say you know. So show some willingness to teach it to us. It wouldn't
be a bad investment for you to be the benefactor of a group as large as
ours. For my own part, I'll tell you that I am not persuaded. I don't believe   *345*
that injustice is more profitable than justice, not even if you give it full
scope and put no obstacles in its way. Suppose that there *is* an unjust
person, and suppose he *does* have the power to do injustice, whether by
trickery or open warfare; nonetheless, he doesn't persuade me that injustice is more profitable than justice. Perhaps someone here, besides myself,   *b*
feels the same as I do. So come now, and persuade us that we are wrong
to esteem justice more highly than injustice in planning our lives.

And how am I to persuade you, if you aren't persuaded by what I said
just now? What more can I do? Am I to take my argument and pour it into
your very soul?

God forbid! Don't do that! But, first, stick to what you've said, and
then, if you change your position, do it openly and don't deceive us. You
see, Thrasymachus, that having defined the true doctor—to continue
examining the things you said before—you didn't consider it necessary   *c*
later to keep a precise guard on the true shepherd. You think that, insofar
as he's a shepherd, he fattens sheep, not looking to what is best for the
sheep but to a banquet, like a guest about to be entertained at a feast, or
to a future sale, like a money-maker rather than a shepherd. Shepherding
is concerned only to provide what is best for the things it is set over, and   *d*
it is itself adequately provided with all it needs to be at its best when it
doesn't fall short in any way of being the craft of shepherding. That's why
I thought it necessary for us to agree before[20] that every kind of rule,
insofar as it rules, doesn't seek anything other than what is best for the
things it rules and cares for, and this is true both of public and private
kinds of rule. But do you think that those who rule cities, the true rulers,   *e*
rule willingly?

I don't think it, by god, I know it.

But, Thrasymachus, don't you realize that in other kinds of rule no one
wants to rule for its own sake, but they ask for pay, thinking that their
ruling will benefit not themselves but their subjects? Tell me, doesn't
every craft differ from every other in having a different function? Please   *346*

20. See 341e–342e.

don't answer contrary to what you believe, so that we can come to some definite conclusion.

Yes, that's what differentiates them.

And each craft benefits us in its own peculiar way, different from the others. For example, medicine gives us health, navigation gives us safety while sailing, and so on with the others?

Certainly.

And wage-earning gives us wages, for this is its function? Or would you
b call medicine the same as navigation? Indeed, if you want to define matters precisely, as you proposed, even if someone who is a ship's captain becomes healthy because sailing is advantageous to his health, you wouldn't for that reason call his craft medicine?

Certainly not.

Nor would you call wage-earning medicine, even if someone becomes healthy while earning wages?

Certainly not.

Nor would you call medicine wage-earning, even if someone earns pay while healing?
c No.

We are agreed, then, that each craft brings its own peculiar benefit?

It does.

Then whatever benefit all craftsmen receive in common must clearly result from their joint practice of some additional craft that benefits each of them?

So it seems.

And we say that the additional craft in question, which benefits the craftsmen by earning them wages, is the craft of wage-earning?

He reluctantly agreed.

Then this benefit, receiving wages, doesn't result from their own craft,
d but rather, if we're to examine this precisely, medicine provides health, and wage-earning provides wages; house-building provides a house, and wage-earning, which accompanies it, provides a wage; and so on with the other crafts. Each of them does its own work and benefits the things it is set over. So, if wages aren't added, is there any benefit that the craftsman gets from his craft?

Apparently none.
e But he still provides a benefit when he works for nothing?

Yes, I think he does.

Then, it is clear now, Thrasymachus, that no craft or rule provides for its own advantage, but, as we've been saying for some time, it provides and orders for its subject and aims at its advantage, that of the weaker, not of the stronger. That's why I said just now, Thrasymachus, that no one willingly chooses to rule and to take other people's troubles in hand and straighten them out, but each asks for wages; for anyone who intends *347* to practice his craft well never does or orders what is best for himself— at least not when he orders as his craft prescribes—but what is best for his subject. It is because of this, it seems, that wages must be provided to a person if he's to be willing to rule, whether in the form of money or honor or a penalty if he refuses.

What do you mean, Socrates? said Glaucon. I know the first two kinds of wages, but I don't understand what penalty you mean or how you can call it a wage.

Then you don't understand the best people's kind of wages, the kind that moves the most decent to rule, when they are willing to rule at all. Don't you know that the love of honor and the love of money are despised,   *b* and rightly so?

I do.

Therefore good people won't be willing to rule for the sake of either money or honor. They don't want to be paid wages openly for ruling and get called hired hands, nor to take them in secret from their rule and be called thieves. And they won't rule for the sake of honor, because they aren't ambitious honor-lovers. So, if they're to be willing to rule, some   *c* compulsion or punishment must be brought to bear on them—perhaps that's why it is thought shameful to seek to rule before one is compelled to. Now, the greatest punishment, if one isn't willing to rule, is to be ruled by someone worse than oneself. And I think that it's fear of this that makes decent people rule when they do. They approach ruling not as something good or something to be enjoyed, but as something necessary, since it can't be entrusted to anyone better than—or even as good as—themselves.   *d* In a city of good men, if it came into being, the citizens would fight in order *not to rule*, just as they do now in order to rule. There it would be quite clear that anyone who is really a true ruler doesn't by nature seek his own advantage but that of his subjects. And everyone, knowing this, would rather be benefited by others than take the trouble to benefit them. So I can't at all agree with Thrasymachus that justice is the advantage of the stronger—but we'll look further into that another time. What   *e* Thrasymachus is now saying—that the life of an unjust person is better than that of a just one—seems to be of far greater importance. Which life would you choose, Glaucon? And which of our views do you consider truer?

I certainly think that the life of a just person is more profitable.

Did you hear all of the good things Thrasymachus listed a moment ago *348* for the unjust life?

I heard, but I wasn't persuaded.

Then, do you want us to persuade him, if we're able to find a way, that what he says isn't true?

Of course I do.

If we oppose him with a parallel speech about the blessings of the just life, and then he replies, and then we do, we'd have to count and measure the good things mentioned on each side, and we'd need a jury to decide

b   the case. But if, on the other hand, we investigate the question, as we've been doing, by seeking agreement with each other, we ourselves can be both jury and advocates at once.

Certainly.

Which approach do you prefer? I asked.

The second.

Come, then, Thrasymachus, I said, answer us from the beginning. You say that complete injustice is more profitable than complete justice?

c   I certainly do say that, and I've told you why.

Well, then, what do you say about this? Do you call one of the two a virtue and the other a vice?

Of course.

That is to say, you call justice a virtue and injustice a vice?

That's hardly likely, since I say that injustice is profitable and justice isn't.

Then, what exactly do you say?

The opposite.

That justice is a vice?

No, just very high-minded simplicity.

d   Then do you call being unjust being low-minded?

No, I call it good judgment.

You consider unjust people, then, Thrasymachus, to be clever and good?

Yes, those who are completely unjust, who can bring cities and whole communities under their power. Perhaps, you think I meant pickpockets? Not that such crimes aren't also profitable, if they're not found out, but they aren't worth mentioning by comparison to what I'm talking about.

e   I'm not unaware of what you want to say. But I wonder about this: Do you really include injustice with virtue and wisdom, and justice with their opposites?

I certainly do.

That's harder, and it isn't easy now to know what to say. If you had declared that injustice is more profitable, but agreed that it is a vice or shameful, as some others do, we could have discussed the matter on the basis of conventional beliefs. But now, obviously, you'll say that injustice is fine and strong and apply to it all the attributes we used to apply to

349 justice, since you dare to include it with virtue and wisdom.

You've divined my views exactly.

Nonetheless, we mustn't shrink from pursuing the argument and look- ing into this, just as long as I take you to be saying what you really think. And I believe that you aren't joking now, Thrasymachus, but are saying what you believe to be the truth.

What difference does it make to you, whether *I* believe it or not? It's *my account* you're supposed to be refuting.

It makes no difference. But try to answer this further question: Do you think that a just person wants to outdo[21] someone else who's just?   b

Not at all, for he wouldn't then be as polite and innocent as he is.

Or to outdo someone who does a just action?

No, he doesn't even want to do that.

And does he claim that he deserves to outdo an unjust person and believe that it is just for him to do so, or doesn't he believe that?

He'd want to outdo him, and he'd claim to deserve to do so, but he wouldn't be able.

That's not what I asked, but whether a just person wants to outdo an unjust person but not a just one, thinking that this is what he deserves?   c

He does.

What about an unjust person? Does he claim that he deserves to outdo a just person or someone who does a just action?

Of course he does; he thinks he deserves to outdo everyone.

Then will an unjust person also outdo an *unjust* person or someone who does an *unjust* action, and will he strive to get the most he can for himself from everyone?

He will.

Then, let's put it this way: A just person doesn't outdo someone like himself but someone unlike himself, whereas an unjust person outdoes both like and unlike.   d

Very well put.

An unjust person is clever and good, and a just one is neither?

That's well put, too.

It follows, then, that an unjust person is like clever and good people, while the other isn't?

Of course that's so. How could he fail to be like them when he has their qualities, while the other isn't like them?

Fine. Then each of them has the qualities of the people he's like?

Of course.

All right, Thrasymachus. Do you call one person musical and another   e
nonmusical?

I do.

21. *Pleon echein.* See 344a n. 18.

Which of them is clever in music, and which isn't?

The musical one is clever, of course, and the other isn't.

And the things he's clever in, he's good in, and the things he isn't clever in, he's bad in?

Yes.

Isn't the same true of a doctor?

It is.

Do you think that a musician, in tuning his lyre and in tightening and loosening the strings, wants to outdo another musician, claiming that this is what he deserves?[22]

I do not.

But he does want to outdo a nonmusician?

Necessarily.

What about a doctor? Does he, when prescribing food and drink, want
350 to outdo another doctor or someone who does the action that medicine prescribes?

Certainly not.

But he does want to outdo a nondoctor?

Yes.

In any branch of knowledge or ignorance, do you think that a knowledgeable person would intentionally try to outdo other knowledgeable people or say something better or different than they do, rather than doing or saying the very same thing as those like him?

Well, perhaps it must be as you say.

And what about an ignorant person? Doesn't he want to outdo both a
b   knowledgeable person and an ignorant one?

Probably.

A knowledgeable person is clever?

I agree.

And a clever one is good?

I agree.

Therefore, a good and clever person doesn't want to outdo those like himself but those who are unlike him and his opposite.

So it seems.

But a bad and ignorant person wants to outdo both his like and his opposite.

---

22. Socrates' point may seem obscure, but what he has in mind is explained at 350a. All expert musicians try to get the same thing, perfect harmony, so they tighten and loosen their strings to exactly the same degree, namely, the one that will produce the right pitch. In the same way, all doctors who are masters of medicine prescribe the same diet for people with the same diseases, namely, the one that will best restore them to health.

Apparently.

Now, Thrasymachus, we found that an unjust person tries to outdo those like him and those unlike him? Didn't you say that?

I did.

And that a just person won't outdo his like but his unlike? *c*

Yes.

Then, a just person is like a clever and good one, and an unjust is like an ignorant and bad one.

It looks that way.

Moreover, we agreed that each has the qualities of the one he resembles.

Yes, we did.

Then, a just person has turned out to be good and clever, and an unjust one ignorant and bad.

Thrasymachus agreed to all this, not easily as I'm telling it, but reluctantly, with toil, trouble, and—since it was summer—a quantity of sweat *d* that was a wonder to behold. And then I saw something I'd never seen before—Thrasymachus blushing. But, in any case, after we'd agreed that justice is virtue and wisdom and that injustice is vice and ignorance, I said: All right, let's take that as established. But we also said that injustice is powerful, or don't you remember that, Thrasymachus?

I remember, but I'm not satisfied with what you're now saying. I could make a speech about it, but, if I did, I know that you'd accuse me of engaging in oratory. So either allow me to speak, or, if you want to ask *e* questions, go ahead, and I'll say, "All right," and nod yes and no, as one does to old wives' tales.

Don't do that, contrary to your own opinion.

I'll answer so as to please you, since you won't let me make a speech. What else do you want?

Nothing, by god. But if that's what you're going to do, go ahead and do it. I'll ask my questions.

Ask ahead.

I'll ask what I asked before, so that we may proceed with our argument *351* about justice and injustice in an orderly fashion, for surely it was claimed that injustice is stronger and more powerful than justice. But, now, if justice is indeed wisdom and virtue, it will easily be shown to be stronger than injustice, since injustice is ignorance (no one could now be ignorant of that). However, I don't want to state the matter so unconditionally, Thrasymachus, but to look into it in some such way as this. Would you *b* say that it is unjust for a city to try to enslave other cities unjustly and to hold them in subjection when it has enslaved many of them?

Of course, that's what the best city will especially do, the one that is most completely unjust.

I understand that's your position, but the point I want to examine is this: Will the city that becomes stronger than another achieve this power without justice, or will it need the help of justice?

c   If what you said a moment ago stands, and justice is cleverness or wisdom, it will need the help of justice, but if things are as I stated, it will need the help of injustice.

I'm impressed, Thrasymachus, that you don't merely nod yes or no but give very fine answers.

That's because I'm trying to please you.

You're doing well at it, too. So please me some more by answering this question: Do you think that a city, an army, a band of robbers or thieves, or any other tribe with a common unjust purpose would be able to achieve it if they were unjust to each other?

d   No, indeed.

What if they weren't unjust to one another? Would they achieve more?
Certainly.

Injustice, Thrasymachus, causes civil war, hatred, and fighting among themselves, while justice brings friendship and a sense of common purpose. Isn't that so?

Let it be so, in order not to disagree with you.

You're still doing well on that front. So tell me this: If the effect of injustice is to produce hatred wherever it occurs, then, whenever it arises, whether among free men or slaves, won't it cause them to hate one another, engage in civil war, and prevent them from achieving any common
e   purpose?

Certainly.

What if it arises between two people? Won't they be at odds, hate each other, and be enemies to one another and to just people?

They will.

Does injustice lose its power to cause dissension when it arises within a single individual, or will it preserve it intact?

Let it preserve it intact.

Apparently, then, injustice has the power, first, to make whatever it arises in—whether it is a city, a family, an army, or anything else—
352 incapable of achieving anything as a unit, because of the civil wars and differences it creates, and, second, it makes that unit an enemy to itself and to what is in every way its opposite, namely, justice. Isn't that so?

Certainly.

And even in a single individual, it has by its nature the very same effect. First, it makes him incapable of achieving anything, because he is in a state of civil war and not of one mind; second, it makes him his own enemy, as well as the enemy of just people. Hasn't it that effect?

Yes.

And the gods too are just?

Let it be so.

So an unjust person is also an enemy of the gods, Thrasymachus, while   *b*
a just person is their friend?

Enjoy your banquet of words! Have no fear, I won't oppose you. That
would make these people hate me.

Come, then, complete the banquet for me by continuing to answer as
you've been doing. We have shown that just people are cleverer and more
capable of doing things, while unjust ones aren't even able to act together,
for when we speak of a powerful achievement by unjust men acting   *c*
together, what we say isn't altogether true. They would never have been
able to keep their hands off each other if they were completely unjust. But
clearly there must have been some sort of justice in them that at least
prevented them from doing injustice among themselves at the same time
as they were doing it to others. And it was this that enabled them to achieve
what they did. When they started doing unjust things, they were only
halfway corrupted by their injustice (for those who are all bad and completely unjust are completely incapable of accomplishing anything). These
are the things I understand to hold, not the ones you first maintained. We
must now examine, as we proposed before,[23] whether just people also live   *d*
better and are happier than unjust ones. I think it's clear already that this
is so, but we must look into it further, since the argument concerns no
ordinary topic but the way we ought to live.

Go ahead and look.

I will. Tell me, do you think there is such a thing as the function of a
horse?

I do.   *e*

And would you define the function of a horse or of anything else as that
which one can do only with it or best with it?

I don't understand.

Let me put it this way: Is it possible to see with anything other than
eyes?

Certainly not.

Or to hear with anything other than ears?

No.

Then, we are right to say that seeing and hearing are the functions of
eyes and ears?

Of course.

23. See 347e.

What about this? Could you use a dagger or a carving knife or lots of
353 other things in pruning a vine?

Of course.

But wouldn't you do a finer job with a pruning knife designed for the
purpose than with anything else?

You would.

Then shall we take pruning to be its function?

Yes.

Now, I think you'll understand what I was asking earlier when I asked
whether the function of each thing is what it alone can do or what it does
better than anything else.

b I understand, and I think that this is the function of each.

All right. Does each thing to which a particular function is assigned
also have a virtue?[24] Let's go over the same ground again. We say that eyes
have some function?

They do.

So there is also a virtue of eyes?

There is.

And ears have a function?

Yes.

So there is also a virtue of ears?

There is.

And all other things are the same, aren't they?

They are.

c And could eyes perform their function well if they lacked their peculiar
virtue and had the vice instead?

How could they, for don't you mean if they had blindness instead of
sight?

Whatever their virtue is, for I'm not now asking about that but about
whether anything that has a function performs it well by means of its own
peculiar virtue and badly by means of its vice?

That's true, it does.

So ears, too, deprived of their own virtue, perform their function badly?

That's right.

d And the same could be said about everything else?

So it seems.

Come, then, and let's consider this: Is there some function of a soul
that you couldn't perform with anything else, for example, taking care of
things, ruling, deliberating, and the like? Is there anything other than a

24. See 335b n. 12.

soul to which you could rightly assign these, and say that they are its peculiar function?

No, none of them.

What of living? Isn't that a function of a soul?

It certainly is.

And don't we also say that there is a virtue of a soul?

We do.

Then, will a soul ever perform its function well, Thrasymachus, if it is *e* deprived of its own peculiar virtue, or is that impossible?

It's impossible.

Doesn't it follow, then, that a bad soul rules and takes care of things badly and that a good soul does all these things well?

It does.

Now, we agreed that justice is a soul's virtue, and injustice its vice?

We did.

Then, it follows that a just soul and a just man will live well, and an unjust one badly.

Apparently so, according to your argument.

And surely anyone who lives well is blessed and happy, and anyone who *354* doesn't is the opposite.

Of course.

Therefore, a just person is happy, and an unjust one wretched.

So be it.

It profits no one to be wretched but to be happy.

Of course.

And so, Thrasymachus, injustice is never more profitable than justice.

Let that be your banquet, Socrates, at the feast of Bendis.

Given by you, Thrasymachus, after you became gentle and ceased to give me rough treatment. Yet I haven't had a fine banquet. But that's my fault not yours. I seem to have behaved like a glutton, snatching at every *b* dish that passes and tasting it before properly savoring its predecessor. Before finding the answer to our first inquiry about what justice is, I let that go and turned to investigate whether it is a kind of vice and ignorance or a kind of wisdom and virtue. Then an argument came up about injustice being more profitable than justice, and I couldn't refrain from abandoning the previous one and following up on that. Hence the result of the discussion, as far as I'm concerned, is that I know nothing, for when I don't *c* know what justice is, I'll hardly know whether it is a kind of virtue or not, or whether a person who has it is happy or unhappy.

BOOK II

Glaucon introduces a sophisticated division of goods into three classes and asks Socrates to which class justice belongs. Socrates places it in the highest class, consisting of things valued both because of themselves and because of their consequences (357a–358a). This conflicts with the general view that justice belongs in the lowest class, consisting of things harsh in themselves and valued only for their consequences. It is this view that Glaucon, with the help of Adeimantus, challenges Socrates to defeat. He is to show that justice itself (justice stripped of its consequences) makes its possessor happier than injustice itself (injustice stripped of its consequences), for this is what the general view denies. Socrates does not complete his response to this challenge until the end of Book IX.

The first step in his response is to shift the debate from individual justice to political justice. He will construct an ideal or completely good polis *or* city—the kallipolis—in theory, knowing, on the basis of the argument that concludes Book I, that such a city would have to be completely virtuous and so completely just (352d–354a). Having located justice in that city, he will then look for it in the soul. If the same thing is justice in both, he will feel secure that what he has identified in them is indeed justice (434d–435a).*

The construction of the ideal city proceeds in stages. Socrates first introduces a city of people—the first city—whose souls are ruled by their necessary appetites (defined at 558d–559c). That is why they eat, drink, and have sex (372a–c), but neither fight for honor nor philosophize to come to know the truth. But this city is not, given human psychology, a real possibility, for unnecessary appetites exist in all of us by nature (571b). The introduction of the second stage in the construction of the kallipolis—the luxurious city—seems to be introduced to make this point (373a, b, d).

The result of the introduction of unnecessary appetites is war, both civil and intercity (373d–e). To prevent this from destroying the kallipolis, soldier-police are needed to constrain both internal and external enemies (414b): These are the guardians. And like all the citizens of the kallipolis, they must specialize in their job, for Socrates argues that a completely good city would require all its members to specialize in the one craft for which they have the highest natural aptitude (see 370a–b, 374a–c, 394e, 423c–d, 433a, 443b, 453b).

The natural assets that a good guardian needs and the education he must have

32

to develop them in the best possible way are, therefore, the next topic. The almost exclusively "moral" focus of the discussion is at first somewhat difficult to justify or understand. But if one asks oneself, What sort of soldier-police would I want to have in the city of which I was a citizen? this focus becomes more readily intelligible, for who would want to live in a city whose soldier-police were unjust and intemperate cowards?

The appropriate basic education for future guardians, Socrates claims, is the traditional one consisting of music and poetry, on the one hand, and physical training, on the other.[1] Since education in music and poetry begins before physical training, its content—more specifically the kinds of stories that the future guardians should hear about gods and heroes—is his first topic (377e). His discussion of it continues into Book III.

When I said this, I thought I had done with the discussion, but it turned out to have been only a prelude. Glaucon showed his characteristic courage *357* on this occasion too and refused to accept Thrasymachus' abandonment of the argument. Socrates, he said, do you want to seem to have persuaded us that it is better in every way to be just than unjust, or do you want truly to convince us of this?   *b*

I want truly to convince you, I said, if I can.

Well, then, you certainly aren't doing what you want. Tell me, do you think there is a kind of good we welcome, not because we desire what comes from it, but because we welcome it for its own sake—joy, for example, and all the harmless pleasures that have no results beyond the joy of having them?

Certainly, I think there are such things.

And is there a kind of good we like for its own sake and also for the sake of what comes from it—knowing, for example, and seeing and being   *c* healthy? We welcome such things, I suppose, on both counts.

Yes.

And do you also see a third kind of good, such as physical training, medical treatment when sick, medicine itself, and the other ways of making money? We'd say that these are onerous but beneficial to us, and we wouldn't choose them for their own sakes, but for the sake of the rewards and other things that come from them.   *d*

---

1. "Music" or "music and poetry" and "physical training" are more transliterations than translations of *mousikē* and *gymnastikē*, which have no English equivalents. It is clear from Plato's discussion, for example, that *mousikē* includes poetry and stories, as well as music proper, and that *gymnastikē* includes dance and training in warfare, as well as what we call physical training. The aims of *mousikē* and *gymnastikē* are characterized at 522a. For further discussion see F.A.G. Beck, *Greek Education 430–350 B.C.* (London: Methuen, 1964).

There is also this third kind. But what of it?

Where do you put justice?

I myself put it among the finest goods, as something to be valued by
358 anyone who is going to be blessed with happiness, both because of itself
and because of what comes from it.

That isn't most people's opinion. They'd say that justice belongs to the
onerous kind, and is to be practiced for the sake of the rewards and
popularity that come from a reputation for justice, but is to be avoided
because of itself as something burdensome.

I know that's the general opinion. Thrasymachus faulted justice on
these grounds a moment ago and praised injustice, but it seems that I'm
a slow learner.

b   Come, then, and listen to me as well, and see whether you still have
that problem, for I think that Thrasymachus gave up before he had to,
charmed by you as if he were a snake. But I'm not yet satisfied by the
argument on either side. I want to know what justice and injustice are and
what power each itself has when it's by itself in the soul. I want to leave
out of account their rewards and what comes from each of them. So, if
you agree, I'll renew the argument of Thrasymachus. First, I'll state what
c   kind of thing people consider justice to be and what its origins are. Second,
I'll argue that all who practice it do so unwillingly, as something necessary,
not as something good. Third, I'll argue that they have good reason to act
as they do, for the life of an unjust person is, they say, much better than
that of a just one.

It isn't, Socrates, that I believe any of that myself. I'm perplexed, indeed,
and my ears are deafened listening to Thrasymachus and countless others.
But I've yet to hear anyone defend justice in the way I want, proving that
d   it is better than injustice. I want to hear it praised *by itself*, and I think that
I'm most likely to hear this from you. Therefore, I'm going to speak at
length in praise of the unjust life, and in doing so I'll show you the way
I want to hear you praising justice and denouncing injustice. But see
whether you want me to do that or not.

I want that most of all. Indeed, what subject could someone with any
understanding enjoy discussing more often?

e   Excellent. Then let's discuss the first subject I mentioned—what justice
is and what its origins are.

They say that to do injustice is naturally good and to suffer injustice
bad, but that the badness of suffering it so far exceeds the goodness of
doing it that those who have done and suffered injustice and tasted both,
but who lack the power to do it and avoid suffering it, decide that it is
359 profitable to come to an agreement with each other neither to do injustice
nor to suffer it. As a result, they begin to make laws and covenants, and

what the law commands they call lawful and just. This, they say, is the origin and essence of justice. It is intermediate between the best and the worst. The best is to do injustice without paying the penalty; the worst is to suffer it without being able to take revenge. Justice is a mean between these two extremes. People value it not as a good but because they are too weak to do injustice with impunity. Someone who has the power to do this, however, and is a true man wouldn't make an agreement with anyone   b not to do injustice in order not to suffer it. For him that would be madness. This is the nature of justice, according to the argument, Socrates, and these are its natural origins.

We can see most clearly that those who practice justice do it unwillingly and because they lack the power to do injustice, if in our thoughts we   c grant to a just and an unjust person the freedom to do whatever they like. We can then follow both of them and see where their desires would lead. And we'll catch the just person red-handed travelling the same road as the unjust. The reason for this is the desire to outdo others and get more and more.[2] This is what anyone's nature naturally pursues as good, but nature is forced by law into the perversion of treating fairness with respect.

The freedom I mentioned would be most easily realized if both people had the power they say the ancestor of Gyges of Lydia possessed. The story goes that he was a shepherd in the service of the ruler of Lydia.   d There was a violent thunderstorm, and an earthquake broke open the ground and created a chasm at the place where he was tending his sheep. Seeing this, he was filled with amazement and went down into it. And there, in addition to many other wonders of which we're told, he saw a hollow bronze horse. There were windowlike openings in it, and, peeping in, he saw a corpse, which seemed to be of more than human size, wearing nothing but a gold ring on its finger. He took the ring and came out of   e the chasm. He wore the ring at the usual monthly meeting that reported to the king on the state of the flocks. And as he was sitting among the others, he happened to turn the setting of the ring towards himself to the inside of his hand. When he did this, he became invisible to those sitting near him, and they went on talking as if he had gone. He wondered at   360 this, and, fingering the ring, he turned the setting outwards again and became visible. So he experimented with the ring to test whether it indeed had this power—and it did. If he turned the setting inward, he became invisible; if he turned it outward, he became visible again. When he realized this, he at once arranged to become one of the messengers sent to report to the king. And when he arrived there, he seduced the king's

2. *Pleonexian.* See 343e n. 18.

b wife, attacked the king with her help, killed him, and took over the kingdom.

Let's suppose, then, that there were two such rings, one worn by a just and the other by an unjust person. Now, no one, it seems, would be so incorruptible that he would stay on the path of justice or stay away from other people's property, when he could take whatever he wanted from the marketplace with impunity, go into people's houses and have sex with
c anyone he wished, kill or release from prison anyone he wished, and do all the other things that would make him like a god among humans. Rather his actions would be in no way different from those of an unjust person, and both would follow the same path. This, some would say, is a great proof that one is never just willingly but only when compelled to be. No one believes justice to be a good when it is kept private, since, wherever either person thinks he can do injustice with impunity, he does it. Indeed, every man believes that injustice is far more profitable to himself than
d justice. And any exponent of this argument will say he's right, for someone who didn't want to do injustice, given this sort of opportunity, and who didn't touch other people's property would be thought wretched and stupid by everyone aware of the situation, though, of course, they'd praise him in public, deceiving each other for fear of suffering injustice. So much for my second topic.

As for the choice between the lives we're discussing, we'll be able to
e make a correct judgment about that only if we separate the most just and the most unjust. Otherwise we won't be able to do it. Here's the separation I have in mind. We'll subtract nothing from the injustice of an unjust person and nothing from the justice of a just one, but we'll take each to be complete in his own way of life. First, therefore, we must suppose that an unjust person will act as clever craftsmen do: A first-rate captain or
361 doctor, for example, knows the difference between what his craft can and can't do. He attempts the first but lets the second go by, and if he happens to slip, he can put things right. In the same way, an unjust person's successful attempts at injustice must remain undetected, if he is to be fully unjust. Anyone who is caught should be thought inept, for the extreme of injustice is to be believed to be just without being just. And our completely unjust person must be given complete injustice; nothing may be subtracted from it. We must allow that, while doing the greatest injustice, he has nonetheless provided himself with the greatest reputation for justice. If
b he happens to make a slip, he must be able to put it right. If any of his unjust activities should be discovered, he must be able to speak persuasively or to use force. And if force is needed, he must have the help of courage and strength and of the substantial wealth and friends with which he has provided himself.

Having hypothesized such a person, let's now in our argument put beside him a just man, who is simple and noble and who, as Aeschylus says, doesn't want to be believed to be good but to be so.[3] We must take away his reputation, for a reputation for justice would bring him honor   *c* and rewards, so that it wouldn't be clear whether he is just for the sake of justice itself or for the sake of those honors and rewards. We must strip him of everything except justice and make his situation the opposite of an unjust person's. Though he does no injustice, he must have the greatest reputation for it, so that his justice may be tested full-strength and not diluted by wrong-doing and what comes from it. Let him stay like that unchanged until he dies—just, but all his life believed to be unjust. In this   *d* way, both will reach the extremes, the one of justice and the other of injustice, and we'll be able to judge which of them is happier.

Whew! Glaucon, I said, how vigorously you've scoured each of the men for our competition, just as you would a pair of statues for an art competition.

I do the best I can, he replied. Since the two are as I've described, in any case, it shouldn't be difficult to complete the account of the kind of life that awaits each of them, but it must be done. And if what I say sounds crude, Socrates, remember that it isn't I who speak but those who praise   *e* injustice at the expense of justice. They'll say that a just person in such circumstances will be whipped, stretched on a rack, chained, blinded with fire, and, at the end, when he has suffered every kind of evil, he'll be impaled, and will realize then that one shouldn't want to be just but to be believed to be just. Indeed, Aeschylus' words are far more correctly applied   *362* to unjust people than to just ones, for the supporters of injustice will say that a really unjust person, having a way of life based on the truth about things and not living in accordance with opinion, doesn't want simply to be believed to be unjust but actually to be so—

Harvesting a deep furrow in his mind,
Where wise counsels propagate.   *b*

He rules his city because of his reputation for justice; he marries into any family he wishes; he gives his children in marriage to anyone he wishes; he has contracts and partnerships with anyone he wants; and besides benefiting himself in all these ways, he profits because he has no scruples about doing injustice. In any contest, public or private, he's the winner

---

3. In *Seven Against Thebes*, 592–94, it is said of Amphiaraus that "he did not wish to be believed to be the best but to be it." The passage continues with the words Glaucon quotes below at 362a–b.

and outdoes[4] his enemies. And by outdoing them, he becomes wealthy, benefiting his friends and harming his enemies. He makes adequate
c   sacrifices to the gods and sets up magnificent offerings to them. He takes better care of the gods, therefore, (and, indeed, of the human beings he's fond of) than a just person does. Hence it's likely that the gods, in turn, will take better care of him than of a just person. That's what they say, Socrates, that gods and humans provide a better life for unjust people than for just ones.

d   When Glaucon had said this, I had it in mind to respond, but his brother Adeimantus intervened: You surely don't think that the position has been adequately stated?

Why not? I said.

The most important thing to say hasn't been said yet.

Well, then, I replied, a man's brother must stand by him, as the saying goes.[5] If Glaucon has omitted something, you must help him. Yet what he has said is enough to throw me to the canvas and make me unable to come to the aid of justice.

Nonsense, he said. Hear what more I have to say, for we should also fully explore the arguments that are opposed to the ones Glaucon gave,
e   the ones that praise justice and find fault with injustice, so that what I take to be his intention may be clearer.

When fathers speak to their sons, they say that one must be just, as do all the others who have charge of anyone. But they don't praise justice
363 itself, only the high reputations it leads to and the consequences of being thought to be just, such as the public offices, marriages, and other things Glaucon listed. But they elaborate even further on the consequences of reputation. By bringing in the esteem of the gods, they are able to talk about the abundant good things that they themselves and the noble Hesiod and Homer say that the gods give to the pious,[6] for Hesiod says that the
b   gods make the oak trees

> Bear acorns at the top and bees in the middle
> And make fleecy sheep heavy laden with wool

for the just, and tells of many other good things akin to these. And Homer is similar:

> When a good king, in his piety,
> Upholds justice, the black earth bears

---

4. *pleonektein.* See 343e n. 18.

5. See Homer, *Odyssey* 16.97–98.

6. The two quotations which follow are from Hesiod, *Works and Days* 332–33, and Homer, *Odyssey* 19.109.

Wheat and barley for him, and his trees are heavy with fruit.   *c*
His sheep bear lambs unfailingly, and the sea yields up its fish.

Musaeus and his son make the gods give the just more headstrong goods than these.[7] In their stories, they lead the just to Hades, seat them on couches, provide them with a symposium of pious people, crown them with wreaths, and make them spend all their time drinking—as if they thought drunkenness was the finest wage of virtue. Others stretch even   *d* further the wages that virtue receives from the gods, for they say that someone who is pious and keeps his promises leaves his children's children and a whole race behind him. In these and other similar ways, they praise justice. They bury the impious and unjust in mud in Hades; force them to carry water in a sieve; bring them into bad repute while they're still alive, and all those penalties that Glaucon gave to the just person they give to the unjust. But they have nothing else to say. This, then, is the way   *e* people praise justice and find fault with injustice.

Besides this, Socrates, consider another form of argument about justice and injustice employed both by private individuals and by poets. All go on repeating with one voice that justice and moderation are fine things, but hard and onerous, while licentiousness and injustice are sweet and easy   *364* to acquire and are shameful only in opinion and law. They add that unjust deeds are for the most part more profitable than just ones, and, whether in public or private, they willingly honor vicious people who have wealth and other types of power and declare them to be happy. But they dishonor and disregard the weak and the poor, even though they agree that they are better than the others.   *b*

But the most wonderful of all these arguments concerns what they have to say about the gods and virtue. They say that the gods, too, assign misfortune and a bad life to many good people, and the opposite fate to their opposites. Begging priests and prophets frequent the doors of the rich and persuade them that they possess a god-given power founded on sacrifices and incantations. If the rich person or any of his ancestors has   *c* committed an injustice, they can fix it with pleasant rituals. Moreover, if he wishes to injure some enemy, then, at little expense, he'll be able to harm just and unjust alike, for by means of spells and enchantments they can persuade the gods to serve them. And the poets are brought forward as witnesses to all these accounts. Some harp on the ease of vice, as follows:

Vice in abundance is easy to get;
The road is smooth and begins beside you,   *d*

---

7. Musaeus was a legendary poet closely associated with the mystery religion of Orphism.

But the gods have put sweat between us and virtue,

and a road that is long, rough, and steep.[8] Others quote Homer to bear
witness that the gods can be influenced by humans, since he said:

> *The gods themselves can be swayed by prayer,*
> *And with sacrifices and soothing promises,*
e > *Incense and libations, human beings turn them from their purpose*
> *When someone has transgressed and sinned.*[9]

And they present a noisy throng of books by Musaeus and Orpheus,
offspring as they say of Selene and the Muses, in accordance with which
they perform their rituals.[10] And they persuade not only individuals but
whole cities that the unjust deeds of the living or the dead can be absolved
365 or purified through sacrifices and pleasant games. These initiations, as
they call them, free people from punishment hereafter, while a terrible
fate awaits the uninitiated.

When all such sayings about the attitudes of gods and humans to virtue
and vice are so often repeated, Socrates, what effect do you suppose they
have on the souls of young people? I mean those who are clever and are
able to flit from one of these sayings to another, so to speak, and gather
from them an impression of what sort of person he should be and of how
b best to travel the road of life. He would surely ask himself Pindar's
question, "Should I by justice or by crooked deceit scale this high wall
and live my life guarded and secure?" And he'll answer: "The various
sayings suggest that there is no advantage in my being just if I'm not also
thought just, while the troubles and penalties of being just are apparent.
But they tell me that an unjust person, who has secured for himself a
reputation for justice, lives the life of a god. Since, then, 'opinion forcibly
c overcomes truth' and 'controls happiness,' as the wise men say, I must
surely turn entirely to it.[11] I should create a façade of illusory virtue around
me to deceive those who come near, but keep behind it the greedy and
crafty fox of the wise Archilochus."[12]

"But surely," someone will object, "it isn't easy for vice to remain always

---

8. *Works and Days* 287–89, with minor alterations.

9. *Iliad* 9.497–501, with minor alterations.

10. It is not clear whether Orpheus was a real person or a mythical figure. His fame
in Greek myth rests on the poems in which the doctrines of the Orphic religion are set
forth. These are discussed in W. Burkert, *Greek Religion* (Cambridge: Harvard University Press, 1985). Musaeus was a mythical singer closely related to Orpheus. Selene is
the Moon.

11. The quotation is attributed to Simonides, whom Polemarchus cites in Book I.

12. Archilochus of Paros (c. 756–16 B.C.), was an iambic and elegiac poet who composed a famous fable about the fox and the hedgehog.

hidden." We'll reply that nothing great is easy. And, in any case, if we're
to be happy, we must follow the path indicated in these accounts. To   *d*
remain undiscovered we'll form secret societies and political clubs. And
there are teachers of persuasion to make us clever in dealing with assemblies and law courts. Therefore, using persuasion in one place and force
in another, we'll outdo others[13] without paying a penalty.

"What about the gods? Surely, we can't hide from them or use violent
force against them!" Well, if the gods don't exist or don't concern themselves with human affairs, why should we worry at all about hiding from
them? If they do exist and do concern themselves with us, we've learned   *e*
all we know about them from the laws and the poets who give their
genealogies—nowhere else. But these are the very people who tell us that
the gods can be persuaded and influenced by sacrifices, gentle prayers,
and offerings. Hence, we should believe them on both matters or neither.
If we believe them, we should be unjust and offer sacrifices from the fruits
of our injustice. If we are just, our only gain is not to be punished by the *366*
gods, since we lose the profits of injustice. But if we are unjust, we get
the profits of our crimes and transgressions and afterwards persuade the
gods by prayer and escape without punishment.

"But in Hades won't we pay the penalty for crimes committed here,
either ourselves or our children's children?" "My friend," the young man
will say as he does his calculation, "mystery rites have great power and
the gods have great power of absolution. The greatest cities tell us this,
as do those children of the gods who have become poets and prophets."   *b*

Why, then, should we still choose justice over the greatest injustice?
Many eminent authorities agree that, if we practice such injustice with a
false façade, we'll do well at the hands of gods and humans, living and
dying as we've a mind to. So, given all that has been said, Socrates, how
is it possible for anyone of any power—whether of mind, wealth, body, or *c*
birth—to be willing to honor justice and not laugh aloud when he hears
it praised? Indeed, if anyone can show that what we've said is false and
has adequate knowledge that justice is best, he'll surely be full not of anger
but of forgiveness for the unjust. He knows that, apart from someone of
godlike character who is disgusted by injustice or one who has gained
knowledge and avoids injustice for that reason, no one is just willingly.   *d*
Through cowardice or old age or some other weakness, people do indeed
object to injustice. But it's obvious that they do so only because they lack
the power to do injustice, for the first of them to acquire it is the first to
do as much injustice as he can.

And all of this has no other cause than the one that led Glaucon and
me to say to you: "Socrates, of all of you who claim to praise justice, from

13. *Pleonektountes.* See 343e n. 18.

the original heroes of old whose words survive, to the men of the present
e   day, not one has ever blamed injustice or praised justice except by mentioning the reputations, honors, and rewards that are their consequences.
No one has ever adequately described what each itself does of its own
power by its presence in the soul of the person who possesses it, even if
it remains hidden from gods and humans. No one, whether in poetry or
in private conversations, has adequately argued that injustice is the worst
thing a soul can have in it and that justice is the greatest good. If you had
treated the subject in this way and persuaded us from youth, we wouldn't
367 now be guarding against one another's injustices, but each would be his
own best guardian, afraid that by doing injustice he'd be living with the
worst thing possible."

Thrasymachus or anyone else might say what we've said, Socrates, or
maybe even more, in discussing justice and injustice—crudely inverting
their powers, in my opinion. And, frankly, it's because I want to hear the
b   opposite from you that I speak with all the force I can muster. So don't
merely give us a theoretical argument that justice is stronger than injustice,
but tell us what each itself does, because of its own powers, to someone who
possesses it, that makes injustice bad and justice good. Follow Glaucon's
advice, and don't take reputations into account, for if you don't deprive
justice and injustice of their true reputations and attach false ones to them,
we'll say that you are not praising them but their reputations and that
c   you're encouraging us to be unjust in secret. In that case, we'll say that
you agree with Thrasymachus that justice is the good of another, the
advantage of the stronger, while injustice is one's own advantage and
profit, though not the advantage of the weaker.

You agree that justice is one of the greatest goods, the ones that are
worth getting for the sake of what comes from them, but much more so
d   for their own sake, such as seeing, hearing, knowing, being healthy, and
all other goods that are fruitful by their own nature and not simply because
of reputation. Therefore, praise justice as a good of that kind, explaining
how—because of its very self—it benefits its possessors and how injustice
harms them. Leave wages and reputations for others to praise.

Others would satisfy me if they praised justice and blamed injustice in
that way, extolling the wages of one and denigrating those of the other.
But you, unless you order me to be satisfied, wouldn't, for you've spent
e   your whole life investigating this and nothing else. Don't, then, give us
only a theoretical argument that justice is stronger than injustice, but show
what effect each has because of itself on the person who has it—the one
for good and the other for bad—whether it remains hidden from gods
and human beings or not.

While I'd always admired the natures of Glaucon and Adeimantus, I

was especially pleased on this occasion, and I said: You are the sons of a *368*
great man, and Glaucon's lover began his elegy well when he wrote,
celebrating your achievements at the battle of Megara,

> *Sons of Ariston, godlike offspring of a famous man.*

That's well said in my opinion, for you must indeed be affected by the
divine if you're not convinced that injustice is better than justice and yet
can speak on its behalf as you have done. And I believe that you really are
unconvinced by your own words. I infer this from the way you live, for if   *b*
I had only your words to go on, I wouldn't trust you. The more I trust
you, however, the more I'm at a loss as to what to do. I don't see how I
can be of help. Indeed, I believe I'm incapable of it. And here's my
evidence. I thought what I said to Thrasymachus showed that justice is
better than injustice, but you won't accept it from me. On the other hand,
I don't see how I can refuse my help, for I fear that it may even be impious
to have breath in one's body and the ability to speak and yet to stand idly
by and not defend justice when it is being prosecuted. So the best course
is to give justice any assistance I can.   *c*

Glaucon and the others begged me not to abandon the argument but to
help in every way to track down what justice and injustice are and what
the truth about their benefits is. So I told them what I had in mind: The
investigation we're undertaking is not an easy one but requires keen eyesight. Therefore, since we aren't clever people, we should adopt the   *d*
method of investigation that we'd use if, lacking keen eyesight, we were
told to read small letters from a distance and then noticed that the same
letters existed elsewhere in a larger size and on a larger surface. We'd consider it a godsend, I think, to be allowed to read the larger ones first and
then to examine the smaller ones, to see whether they really are the same.

That's certainly true, said Adeimantus, but how is this case similar to
our investigation of justice?   *e*

I'll tell you. We say, don't we, that there is the justice of a single man
and also the justice of a whole city?

Certainly.

And a city is larger than a single man?

It is larger.

Perhaps, then, there is more justice in the larger thing, and it will be
easier to learn what it is. So, if you're willing, let's first find out what sort
of thing justice is in a city and afterwards look for it in the individual, *369*
observing the ways in which the smaller is similar to the larger.

That seems fine to me.

If we could watch a city coming to be in theory, wouldn't we also see
its justice coming to be, and its injustice as well?

Probably so.

And when that process is completed, we can hope to find what we are looking for more easily?

b   Of course.

Do you think we should try to carry it out, then? It's no small task, in my view. So think it over.

We have already, said Adeimantus. Don't even consider doing anything else.

I think a city comes to be because none of us is self-sufficient, but we all need many things. Do you think that a city is founded on any other principle?

No.

And because people need many things, and because one person calls
c on a second out of one need and on a third out of a different need, many people gather in a single place to live together as partners and helpers. And such a settlement is called a city.[14] Isn't that so?

It is.

And if they share things with one another, giving and taking, they do so because each believes that this is better for himself?

That's right.

Come, then, let's create a city in theory from its beginnings. And it's our needs, it seems, that will create it.

It is, indeed.

d   Surely our first and greatest need is to provide food to sustain life.

Certainly.

Our second is for shelter, and our third for clothes and such.

That's right.

How, then, will a city be able to provide all this? Won't one person have to be a farmer, another a builder, and another a weaver? And shouldn't we add a cobbler and someone else to provide medical care?

All right.

So the essential minimum for a city is four or five men?

e   Apparently.

And what about this? Must each of them contribute his own work for the common use of all? For example, will a farmer provide food for everyone, spending quadruple the time and labor to provide food to be shared by them all? Or will he not bother about that, producing one quarter
370 the food in one quarter the time, and spending the other three quarters, one in building a house, one in the production of clothes, and one in

---

14. Notice that a city (*polis*) is a collection of people, not a collection of buildings.

making shoes, not troubling to associate with the others, but minding his own business on his own?

Perhaps, Socrates, Adeimantus replied, the way you suggested first would be easier than the other.

That certainly wouldn't be surprising, for, even as you were speaking it occurred to me that, in the first place, we aren't all born alike, but each of us differs somewhat in nature from the others, one being suited to one task, another to another. Or don't you think so? *b*

I do.

Second, does one person do a better job if he practices many crafts or—since he's one person himself—if he practices one?

If he practices one.

It's clear, at any rate, I think, that if one misses the right moment in anything, the work is spoiled.

It is.

That's because the thing to be done won't wait on the leisure of the doer but the doer, must of necessity pay close attention to his work rather than treating it as a secondary occupation. *c*

Yes, he must.

The result, then, is that more plentiful and better-quality goods are more easily produced if each person does one thing for which he is naturally suited, does it at the right time, and is released from having to do any of the others.

Absolutely.

Then, Adeimantus, we're going to need more than four citizens to provide the things we've mentioned, for a farmer won't make his own plough, not if it's to be a good one, nor his hoe, nor any of his other farming tools. Neither will a builder—and he, too, needs lots of things. *d* And the same is true of a weaver and a cobbler, isn't it?

It is.

Hence, carpenters, metal workers, and many other craftsmen of that sort will share our little city and make it bigger.

That's right.

Yet it won't be a huge settlement even if we add cowherds, shepherds, and other herdsmen in order that the farmers have cows to do their ploughing, the builders have oxen to share with the farmers in hauling *e* their materials, and the weavers and cobblers have hides and fleeces to use.

It won't be a small one either, if it has to hold all those.

Moreover, it's almost impossible to establish a city in a place where nothing has to be imported.

Indeed it is.

So we'll need yet further people to import from other cities whatever is needed.

Yes.

And if an importer goes empty-handed to another city, without a cargo of the things needed by the city from which he's to bring back what his 371 own city needs, he'll come away empty-handed, won't he?

So it seems.

Therefore our citizens must not only produce enough for themselves at home but also goods of the right quality and quantity to satisfy the requirements of others.

They must.

So we'll need more farmers and other craftsmen in our city.

Yes.

And others to take care of imports and exports. And they're called merchants, aren't they?

Yes.

So we'll need merchants, too.

Certainly.

And if the trade is by sea, we'll need a good many others who know
b   how to sail.

A good many, indeed.

And how will those in the city itself share the things that each produces? It was for the sake of this that we made their partnership and founded their city.

Clearly, they must do it by buying and selling.

Then we'll need a marketplace and a currency for such exchange.

Certainly.

c   If a farmer or any other craftsman brings some of his products to market, and he doesn't arrive at the same time as those who want to exchange things with him, is he to sit idly in the marketplace, away from his own work?

Not at all. There'll be people who'll notice this and provide the requisite service—in well-organized cities they'll usually be those whose bodies are weakest and who aren't fit to do any other work. They'll stay around the
d   market exchanging money for the goods of those who have something to sell and then exchanging those goods for the money of those who want them.

Then, to fill this need there will have to be retailers in our city, for aren't those who establish themselves in the marketplace to provide this service of buying and selling called retailers, while those who travel between cities are called merchants?

That's right.

There are other servants, I think, whose minds alone wouldn't qualify

them for membership in our society but whose bodies are strong enough   *e*
for labor. These sell the use of their strength for a price called a wage and
hence are themselves called wage-earners. Isn't that so?

Certainly.

So wage-earners complete our city?

I think so.

Well, Adeimantus, has our city grown to completeness, then?

Perhaps it has.

Then where are justice and injustice to be found in it? With which of
the things we examined did they come in?

I've no idea, Socrates, unless it was somewhere in some need that these   *372*
people have of one another.

You may be right, but we must look into it and not grow weary. First,
then, let's see what sort of life our citizens will lead when they've been
provided for in the way we have been describing. They'll produce bread,
wine, clothes, and shoes, won't they? They'll build houses, work naked
and barefoot in the summer, and wear adequate clothing and shoes in the   *b*
winter. For food, they'll knead and cook the flour and meal they've made
from wheat and barley. They'll put their honest cakes and loaves on reeds
or clean leaves, and, reclining on beds strewn with yew and myrtle, they'll
feast with their children, drink their wine, and, crowned with wreaths,
hymn the gods. They'll enjoy sex with one another but bear no more
children than their resources allow, lest they fall into either poverty or
war.   *c*

It seems that you make your people feast without any delicacies, Glaucon
interrupted.

True enough, I said, I was forgetting that they'll obviously need salt,
olives, cheese, boiled roots, and vegetables of the sort they cook in the
country. We'll give them desserts, too, of course, consisting of figs,
chickpeas, and beans, and they'll roast myrtle and acorns before the fire,[15]
drinking moderately. And so they'll live in peace and good health, and   *d*
when they die at a ripe old age, they'll bequeath a similar life to their
children.

If you were founding a city for pigs, Socrates, he replied, wouldn't you
fatten *them* on the same diet?

Then how should I feed these people, Glaucon? I asked.

In the conventional way. If they aren't to suffer hardship, they should
recline on proper couches, dine at a table, and have the delicacies and
desserts that people have nowadays.   *e*

All right, I understand. It isn't merely the origin of a city that we're

---

15. It seems likely that a sexual pun is intended since myrtle (*murton*) and acorn (*phēgos*)
are common slang terms for the female and male genitalia respectively.

considering, it seems, but the origin of a *luxurious* city. And that may not
be a bad idea, for by examining it, we might very well see how justice and
injustice grow up in cities. Yet the true city, in my opinion, is the one we've
described, the healthy one, as it were. But let's study a city with a fever, if
373 that's what you want. There's nothing to stop us. The things I mentioned
earlier and the way of life I described won't satisfy some people, it seems,
but couches, tables, and other furniture will have to be added, and, of
course, all sorts of delicacies, perfumed oils, incense, prostitutes, and pastries. We mustn't provide them only with the necessities[16] we mentioned at
first, such as houses, clothes, and shoes, but painting and embroidery must
be begun, and gold, ivory, and the like acquired. Isn't that so?

b   Yes.

Then we must enlarge our city, for the healthy one is no longer adequate.
We must increase it in size and fill it with a multitude of things that go
beyond what is necessary for a city—hunters, for example, and artists or
imitators, many of whom work with shapes and colors, many with music.
And there'll be poets and their assistants, actors, choral dancers, contrac-
tors, and makers of all kinds of devices, including, among other things,
those needed for the adornment of women. And so we'll need more

c   servants, too. Or don't you think that we'll need tutors, wet nurses, nannies,
beauticians, barbers, chefs, cooks, and swineherds? We didn't need any
of these in our earlier city, but we'll need them in this one. And we'll also
need many more cattle, won't we, if the people are going to eat meat?

Of course.

And if we live like that, we'll have a far greater need for doctors than

d   we did before?

Much greater.

And the land, I suppose, that used to be adequate to feed the population
we had then, will cease to be adequate and become too small. What do
you think?

The same.

Then we'll have to seize some of our neighbors' land if we're to have
enough pasture and ploughland. And won't our neighbors want to seize
part of ours as well, if they too have surrendered themselves to the endless
acquisition of money and have overstepped the limit of their necessities?

e   That's completely inevitable, Socrates.

Then our next step will be war, Glaucon, won't it?

It will.

We won't say yet whether the effects of war are good or bad but only
that we've now found the origins of war. It comes from those same desires

16. See 554a for an explanation.

that are most of all responsible for the bad things that happen to cities
and the individuals in them.

That's right.

Then the city must be further enlarged, and not just by a small number,
either, but by a whole army, which will do battle with the invaders in
defense of the city's substantial wealth and all the other things we men- *374*
tioned.

Why aren't the citizens themselves adequate for that purpose?

They won't be, if the agreement you and the rest of us made when we
were founding the city was a good one, for surely we agreed, if you
remember, that it's impossible for a single person to practice many crafts
or professions well.

That's true.

Well, then, don't you think that warfare is a profession?   *b*

Of course.

Then should we be more concerned about cobbling than about warfare?

Not at all.

But we prevented a cobbler from trying to be a farmer, weaver, or
builder at the same time and said that he must remain a cobbler in order
to produce fine work. And each of the others, too, was to work all his life
at a single trade for which he had a natural aptitude and keep away from
all the others, so as not to miss the right moment to practice his own work   *c*
well. Now, isn't it of the greatest importance that warfare be practiced
well? And is fighting a war so easy that a farmer or a cobbler or any other
craftsman can be a soldier at the same time? Though no one can become
so much as a good player of checkers or dice if he considers it only as a
sideline and doesn't practice it from childhood. Or can someone pick up
a shield or any other weapon or tool of war and immediately perform
adequately in an infantry battle or any other kind? No other tool makes   *d*
anyone who picks it up a craftsman or champion unless he has acquired
the requisite knowledge and has had sufficient practice.

If tools could make anyone who picked them up an expert, they'd be
valuable indeed.

Then to the degree that the work of the guardians is most important,   *e*
it requires most freedom from other things and the greatest skill and
devotion.

I should think so.

And doesn't it also require a person whose nature is suited to that way
of life?

Certainly.

Then our job, it seems, is to select, if we can, the kind of nature suited
to guard the city.

It is.

By god, it's no trivial task that we've taken on. But insofar as we are able, we mustn't shrink from it.

375 No, we mustn't.

Do you think that, when it comes to guarding, there is any difference between the nature of a pedigree young dog and that of a well-born youth?

What do you mean?

Well, each needs keen senses, speed to catch what it sees, and strength in case it has to fight it out with what it captures.

They both need all these things.

And each must be courageous if indeed he's to fight well.

Of course.

And will a horse, a dog, or any other animal be courageous, if he isn't spirited? Or haven't you noticed just how invincible and unbeatable spirit

b is, so that its presence makes the whole soul fearless and unconquerable?

I have noticed that.

The physical qualities of the guardians are clear, then.

Yes.

And as far as their souls are concerned, they must be spirited.

That too.

But if they have natures like that, Glaucon, won't they be savage to each other and to the rest of the citizens?

By god, it will be hard for them to be anything else.

Yet surely they must be gentle to their own people and harsh to the

c enemy. If they aren't, they won't wait around for others to destroy the city but will do it themselves first.

That's true.

What are we to do, then? Where are we to find a character that is both gentle and high-spirited at the same time? After all, a gentle nature is the opposite of a spirited one.

Apparently.

If someone lacks either gentleness or spirit, he can't be a good guardian. Yet it seems impossible to combine them. It follows that a good guardian

d cannot exist.

It looks like it.

I couldn't see a way out, but on reexamining what had gone before, I said: We deserve to be stuck, for we've lost sight of the analogy we put forward.

How do you mean?

We overlooked the fact that there *are* natures of the sort we thought impossible, natures in which these opposites are indeed combined.

Where?

You can see them in other animals, too, but especially in the one to which we compared the guardian, for you know, of course, that a pedigree dog naturally has a character of this sort—he is gentle as can be to those *e* he's used to and knows, but the opposite to those he doesn't know.

I do know that.

So the combination we want is possible after all, and our search for the good guardian is not contrary to nature.

Apparently not.

Then do you think that our future guardian, besides being spirited, must also be by nature philosophical?[17]

How do you mean? I don't understand.   *376*

It's something else you see in dogs, and it makes you wonder at the animal.

What?

When a dog sees someone it doesn't know, it gets angry before anything bad happens to it. But when it knows someone, it welcomes him, even if it has never received anything good from him. Haven't you ever wondered at that?

I've never paid any attention to it, but obviously that is the way a dog behaves.

Surely this is a refined quality in its nature and one that is truly philo- *b* sophical.

In what way philosophical?

Because it judges anything it sees to be either a friend or an enemy, on no other basis than that it knows the one and doesn't know the other. And how could it be anything besides a lover of learning, if it defines what is its own and what is alien to it in terms of knowledge and ignorance?

It couldn't.

But surely the love of learning is the same thing as philosophy or the love of wisdom?

It is.

Then, may we confidently assume in the case of a human being, too, that if he is to be gentle toward his own and those he knows, he must be a lover of learning and wisdom?   *c*

We may.

Philosophy, spirit, speed, and strength must all, then, be combined in the nature of anyone who is to be a fine and good guardian of our city.

---

17. The word *philosophos* is used here in its general sense to refer to intellectual curiosity or wanting to know things without ulterior motives. Plato is not suggesting (below) that pedigree dogs have the traits that he will attribute to full-blown philosophers in Books V–VII.

Absolutely.

Then those are the traits a potential guardian would need at the outset.
But how are we to bring him up and educate him? Will inquiry into that
topic bring us any closer to the goal of our inquiry, which is to discover
d   the origins of justice and injustice in a city? We want our account to be
adequate, but we don't want it to be any longer than necessary.

I certainly expect, Glaucon's brother said, that such inquiry will further
our goal.

Then, by god, Adeimantus, I said, we mustn't leave it out, even if it
turns out to be a somewhat lengthy affair.

No, we mustn't.

Come, then, and just as if we had the leisure to make up stories, let's
describe in theory how to educate our men.
e   All right.

What will their education be? Or is it hard to find anything better than
that which has developed over a long period—physical training for bodies
and music and poetry for the soul?[18]

Yes, it would be hard.

Now, we start education in music and poetry before physical training,
don't we?

Of course.

Do you include stories under music and poetry?

I do.

Aren't there two kinds of story, one true and the other false?

Yes.

377   And mustn't our men be educated in both, but first in false ones?

I don't understand what you mean.

Don't you understand that we first tell stories to children? These are
false, on the whole, though they have some truth in them. And we tell
them to small children before physical training begins.

That's true.

And that's what I meant by saying that we must deal with music and
poetry before physical training.

All right.

You know, don't you, that the beginning of any process is most important, especially for anything young and tender? It's at that time that it is
b   most malleable and takes on any pattern one wishes to impress on it.

Exactly.

Then shall we carelessly allow the children to hear any old stories, told
by just anyone, and to take beliefs into their souls that are for the most

18. See p. 33 n. 1.

part opposite to the ones we think they should hold when they are grown up?

We certainly won't.

Then we must first of all, it seems, supervise the storytellers. We'll select their stories whenever they are fine or beautiful and reject them when they aren't. And we'll persuade nurses and mothers to tell their   *c* children the ones we have selected, since they will shape their children's souls with stories much more than they shape their bodies by handling them. Many of the stories they tell now, however, must be thrown out.

Which ones do you mean?

We'll first look at the major stories, and by seeing how to deal with them, we'll see how to deal with the minor ones as well, for they exhibit the same pattern and have the same effects whether they're famous or not. Don't you think so?   *d*

I do, but I don't know which ones you're calling major.

Those that Homer, Hesiod, and other poets tell us, for surely they composed false stories, told them to people, and are still telling them.

Which stories do you mean, and what fault do you find in them?

The fault one ought to find first and foremost, especially if the falsehood isn't well told.

For example?

When a story gives a bad image of what the gods and heroes are like, the way a painter does whose picture is not at all like the things he's trying   *e* to paint.

You're right to object to that. But what sort of thing in particular do you have in mind?

First, telling the greatest falsehood about the most important things doesn't make a fine story—I mean Hesiod telling us about how Ouranos behaved, how Cronos punished him for it, and how he was in turn punished by his own son.[19] But even if it were true, it should be passed *378* over in silence, not told to foolish young people. And if, for some reason, it has to be told, only a very few people—pledged to secrecy and after sacrificing not just a pig but something great and scarce—should hear it, so that their number is kept as small as possible.

Yes, such stories are hard to deal with.

And they shouldn't be told in our city, Adeimantus. Nor should a young   *b*

---

19. Ouranos prevented his wife Gaia from giving birth to his children, by blocking them up inside her. Gaia gave a sickle to one of these children, Cronos, with which he castrated his father when the latter next had intercourse with her. Cronos ate the children he had by his wife Rheia, until, by deceiving him with a stone, she was able to save Zeus from suffering this fate. Zeus then overthrew his father. See Hesiod, *Theogony* 154–210, 453–506.

person hear it said that in committing the worst crimes he's doing nothing out of the ordinary, or that if he inflicts every kind of punishment on an unjust father, he's only doing the same as the first and greatest of the gods.

No, by god, I don't think myself that these stories are fit to be told.

Indeed, if we want the guardians of our city to think that it's shameful to be easily provoked into hating one another, we mustn't allow *any* stories
c   about gods warring, fighting, or plotting against one another, for they aren't true. The battles of gods and giants, and all the various stories of the gods hating their families or friends, should neither be told nor even woven in embroideries. If we're to persuade our people that no citizen has ever hated another and that it's impious to do so, then *that's* what should be told to children from the beginning by old men and women; and as these children grow older, poets should be compelled to tell them the same
d   sort of thing. We won't admit stories into our city—whether allegorical or not—about Hera being chained by her son, nor about Hephaestus being hurled from heaven by his father when he tried to help his mother, who was being beaten, nor about the battle of the gods in Homer. The young can't distinguish what is allegorical from what isn't, and the opinions they absorb at that age are hard to erase and apt to become unalterable. For these reasons, then, we should probably take the utmost care to insure
e   that the first stories they hear about virtue are the best ones for them to hear.

That's reasonable. But if someone asked us what stories these are, what should we say?

You and I, Adeimantus, aren't poets, but we *are* founding a city. And
379 it's appropriate for the founders to know the patterns on which poets must base their stories and from which they mustn't deviate. But we aren't actually going to compose their poems for them.

All right. But what precisely are the patterns for theology or stories about the gods?

Something like this: Whether in epic, lyric, or tragedy, a god must always be represented as he is.

Indeed, he must.
b   Now, a god is really good, isn't he, and must be described as such? What else?

And surely nothing good is harmful, is it?

I suppose not.

And can what isn't harmful do harm?

Never.

Or can what does no harm do anything bad?

No.

And can what does nothing bad be the cause of anything bad?

How could it?

Moreover, the good is beneficial?

Yes.

It is the cause of doing well?

Yes.

The good isn't the cause of all things, then, but only of good ones; it isn't the cause of bad ones.

I agree entirely.   c

Therefore, since a god is good, he is not—as most people claim—the cause of everything that happens to human beings but of only a few things, for good things are fewer than bad ones in our lives. He alone is responsible for the good things, but we must find some other cause for the bad ones, not a god.

That's very true, and I believe it.

Then we won't accept from anyone the foolish mistake Homer makes about the gods when he says: d

There are two urns at the threshold of Zeus,
One filled with good fates, the other with bad ones. . . .

and the person to whom he gives a mixture of these

Sometimes meets with a bad fate, sometimes with good,

but the one who receives his fate entirely from the second urn,

Evil famine drives him over the divine earth.

We won't grant either that Zeus is for us   e

The distributor of both good and bad.

And as to the breaking of the promised truce by Pandarus, if anyone tells us that it was brought about by Athena and Zeus or that Themis and Zeus were responsible for strife and contention among the gods, we will not praise him. Nor will we allow the young to hear the words of Aeschylus: *380*

A god makes mortals guilty
When he wants utterly to destroy a house.[20]

And if anyone composes a poem about the sufferings of Niobe, such as the one in which these lines occur, or about the house of Pelops, or the

---

20. The first three quotations are from *Iliad* 24. 527–532. The sources for the fourth and for the quotation from Aeschylus are unknown. The story of Athena urging Pandarus to break the truce is told in *Iliad* 4.73–126.

tale of Troy, or anything else of that kind, we must require him to say that these things are not the work of a god. Or, if they are, then poets must look for the kind of account of them that we are now seeking, and say that *b* the actions of the gods are good and just, and that those they punish are benefited thereby. We won't allow poets to say that the punished are made wretched and that it was a god who made them so. But we will allow them to say that bad people are wretched because they are in need of punishment and that, in paying the penalty, they are benefited by the gods. And, as for saying that a god, who is himself good, is the cause of bad things, we'll fight that in every way, and we won't allow anyone to say it in his own city, if it's to be well governed, or anyone to hear it either—whether young or *c* old, whether in verse or prose. These stories are not pious, not advantageous to us, and not consistent with one another.

I like your law, and I'll vote for it.

This, then, is one of the laws or patterns concerning the gods to which speakers and poets must conform, namely, that a god isn't the cause of all things but only of good ones.

And it's a fully satisfactory law.

What about this second law? Do you think that a god is a sorcerer, able *d* to appear in different forms at different times, sometimes changing himself from his own form into many shapes, sometimes deceiving us by making us think that he has done it? Or do you think he's simple and least of all likely to step out of his own form?

I can't say offhand.

Well, what about this? If he steps out of his own form, mustn't he either *e* change himself or be changed by something else?

He must.

But the best things are least liable to alteration or change, aren't they? For example, isn't the healthiest and strongest body least changed by food, drink, and labor, or the healthiest and strongest plant by sun, wind, and the like?

381 Of course.

And the most courageous and most rational soul is least disturbed or altered by any outside affection?

Yes.

And the same account is true of all artifacts, furniture, houses, and clothes. The ones that are good and well made are least altered by time or anything else that happens to them.

That's right.

b Whatever is in good condition, then, whether by nature or craft or both, admits least of being changed by anything else.

So it seems.

Now, surely a god and what belongs to him are in every way in the best condition.

How could they fail to be?

Then a god would be least likely to have many shapes.

Indeed.

Then does he change or alter himself?

Clearly he does, if indeed he is altered at all.

Would he change himself into something better and more beautiful than himself or something worse and uglier?

It would have to be into something worse, if he's changed at all, for   *c* surely we won't say that a god is deficient in either beauty or virtue.

Absolutely right. And do you think, Adeimantus, that anyone, whether god or human, would deliberately make himself worse in any way?

No, that's impossible.

Is it impossible, then, for gods to want to alter themselves? Since they are the most beautiful and best possible, it seems that each always and unconditionally retains his own shape.

That seems entirely necessary to me.

Then let no poet tell us about Proteus or Thetis, or say that   *d*

The gods, in the likeness of strangers from foreign lands,
Adopt every sort of shape and visit our cities.[21]

Nor must they present Hera, in their tragedies or other poems, as a priestess collecting alms for

the life-giving sons of the Argive river Inachus,[22]

or tell us other stories of that sort. Nor must mothers, believing bad stories about the gods wandering at night in the shapes of strangers from foreign   *e* lands, terrify their children with them. Such stories blaspheme the gods and, at the same time, make children more cowardly.

They mustn't be told.

But though the gods are unable to change, do they nonetheless make us believe that they appear in all sorts of ways, deceiving us through sorcery?

Perhaps.

What? Would a god be willing to be false, either in word or deed, by   *382* presenting an illusion?

I don't know.

---

21. *Odyssey* 17.485–86.

22. Inachus was the father of Io, who was persecuted by Hera because Zeus was in love with her. The source for the part of the story Plato quotes is unknown.

Don't you know that a *true* falsehood, if one may call it that, is hated by all gods and humans?

What do you mean?

I mean that no one is willing to tell falsehoods to the most important part of himself about the most important things, but of all places he is most afraid to have falsehood there.

I still don't understand.

b   That's because you think I'm saying something deep. I simply mean that to be false to one's soul about the things that are, to be ignorant and to have and hold falsehood there, is what everyone would least of all accept, for everyone hates a falsehood in that place most of all.

That's right.

Surely, as I said just now, this would be most correctly called true falsehood—ignorance in the soul of someone who has been told a falsehood. Falsehood in words is a kind of imitation of this affection in the soul, an image of it that comes into being after it and is not a pure

c   falsehood. Isn't that so?

Certainly.

And the thing that is really a falsehood is hated not only by the gods but by human beings as well.

It seems so to me.

What about falsehood in words? When and to whom is it useful and so not deserving of hatred? Isn't it useful against one's enemies? And when any of our so-called friends are attempting, through madness or ignorance, to do something bad, isn't it a useful drug for preventing them? It is also useful in the case of those stories we were just talking about, the ones we

d   tell because we don't know the truth about those ancient events involving the gods. By making a falsehood as much like the truth as we can, don't we also make it useful?

We certainly do.

Then in which of these ways could a falsehood be useful to a god? Would he make false likenesses of ancient events because of his ignorance of them?

It would be ridiculous to think that.

Then there is nothing of the false poet in a god?

Not in my view.

Would he be false, then, through fear of his enemies?

e   Far from it.

Because of the ignorance or madness of his family or friends, then?

No one who is ignorant or mad is a friend of the gods.

Then there's no reason for a god to speak falsely?

None.

Therefore the daimonic and the divine are in every way free from falsehood.[23]

Completely.

A god, then, is simple and true in word and deed. He doesn't change himself or deceive others by images, words, or signs, whether in visions or in dreams.

That's what I thought as soon as I heard you say it.   *383*

You agree, then, that this is our second pattern for speaking or composing poems about the gods: They are not sorcerers who change themselves, nor do they mislead us by falsehoods in words or deeds.

I agree.

So, even though we praise many things in Homer, we won't approve of the dream Zeus sent to Agamemnon, nor of Aeschylus when he makes Thetis say that Apollo sang in prophecy at her wedding: *b*

> *About the good fortune my children would have,*
> *Free of disease throughout their long lives,*
> *And of all the blessings that the friendship of the gods would bring me.*
> *I hoped that Phoebus' divine mouth would be free of falsehood,*
> *Endowed as it is with the craft of prophecy.*
> *But the very god who sang, the one at the feast,*
> *The one who said all this, he himself it is*
> *Who killed my son.*[24]

Whenever anyone says such things about a god, we'll be angry with him, refuse him a chorus,[25] and not allow his poetry to be used in the education   *c* of the young, so that our guardians will be as god-fearing and godlike as human beings can be.

I completely endorse these patterns, he said, and I would enact them as laws.

---

23. The daimonic (*to daimonion*) refers to such things as Socrates' famous voice or sign (see *Apology* 26b–28a, 31c8–d4; *Euthydemus* 272e–273a; *Alcibiades 1* 103a; *Theages* 128d–129e). In the *Apology* 27d–e, Socrates says that daimons are gods or children of the gods, and in the *Symposium* 202e, they are described as messengers from the gods.

24. In the *Iliad* 2.1–34, Zeus sends a dream to Agamemnon to promise success if he attacks Troy immediately. The promise is false. The source for the quotation from Aeschylus is unknown.

25. I.e. deny him the funding necessary to hire a chorus of actors and produce his play.

Book III

Having completed his discussion of the content of stories about gods and heroes that the guardians should hear as part of their early training in music and poetry (392a), Socrates turns to the content of stories about human beings, only to postpone his discussion of it till Book X. He explains why this postponement is necessary at 392a–c. His next topic is the appropriate style *for these stories to have and the appropriate* mode *and* rhythm *for lyric odes and songs (392c–403c). In the course of this discussion, he makes important remarks about all the arts (410b–d) and about the right sort of love between mature men and teenage boys (402d–403c). The latter topic may strike us as out of place, but in fact these sorts of relationships were conceived by Plato and his contemporaries as having an educational function. The discussion of physical training is next (403c–412b). It includes an important discussion of the sort of medical treatment that a kallipolis should provide (405a–410a) and a provision for the execution of incurable psychopaths (410a).*

The next topic is the selection of rulers or "complete guardians" from among the class of guardians (412b–414b). Socrates does not explain why he thinks there have to be rulers in the kallipolis. Perhaps, like Thrasymachus, he assumes that, in a world of unequal power, someone will in fact always rule.

The final topic is the housing and life-styles of the rulers (414c–417b). It includes the so-called Myth of the Metals.

The luxurious city (372e) has now been "purified" (399e). This purified city, complete with guardians and rulers, is the second stage in Plato's account of the kallipolis. It contains money-loving producers and honor-loving guardians, but no full-blown Platonic philosophers, for the educational institutions needed to produce such philosophers have not yet been provided for in the city's constitution.

Such, then, I said, are the kinds of stories that I think future guardians
386 should and should not hear about the gods from childhood on, if they are to honor the gods and their parents and not take their friendship with one another lightly.

I'm sure we're right about that, at any rate.

What if they are to be courageous as well? Shouldn't they be told stories

that will make them least afraid of death? Or do you think that anyone
ever becomes courageous if he's possessed by this fear?   *b*

No, I certainly don't.

And can someone be unafraid of death, preferring it to defeat in battle
or slavery, if he believes in a Hades full of terrors?

Not at all.

Then we must supervise such stories and those who tell them, and ask
them not to disparage the life in Hades in this unconditional way, but
rather to praise it, since what they now say is neither true nor beneficial
to future warriors.   *c*

We must.

Then we'll expunge all that sort of disparagement, beginning with the
following lines:

> *I would rather labor on earth in service to another,*
> *To a man who is landless, with little to live on,*
> *Than be king over all the dead.*[1]

and also these:

> *He feared that his home should appear to gods and men*   *d*
> *Dreadful, dank, and hated even by the gods.*[2]

and

> *Alas, there survives in the Halls of Hades*
> *A soul, a mere phantasm, with its wits completely gone.*[3]

and this:

> *And he alone could think; the others are flitting shadows.*[4]

and

> *The soul, leaving his limbs, made its way to Hades,*
> *Lamenting its fate, leaving manhood and youth behind.*[5]

---

1. *Odyssey* 11.489–91. Odysseus is being addressed by the dead Achilles in Hades.

2. *Iliad* 20.64–65. The speaker is Hades—god of Hades or the underworld—who is afraid that the earth will split open and reveal that his home is dreadful, etc.

3. *Iliad* 23.103–4. Achilles speaks these lines as the soul of the dead Patroclus leaves for Hades.

4. *Odyssey* 10.493–95. Circe is speaking to Odysseus about the prophet Tiresias.

5. *Iliad* 16.856–57. The words refer to Patroclus, who has just been mortally wounded by Hector.

387 and these:

> *His soul went below the earth like smoke,*
> *Screeching as it went . . .*[6]

and

> *As when bats in an awful cave*
> *Fly around screeching if one of them falls*
> *From the cluster on the ceiling, all clinging to one another,*
> *So their souls went screeching . . .*[7]

We'll ask Homer and the other poets not to be angry if we delete these passages and all similar ones. It isn't that they aren't poetic and pleasing to the majority of hearers but that, the more poetic they are, the less they should be heard by children or by men who are supposed to be free and to fear slavery more than death.

Most certainly.

And the frightening and dreadful names for the underworld must be struck out, for example, "Cocytus" and "Styx,"[8] and also the names for the dead, for example, "those below" and "the sapless ones," and all those names of things in the underworld that make everyone who hears them shudder. They may be all well and good for other purposes, but we are afraid that our guardians will be made softer and more malleable by such shudders.

And our fear is justified.

Then such passages are to be struck out?

Yes.

And poets must follow the opposite pattern in speaking and writing?

Clearly.

Must we also delete the lamentations and pitiful speeches of famous men?

We must, if indeed what we said before is compelling.

Consider though whether we are right to delete them or not. We surely say that a decent man doesn't think that death is a terrible thing for someone decent to suffer—even for someone who happens to be his friend.

We do say that.

---

6. *Iliad* 23.100. The soul referred to is Patroclus'.

7. *Odyssey* 24.6–9. The souls are those of the suitors of Penelope, whom Odysseus has killed.

8. "Cocytus" means river of wailing or lamenting; "Styx" means river of hatred or gloom.

Then he won't mourn for him as for someone who has suffered a terrible fate.

Certainly not.

We also say that a decent person is most self-sufficient in living well and, above all others, has the least need of anyone else.   *e*

That's true.

Then it's less dreadful for him than for anyone else to be deprived of his son, brother, possessions, or any other such things.

Much less.

Then he'll least give way to lamentations and bear misfortune most quietly when it strikes.

Certainly.

We'd be right, then, to delete the lamentations of famous men, leaving them to women (and not even to good women, either) and to cowardly men, so that those we say we are training to guard our city will disdain to *388* act like that.

That's right.

Again, then, we'll ask Homer and the other poets not to represent Achilles, the son of a goddess, as

> *Lying now on his side, now on his back, now again*
> *On his belly; then standing up to wander distracted*
> *This way and that on the shore of the unharvested sea.*[9]

Nor to make him pick up ashes in both hands and pour them over his head, weeping and lamenting in the ways he does in Homer.[10] Nor to   *b* represent Priam, a close descendant of the gods, as entreating his men and

> *Rolling around in dung,*
> *Calling upon each man by name.*[11]

And we'll ask them even more earnestly not to make the gods lament and say:

> *Alas, unfortunate that I am, wretched mother of a great son.*[12]   *c*

But, if they do make the gods do such things, at least they mustn't dare to represent the greatest of the gods as behaving in so unlikely a fashion as to say:

9. *Iliad* 24.3–12.
10. *Iliad* 18.23–24.
11. *Iliad* 22.414–15.
12. *Iliad* 18.54. Thetis, the mother of Achilles, is mourning his fate among the Nereids.

> *Alas, with my own eyes I see a man who is most dear to me*
> *Chased around the city, and my heart laments*[13]

or

> *Woe is me, that Sarpedon, who is most dear to me, should be*
> *Fated to be killed by Patroclus, the son of Menoetius . . .*[14]

d

If our young people, Adeimantus, listen to these stories without ridiculing them as not worth hearing, it's hardly likely that they'll consider the things described in them to be unworthy of mere human beings like themselves or that they'll rebuke themselves for doing or saying similar things when misfortune strikes. Instead, they'll feel neither shame nor restraint but groan and lament at even insignificant misfortunes.

e   What you say is completely true.

Then, as the argument has demonstrated—and we must remain persuaded by it until someone shows us a better one—they mustn't behave like that.

No, they mustn't.

Moreover, they mustn't be lovers of laughter either, for whenever anyone indulges in violent laughter, a violent change of mood is likely to follow.

So I believe.

Then, if someone represents worthwhile people as overcome by laughter, we won't approve, and we'll approve even less if they represent gods
389 that way.

Much less.

Then we won't approve of Homer saying things like this about the gods:

> *And unquenchable laughter arose among the blessed gods*
> *As they saw Hephaestus limping through the hall.*[15]

According to your argument, such things must be rejected.

b   If you want to call it mine, but they must be rejected in any case.

Moreover, we have to be concerned about truth as well, for if what we said just now is correct, and falsehood, though of no use to the gods, is useful to people as a form of drug, clearly we must allow only doctors to use it, not private citizens.

Clearly.

Then if it is appropriate for anyone to use falsehoods for the good of

---

13. *Iliad* 22.168–69. Zeus is watching Hector being pursued by Achilles.
14. *Iliad* 16.433–34.
15. *Iliad* 1.599–600.

the city, because of the actions of either enemies or citizens, it is the rulers.
But everyone else must keep away from them, because for a private citizen
to lie to a ruler is just as bad a mistake as for a sick person or athlete not   *c*
to tell the truth to his doctor or trainer about his physical condition or for
a sailor not to tell the captain the facts about his own condition or that of
the ship and the rest of its crew—indeed it is a worse mistake than either
of these.

That's completely true.

And if the ruler catches someone else telling falsehoods in the city—   *d*

> *Any one of the craftsmen,*
> *Whether a prophet, a doctor who heals the sick, or a maker of spears*[16]

—he'll punish him for introducing something as subversive and destructive
to a city as it would be to a ship.

He will, if practice is to follow theory.

What about moderation? Won't our young people also need that?

Of course.

And aren't these the most important aspects of moderation for the
majority of people, namely, to obey the rulers and to rule the pleasures of
drink, sex, and food for themselves?   *e*

That's my opinion at any rate.

Then we'll say that the words of Homer's Diomedes are well put:

> *Sit down in silence, my friend, and be persuaded by me.*[17]

and so is what follows:

> *The Achaeans, breathing eagerness for battle,*
> *Marched in silence, fearing their commanders.*[18]

and all other such things.

Those *are* well put.

But what about this?

> *Wine-bibber, with the eyes of a dog and the heart of a deer*[19]

and the rest, is it—or any other headstrong words spoken in prose or
poetry by private citizens against their rulers—well put?   *390*

---

16. *Odyssey* 17.384.
17. *Iliad* 4.412. Agamemnon has unfairly rebuked Diomedes for cowardice. Diomedes'
squire protests, but Diomedes quiets him with these words. By obeying, the squire
exhibits the kind of moderation that the majority of people can come to possess.
18. *Iliad* 3.8 and 4.443 respectively.
19. *Iliad* 1.225. Achilles is insulting his commander, Agamemnon.

No, they aren't.

I don't think they are suitable for young people to hear—not, in any case, with a view to making them moderate. Though it isn't surprising that they are pleasing enough in other ways. What do you think?

The same as you.

What about making the cleverest man say that the finest thing of all is when

> *The tables are well laden*
b > *With bread and meat, and the winebearer*
> *Draws wine from the mixing bowl and pours it in the cups.*[20]

or

> *Death by starvation is the most pitiful fate.*[21]

Do you think that such things make for self-control in young people? Or what about having Zeus, when all the other gods are asleep and he alone c is awake, easily forget all his plans because of sexual desire and be so overcome by the sight of Hera that he doesn't even want to go inside but wants to possess her there on the ground, saying that his desire for her is even greater than it was when—without their parents' knowledge—they were first lovers? Or what about the chaining together of Ares and Aphrodite by Hephaestus[22]—also the result of sexual passion?

No, by god, none of that seems suitable to me.

But if, on the other hand, there are words or deeds of famous men, who d are exhibiting endurance in the face of everything, surely they must be seen or heard. For example,

> *He struck his chest and spoke to his heart:*
> *"Endure, my heart, you've suffered more shameful things than this."*[23]

They certainly must.

Now, we mustn't allow our men to be money-lovers or to be bribable with gifts.

e Certainly not.

Then the poets mustn't sing to them:

20. *Odyssey* 9.8–10.
21. *Odyssey* 12.342. Eurylochus urges the men to slay the cattle of Helios in Odysseus' absence.
22. *Odyssey* 8.266 ff.
23. *Odyssey* 20.27–28. The speaker is Odysseus.

Gifts persuade gods, and gifts persuade revered kings.[24]

Nor must Phoenix, the tutor of Achilles, be praised as speaking with moderation when he advises him to take the gifts and defend the Achaeans, but not to give up his anger without gifts.[25] Nor should we think such things to be worthy of Achilles himself. Nor should we agree that he was such a money-lover that he would accept the gifts of Agamemnon or release the corpse of Hector for a ransom but not otherwise.[26]

It certainly isn't right to praise such things.

It is only out of respect for Homer, indeed, that I hesitate to say that it is positively impious to accuse Achilles of such things or to believe others who say them. Or to make him address Apollo in these words:

You've injured me, Farshooter, most deadly of the gods;
And I'd punish you, if I had the power.[27]

Or to say that he disobeyed the river—a god—and was ready to fight it,[28] or that he consecrated hair to the dead Patroclus, which was already consecrated to a different river, Sphercheios.[29] It isn't to be believed that he did any of these. Nor is it true that he dragged the dead Hector around the tomb of Patroclus[30] or massacred the captives on his pyre.[31] So we'll deny that. Nor will we allow our people to believe that Achilles, who was the son of a goddess and of Peleus (the most moderate of men and the grandson of Zeus) and who was brought up by the most wise Cheiron, was so full of inner turmoil as to have two diseases in his soul—slavishness accompanied by the love of money, on the one hand, and arrogance towards gods and humans, on the other.

That's right.

We certainly won't believe such things, nor will we allow it to be said that Theseus, the son of Poseidon, and Peirithous, the son of Zeus, engaged in terrible kidnappings,[32] or that any other hero and son of a god dared to do any of the terrible and impious deeds that they are now falsely

391

b

c

d

24. The source of the passage is unknown. Cf. Euripides, *Medea* 964.
25. *Iliad* 9.602–3.
26. *Iliad* 24.
27. *Iliad* 22.15, 20.
28. *Iliad* 21.232 ff.
29. *Iliad* 23.141–52.
30. *Iliad* 24.14–18.
31. *Iliad* 23.175.
32. According to some legends, Theseus and Peirithous abducted Helen and tried to abduct Persephone from Hades.

said to have done. We'll compel the poets either to deny that the heroes
did such things or else to deny that they were children of the gods. They
mustn't say both or attempt to persuade our young people that the gods
bring about evil or that heroes are no better than humans. As we said
e   earlier, these things are both impious and untrue, for we demonstrated
that it is impossible for the gods to produce bad things.[33]
Of course.

Moreover, these stories are harmful to people who hear them, for
everyone will be ready to excuse himself when he's bad, if he is persuaded
that similar things both are being done now and have been done in the
past by

> Close descendants of the gods,
> Those near to Zeus, to whom belongs
> The ancestral altar high up on Mount Ida,
> In whom the blood of daimons has not weakened.[34]

For that reason, we must put a stop to such stories, lest they produce in
392 the youth a strong inclination to do bad things.
Absolutely.

Now, isn't there a kind of story whose content we haven't yet discussed?
So far we've said how one should speak about gods, heroes, daimons, and
things in Hades.
We have.

Then what's left is how to deal with stories about human beings, isn't
it?
Obviously.

But we can't settle that matter at present.
Why not?

Because I think we'll say that what poets and prose-writers tell us about
the most important matters concerning human beings is bad. They say
b   that many unjust people are happy and many just ones wretched, that
injustice is profitable if it escapes detection, and that justice is another's
good but one's own loss. I think we'll prohibit these stories and order the
poets to compose the opposite kind of poetry and tell the opposite kind of
tales. Don't you think so?
I know so.

But if you agree that what I said is correct, couldn't I reply that you've
agreed to the very point that is in question in our whole discussion?
And you'd be right to make that reply.
c   Then we'll agree about what stories should be told about human beings

33. See 380d ff.
34. Thought to be from Aeschylus' lost play *Niobe*.

only when we've discovered what sort of thing justice is and how by nature it profits the one who has it, whether he is believed to be just or not.

That's very true.

This concludes our discussion of the content of stories. We should now, I think, investigate their style, for we'll then have fully investigated both what should be said and how it should be said.

I don't understand what you mean, Adeimantus responded.

But you must, I said. Maybe you'll understand it better if I put it this way. Isn't everything said by poets and storytellers a narrative about past, *d* present, or future events?

What else could it be?

And aren't these narratives either narrative alone, or narrative through imitation, or both?

I need a clearer understanding of that as well.

I seem to be a ridiculously unclear teacher. So, like those who are incompetent at speaking, I won't try to deal with the matter as a whole, but I'll take up a part and use it as an example to make plain what I want to say. Tell me, do you know the beginning of the *Iliad*, where the *e* poet tells us that Chryses begs Agamemnon to release his daughter, that Agamemnon harshly rejects him, and that, having failed, Chryses prays to the god against the Achaeans?   *393*

I do.

You know, then, that up to the lines:

> *And he begged all the Achaeans*
> *But especially the two sons of Atreus, the commanders of the army,*

the poet himself is speaking and doesn't attempt to get us to think that the speaker is someone other than himself. After this, however, he speaks as if he were Chryses and tries as far as possible to make us think that the speaker isn't Homer but the priest himself—an old man. And he composes *b* pretty well all the rest of his narrative about events in Troy, Ithaca, and the whole *Odyssey* in this way.

That's right.

Now, the speeches he makes and the parts between them are both narrative?

Of course.

But when he makes a speech as if he were someone else, won't we say that he makes his own style as much like that of the indicated speaker as *c* possible?

We certainly will.

Now, to make oneself like someone else in voice or appearance is to imitate the person one makes oneself like.

Certainly.

In these passages, then, it seems that he and the other poets effect their narrative through imitation.

That's right.

d   If the poet never hid himself, the whole of his poem would be narrative without imitation. In order to prevent you from saying again that you don't understand, I'll show you what this would be like. If Homer said that Chryses came with a ransom for his daughter to supplicate the Achaeans, especially the kings, and after that didn't speak as if he had become Chryses, but still as Homer, there would be no imitation but rather simple narrative. It would have gone something like this—I'll speak without meter since I'm no poet: "And the priest came and prayed that the gods would
e   allow them to capture Troy and be safe afterwards, that they'd accept the ransom and free his daughter, and thus show reverence for the god. When he'd said this, the others showed their respect for the priest and consented. But Agamemnon was angry and ordered him to leave and never to return, lest his priestly wand and the wreaths of the god should fail to protect him. He said that, before freeing the daughter, he'd grow old in Argos by her side. He told Chryses to go away and not to make him angry, if he
394 wanted to get home safely. When the old man heard this, he was frightened and went off in silence. But when he'd left the camp he prayed at length to Apollo, calling him by his various titles and reminding him of his own services to him. If any of those services had been found pleasing, whether it was the building of temples or the sacrifice of victims, he asked in return that the arrows of the god should make the Achaeans pay for his tears."
b   That is the way we get simple narrative without imitation.

I understand.

Then also understand that the opposite occurs when one omits the words between the speeches and leaves the speeches by themselves.

I understand that too. Tragedies are like that.

c   That's absolutely right. And now I think that I can make clear to you what I couldn't before. One kind of poetry and story-telling employs only imitation—tragedy and comedy, as you say. Another kind employs only narration by the poet himself—you find this most of all in dithyrambs.[35] A third kind uses both—as in epic poetry and many other places, if you follow me.

Now I understand what you were trying to say.

Remember, too, that before all that we said that we had dealt with *what* must be said in stories, but that we had yet to investigate *how* it must be said.

Yes, I remember.

35. Choral songs to the god Dionysus.

Well, this, more precisely, is what I meant: We need to come to an *d* agreement about whether we'll allow poets to narrate through imitation, and, if so, whether they are to imitate some things but not others—and what things these are, or whether they are not to imitate at all.

I divine that you're looking into the question of whether or not we'll allow tragedy and comedy into our city.

Perhaps, and perhaps even more than that, for I myself really don't know yet, but whatever direction the argument blows us, that's where we must go.

Fine.

Then, consider, Adeimantus, whether our guardians should be imitators or not. Or does this also follow from our earlier statement that each *e* individual would do a fine job of one occupation, not of many, and that if he tried the latter and dabbled in many things, he'd surely fail to achieve distinction in any of them?

He would indeed.

Then, doesn't the same argument also hold for imitation—a single individual can't imitate many things as well as he can imitate one?

No, he can't.

Then, he'll hardly be able to pursue any worthwhile way of life while at the same time imitating many things and being an imitator. Even in the *395* case of two kinds of imitation that are thought to be closely akin, such as tragedy and comedy, the same people aren't able to do both of them well. Did you not just say that these were both imitations?

I did, and you're quite right that the same people can't do both.

Nor can they be both rhapsodes and actors.

True.

Indeed, not even the same actors are used for tragedy and comedy. Yet all these are imitations, aren't they? *b*

They are.

And human nature, Adeimantus, seems to me to be minted in even smaller coins than these, so that it can neither imitate many things well nor do the actions themselves, of which those imitations are likenesses.

That's absolutely true.

Then, if we're to preserve our first argument, that our guardians must be kept away from all other crafts so as to be the craftsmen of the city's freedom, and be exclusively that, and do nothing at all except what *c* contributes to it, they must neither do nor imitate anything else. If they do imitate, they must imitate from childhood what is appropriate for them, namely, people who are courageous, self-controlled, pious, and free, and their actions. They mustn't be clever at doing or imitating slavish or shameful actions, lest from enjoying the imitation, they come to enjoy the *d*   reality. Or haven't you noticed that imitations practiced from youth become part of nature and settle into habits of gesture, voice, and thought?

I have indeed.

Then we won't allow those for whom we profess to care, and who must grow into good men, to imitate either a young woman or an older one, or one abusing her husband, quarreling with the gods, or bragging because she thinks herself happy, or one suffering misfortune and possessed by

e   sorrows and lamentations, and even less one who is ill, in love, or in labor.

That's absolutely right.

Nor must they imitate either male or female slaves doing slavish things.

No, they mustn't.

Nor bad men, it seems, who are cowards and are doing the opposite of what we described earlier, namely, libelling and ridiculing each other, using shameful language while drunk or sober, or wronging themselves and others, whether in word or deed, in the various other ways that

396 are typical of such people. They mustn't become accustomed to making themselves like madmen in either word or deed, for, though they must know about mad and vicious men and women, they must neither do nor imitate anything they do.

That's absolutely true.

Should they imitate metal workers or other craftsmen, or those who row in triremes, or their time-keepers, or anything else connected with

b   ships?

How could they, since they aren't to concern themselves with any of those occupations?

And what about this? Will they imitate neighing horses, bellowing bulls, roaring rivers, the crashing sea, thunder, or anything of that sort?

They are forbidden to be mad or to imitate mad people.

If I understand what you mean, there is one kind of style and narrative that someone who is really a gentleman would use whenever he wanted to narrate something, and another kind, unlike this one, which his opposite

c   by nature and education would favor, and in which he would narrate.

Which styles are those?

Well, I think that when a moderate man comes upon the words or actions of a good man in his narrative, he'll be willing to report them as if he were that man himself, and he won't be ashamed of that kind of imitation. He'll imitate this good man most when he's acting in a faultless

d   and intelligent manner, but he'll do so less, and with more reluctance, when the good man is upset by disease, sexual passion, drunkenness, or some other misfortune. When he comes upon a character unworthy of himself, however, he'll be unwilling to make himself seriously resemble that inferior character—except perhaps for a brief period in which he's doing something good. Rather he'll be ashamed to do something like that, both because he's unpracticed in the imitation of such people and because he can't stand to shape and mould himself according to a worse pattern. He despises this in his mind, unless it's just done in play.   *e*

That seems likely.

He'll therefore use the kind of narrative we described in dealing with the Homeric epics a moment ago. His style will participate both in imitation and in the other kind of narrative, but there'll be only a little bit of imitation in a long story? Or is there nothing in what I say?

That's precisely how the pattern for such a speaker must be.

As for someone who is not of this sort, the more inferior he is, the more   *397* willing he'll be to narrate anything and to consider nothing unworthy of himself. As a result, he'll undertake to imitate seriously and before a large audience all the things we just mentioned—thunder, the sounds of wind, hail, axles, pulleys, trumpets, flutes, pipes, and all the other instruments, even the cries of dogs, sheep, and birds. And this man's style will consist entirely of imitation in voice and gesture, or else include only a small bit   *b* of plain narrative.

That too is certain.

These, then, are the two kinds of style I was talking about.

There are these two.

The first of these styles involves little variation, so that if someone provides a musical mode and rhythm appropriate to it, won't the one who speaks correctly remain—with a few minor changes—pretty well within that mode and rhythm throughout?   *c*

That's precisely what he'll do.

What about the other kind of style? Doesn't it require the opposite if it is to speak appropriately, namely, all kinds of musical modes and all kinds of rhythms, because it contains every type of variation?

That's exactly right.

Do all poets and speakers adopt one or other of these patterns of style or a mixture of both?

Necessarily.

What are we to do, then? Shall we admit all these into our city, only   *d* one of the pure kinds, or the mixed one?

If my opinion is to prevail, we'll admit only the pure imitator of a decent person.

And yet, Adeimantus, the mixed style is pleasant. Indeed, it is by far the most pleasing to children, their tutors, and the vast majority of people.

Yes, it is the most pleasing.

But perhaps you don't think that it harmonizes with our constitution, because no one in our city is two or more people simultaneously, since each does only one job.   *e*

Indeed, it doesn't harmonize.

And isn't it because of this that it's only in our city that we'll find a cobbler who is a cobbler and not also a captain along with his cobbling, and a farmer who is a farmer and not also a juror along with his farming, and a soldier who is a soldier and not a money-maker in addition to his soldiering, and so with them all?

That's true.

It seems, then, that if a man, who through clever training can become 398 anything and imitate anything, should arrive in our city, wanting to give a performance of his poems, we should bow down before him as someone holy, wonderful, and pleasing, but we should tell him that there is no one like him in our city and that it isn't lawful for there to be. We should pour myrrh on his head, crown him with wreaths, and send him away to another city. But, for our own good, we ourselves should employ a more austere b and less pleasure-giving poet and storyteller, one who would imitate the speech of a decent person and who would tell his stories in accordance with the patterns we laid down when we first undertook the education of our soldiers.

That is certainly what we'd do if it were up to us.

It's likely, then, that we have now completed our discussion of the part of music and poetry that concerns speech and stories, for we've spoken both of what is to be said and of how it is to be said.

I agree.

c   Doesn't it remain, then, tо discuss lyric odes and songs?

Clearly.

And couldn't anyone discover what we would say about them, given that it has to be in tune with what we've already said?

Glaucon laughed and said: I'm afraid, Socrates, that I'm not to be included under "anyone," for I don't have a good enough idea at the moment of what we're to say. Of course, I have my suspicions.

Nonetheless, I said, you know that, in the first place, a song consists of d   three elements—words, harmonic mode, and rhythm.

Yes, I do know that.

As far as words are concerned, they are no different in songs than they are when not set to music, so mustn't they conform in the same way to the patterns we established just now?

They must.

Further, the mode and rhythm must fit the words.

Of course.

And we said that we no longer needed dirges and lamentations among our words.

We did, indeed.

e   What are the lamenting modes, then? You tell me, since you're musical.

The mixo-Lydian, the syntono-Lydian, and some others of that sort.
Aren't they to be excluded, then? They're useless even to decent women,
let alone to men.

Certainly.

Drunkenness, softness, and idleness are also most inappropriate for our
guardians.

How could they not be?

What, then, are the soft modes suitable for drinking-parties?

The Ionian and those Lydian modes that are said to be relaxed.

Could you ever use these to make people warriors?   *399*

Never. And now all you have left is the Dorian and Phrygian modes.

I don't know all the musical modes. Just leave me the mode that would
suitably imitate the tone and rhythm of a courageous person who is active
in battle or doing other violent deeds, or who is failing and facing wounds,
death, or some other misfortune, and who, in all these circumstances, is   *b*
fighting off his fate steadily and with self-control. Leave me also another
mode, that of someone engaged in a peaceful, unforced, voluntary action,
persuading someone or asking a favor of a god in prayer or of a human
being through teaching and exhortation, or, on the other hand, of someone
submitting to the supplications of another who is teaching him and trying
to get him to change his mind, and who, in all these circumstances, is
acting with moderation and self-control, not with arrogance but with
understanding, and is content with the outcome. Leave me, then, these   *c*
two modes, which will best imitate the violent or voluntary tones of voice
of those who are moderate and courageous, whether in good fortune or
in bad.

The modes you're asking for are the very ones I mentioned.

Well, then, we'll have no need for polyharmonic or multistringed instruments to accompany our odes and songs.

It doesn't seem so to me at least.

Then we won't need the craftsmen who make triangular lutes, harps,
and all other such multistringed and polyharmonic instruments.   *d*

Apparently not.

What about flute-makers and flute-players? Will you allow them into
the city? Or isn't the flute the most "many-stringed" of all? And aren't the
panharmonic instruments all imitations of it?[36]

Clearly.

---

36. The instrument being discussed is the *aulos*, which unlike the modern flute was a
reed instrument, like an oboe. The description of it as "many-stringed" seems to refer
only to the number of different notes which the *aulos* was capable of producing. The
aulos was thought to be especially good at conveying emotion.

The lyre and the cithara are left, then, as useful in the city, while in the country, there'd be some sort of pipe for the shepherds to play.

That is what our argument shows, at least.

e   Well, we certainly aren't doing anything new in preferring Apollo and his instruments to Marsyas and his.[37]

By god, it doesn't seem as though we are.

And, by the dog,[38] without being aware of it, we've been purifying the city we recently said was luxurious.

That's because we're being moderate.

Then let's purify the rest. The next topic after musical modes is the regulation of meter. We shouldn't strive to have either subtlety or great variety in meter. Rather, we should try to discover what are the rhythms of someone who leads an ordered and courageous life and then adapt the
400 meter and the tune to his words, not his words to them. What these rhythms actually are is for you to say, just as in the case of the modes.

I really don't know what to say. I can tell you from observation that there are three basic kinds of metrical feet out of which the others are constructed, just as there are four in the case of modes. But I can't tell you which sort imitates which sort of life.[39]

b   Then we'll consult with Damon[40] as to which metrical feet are suited to slavishness, insolence, madness, and the other vices and which are suited to their opposites. I think I've heard him talking about an enoplion,[41] which is a composite metrical phrase (although I'm not clear on this), and also about dactylic or heroic meter, which he arranged, I don't know how, to be equal up and down in the interchange of long and short. I think he
c   called one foot an iambus, another a trochee, assigning a long and a short to both of them. In the case of some of these, I think he approved or disapproved of the tempo of the foot as much as of the rhythm itself, or of some combination of the two—I can't tell you which. But, as I said,

---

37. After Athena had invented the flute, she discarded it because it distorted her features to play it. It was picked up by the satyr Marsyas, who was foolish enough to challenge Apollo (inventor of the lyre) to a musical contest. He was defeated, and Apollo flayed him alive. Satyrs were bestial in their behavior and desires—especially their sexual desires.

38. Socrates swears "by the dog" at 592a and "by the dog, the god of the Egyptians" at *Gorgias* 428b.

39. The three kinds are probably those in which the foot is divided in the ratio of (1) 2/2, e.g. the dactyl $(-/\smile\smile)$ and the spondee $(-/-)$, (2) 3/2, e.g. the paeon $(\smile\smile\smile/-)$, and (3) 1/2 or 2/1, e.g. the iambus $(\smile/-)$ and the trochee $(-/\smile)$.

40. Damon was an important fifth-century writer on music and meter. He is referred to at *Laches* 197d–200c.

41. The enoplion (or battle meter) is $\smile-$, $\smile\smile-$, $\smile\smile-$.

we'll leave these things to Damon, since to mark off the different kinds would require a long argument. Or do you think we should try it?

No, I certainly don't.

But you can discern, can't you, that grace and gracelessness follow good and bad rhythm respectively?

Of course.

Further, if, as we said just now, rhythm and mode must conform to the *d* words and not vice versa, then good rhythm follows fine words and is similar to them, while bad rhythm follows the opposite kind of words, and the same for harmony and disharmony.

To be sure, these things must conform to the words.

What about the style and content of the words themselves? Don't they conform to the character of the speaker's soul?

Of course.

And the rest conform to the words?

Yes.

Then fine words, harmony, grace, and rhythm follow simplicity of character—and I do not mean this in the sense in which we use "simplicity" *e* as a euphemism for "simple-mindedness"—but I mean the sort of fine and good character that has developed in accordance with an intelligent plan.

That's absolutely certain.

And must not our young people everywhere aim at these, if they are to do their own work?

They must, indeed.

Now, surely painting is full of these qualities, as are all the crafts similar to it; weaving is full of them, and so are embroidery, architecture, and the *401* crafts that produce all the other furnishings. Our bodily nature is full of them, as are the natures of all growing things, for in all of these there is grace and gracelessness. And gracelessness, bad rhythm, and disharmony are akin to bad words and bad character, while their opposites are akin to and are imitations of the opposite, a moderate and good character.

Absolutely.

Is it, then, only poets we have to supervise, compelling them to make *b* an image of a good character in their poems or else not to compose them among us? Or are we also to give orders to other craftsmen, forbidding them to represent—whether in pictures, buildings, or any other works— a character that is vicious, unrestrained, slavish, and graceless? Are we to allow someone who cannot follow these instructions to work among us, so that our guardians will be brought up on images of evil, as if in a meadow *c* of bad grass, where they crop and graze in many different places every day until, little by little, they unwittingly accumulate a large evil in their

souls? Or must we rather seek out craftsmen who are by nature able to pursue what is fine and graceful in their work, so that our young people will live in a healthy place and be benefited on all sides, and so that something of those fine works will strike their eyes and ears like a breeze that brings health from a good place, leading them unwittingly, from
d childhood on, to resemblance, friendship, and harmony with the beauty of reason?

The latter would be by far the best education for them.

Aren't these the reasons, Glaucon, that education in music and poetry is most important? First, because rhythm and harmony permeate the inner part of the soul more than anything else, affecting it most strongly and bringing it grace, so that if someone is properly educated in music and poetry, it makes him graceful, but if not, then the opposite. Second,
e because anyone who has been properly educated in music and poetry will sense it acutely when something has been omitted from a thing and when it hasn't been finely crafted or finely made by nature. And since he has the right distastes, he'll praise fine things, be pleased by them, receive them into his soul, and, being nurtured by them, become fine and good.
402 He'll rightly object to what is shameful, hating it while he's still young and unable to grasp the reason, but, having been educated in this way, he will welcome the reason when it comes and recognize it easily because of its kinship with himself.

Yes, I agree that those are the reasons to provide education in music and poetry.

It's just the way it was with learning how to read. Our ability wasn't adequate until we realized that there are only a few letters that occur in
b all sorts of different combinations, and that—whether written large or small[42]—they were worthy of our attention, so that we picked them out eagerly wherever they occurred, knowing that we wouldn't be competent readers until we knew our letters.

True.

And isn't it also true that if there are images of letters reflected in mirrors or water, we won't know them until we know the letters themselves, for both abilities are parts of the same craft and discipline?

Absolutely.

c   Then, by the gods, am I not right in saying that neither we, nor the guardians we are raising, will be educated in music and poetry until we know the different forms of moderation, courage, frankness, high-mindedness, and all their kindred, and their opposites too, which are moving around everywhere, and see them in the things in which they are, both themselves and their images, and do not disregard them, whether

42. See 368c–d.

they are written on small things or large, but accept that the knowledge of both large and small letters is part of the same craft and discipline?

That's absolutely essential.

Therefore, if someone's soul has a fine and beautiful character and his body matches it in beauty and is thus in harmony with it, so that both *d* share in the same pattern, wouldn't that be the most beautiful sight for anyone who has eyes to see?

It certainly would.

And isn't what is most beautiful also most loveable?

Of course.

And a musical person would love such people most of all, but he wouldn't love anyone who lacked harmony?

No, he wouldn't, at least not if the defect was in the soul, but if it was only in the body, he'd put up with it and be willing to embrace the boy who had it.[43]   *e*

I gather that you love or have loved such a boy yourself, and I agree with you. Tell me this, however: Is excessive pleasure compatible with moderation?

How can it be, since it drives one mad just as much as pain does?

What about with the rest of virtue?

No.   *403*

Well, then, is it compatible with violence and licentiousness?

Very much so.

Can you think of a greater or keener pleasure than sexual pleasure?

I can't—or a madder one either.

But the right kind of love is by nature the love of order and beauty that has been moderated by education in music and poetry?

That's right.

Therefore, the right kind of love has nothing mad or licentious about it?

No, it hasn't.

Then sexual pleasure mustn't come into it, and the lover and the boy he loves must have no share in it, if they are to love and be loved in the   *b* right way?

By god, no, Socrates, it mustn't come into it.

It seems, then, that you'll lay it down as a law in the city we're establishing that if a lover can persuade a boy to let him, then he may kiss him, be with him, and touch him, as a father would a son, for the sake of what is fine and beautiful, but—turning to the other things—his association with the

43. The best discussion of the kind of erotic relationships between an older man and a younger boy to which Plato is referring here is K. J. Dover, *Greek Homosexuality* (Cambridge: Harvard University Press, 1978).

c   one he cares about must never seem to go any further than this, otherwise
he will be reproached as untrained in music and poetry and lacking in
appreciation for what is fine and beautiful.

That's right.

Does it seem to you that we've now completed our account of education
in music and poetry? Anyway, it has ended where it ought to end, for it
ought to end in the love of the fine and beautiful.

I agree.

After music and poetry, our young people must be given physical
training.

Of course.

In this, too, they must have careful education from childhood through-
d   out life. The matter stands, I believe, something like this—but you, too,
should look into it. It seems to me that a fit body doesn't by its own virtue
make the soul good, but instead that the opposite is true—a good soul by
its own virtue makes the body as good as possible. How does it seem to
you?

The same.

Then, if we have devoted sufficient care to the mind, wouldn't we be
right, in order to avoid having to do too much talking, to entrust it with
the detailed supervision of the body, while we indicate only the general
e   patterns to be followed?

Certainly.

We said that our prospective guardians must avoid drunkenness, for it
is less appropriate for a guardian to be drunk and not to know where on
earth he is than it is for anyone else.

It would be absurd for a guardian to need a guardian.

What about food? Aren't these men athletes in the greatest contest?

They are.

Then would the regimen currently prescribed for athletes in training
404 be suitable for them?

Perhaps it would.

Yet it seems to result in sluggishness and to be of doubtful value for
health. Or haven't you noticed that these athletes sleep their lives away
and that, if they deviate even a little from their orderly regimen, they
become seriously and violently ill?

I have noticed that.

Then our warrior athletes need a more sophisticated kind of training.
They must be like sleepless hounds, able to see and hear as keenly as
possible and to endure frequent changes of water and food, as well as
b   summer and winter weather on their campaigns, without faltering in
health.

That's how it seems to me, too.

Now, isn't the best physical training akin to the simple music and poetry we were describing a moment ago?

How do you mean?

I mean a simple and decent physical training, particularly the kind involved in training for war.

What would it be like?

You might learn about such things from Homer. You know that, when his heroes are campaigning, he doesn't give them fish to banquet on, even though they are by the sea in the Hellespont, nor boiled meat either. Instead, he gives them only roasted meat, which is the kind most easily   c available to soldiers, for it's easier nearly everywhere to use fire alone than to carry pots and pans.

That's right.

Nor, I believe, does Homer mention sweet desserts anywhere. Indeed, aren't even the other athletes aware that, if one's body is to be sound, one must keep away from all such things?

They're right to be aware of it, at any rate, and to avoid such things.

If you think that, then it seems that you don't approve of Syracusan   d cuisine or of Sicilian-style dishes.

I do not.

Then you also object to Corinthian girlfriends for men who are to be in good physical condition.[44]

Absolutely.

What about the reputed delights of Attic pastries?

I certainly object to them, too.

I believe that we'd be right to compare this diet and this entire life-style to the kinds of lyric odes and songs that are composed in all sorts of modes and rhythms.   e

Certainly.

Just as embellishment in the one gives rise to licentiousness, doesn't it give rise to illness in the other? But simplicity in music and poetry makes for moderation in the soul, and in physical training it makes for bodily health?

That's absolutely true.

And as licentiousness and disease breed in the city, aren't many law courts and hospitals opened? And don't medicine and law give themselves   405 solemn airs when even large numbers of free men take them very seriously?

How could it be otherwise?

---

44. In the Classical period Corinthian prostitutes and hetairai enjoyed an international reputation. Plato is here objecting to them as hired female dinner companions.

Yet could you find a greater sign of bad and shameful education in a city than that the need for skilled doctors and lawyers is felt not only by inferior people and craftsmen but by those who claim to have been brought up in the manner of free men? Don't you think it's shameful and a great

b sign of vulgarity to be forced to make use of a justice imposed by others, as masters and judges, because you are unable to deal with the situation yourself?

I think that's the most shameful thing of all.

Yet isn't it even more shameful when someone not only spends a good part of his life in court defending himself or prosecuting someone else but, through inexperience of what is fine, is persuaded to take pride in

c being clever at doing injustice and then exploiting every loophole and trick to escape conviction—and all for the sake of little worthless things and because he's ignorant of how much better and finer it is to arrange one's own life so as to have no need of finding a sleepy or inattentive judge?

This case is even more shameful than the other.

And doesn't it seem shameful to you to need medical help, not for wounds or because of some seasonal illness, but because, through idleness

d and the life-style we've described, one is full of gas and phlegm like a stagnant swamp, so that sophisticated Asclepiad doctors are forced to come up with names like "flatulence" and "catarrh" to describe one's diseases?

It does. And those certainly are strange new names for diseases.

Indeed, I don't suppose that they even existed in the time of Asclepius himself. I take it as a proof of this that his sons at Troy didn't criticize either

e the woman who treated Eurypylus when he was wounded, or Patroclus who prescribed the treatment, which consisted of Pramnian wine with barley meal and grated cheese sprinkled on it, though such treatment is now

406 thought to cause inflammation.[45]

Yet it's a strange drink to give someone in that condition.

Not if you recall that they say that the kind of modern medicine that plays nursemaid to the disease wasn't used by the Asclepiads before Herodicus. He was a physical trainer who became ill, so he mixed physical training with medicine and wore out first himself and then many others

b as well.

How did he do that?

By making his dying a lengthy process. Always tending his mortal illness, he was nonetheless, it seems, unable to cure it, so he lived out his life under medical treatment, with no leisure for anything else whatever. If he

45. At *Iliad* 11.580 ff. Eurypylus is wounded but not treated in this way (see 11.828–36). However, Machaon, the son of Asclepius, receives this treatment at 11.624–50.

departed even a little from his accustomed regimen, he became completely worn out, but because his skill made dying difficult, he lived into old age. That's a fine prize for his skill.

One that's appropriate for someone who didn't know that it wasn't   c
because he was ignorant or inexperienced that Asclepius failed to teach this type of medicine to his sons, but because he knew that everyone in a well-regulated city has his own work to do and that no one has the leisure to be ill and under treatment all his life. It's absurd that we recognize this to be true of craftsmen while failing to recognize that it's equally true of those who are wealthy and supposedly happy.

How is that?

When a carpenter is ill, he expects to receive an emetic or a purge from   d
his doctor or to get rid of his disease through surgery or cautery. If anyone prescribed a lengthy regimen to him, telling him that he should rest with his head bandaged and so on, he'd soon reply that he had no leisure to be ill and that life is no use to him if he has to neglect his work and always be concerned with his illness. After that he'd bid good-bye to his doctor,   e
resume his usual way of life, and either recover his health or, if his body couldn't withstand the illness, he'd die and escape his troubles.

It is believed to be appropriate for someone like that to use medicine in this way.

Is that because his life is of no profit to him if he doesn't do his work?   407
Obviously.

But the rich person, we say, has no work that would make his life unlivable if he couldn't do it.

That's what people say, at least.

That's because you haven't heard the saying of Phocylides that, once you have the means of life, you must practice virtue.[46]

I think he must also practice virtue before that.

We won't quarrel with Phocylides about this. But let's try to find out whether the rich person must indeed practice virtue and whether his life is not worth living if he doesn't or whether tending an illness, while it is an obstacle to applying oneself to carpentry and the other crafts, is no   b
obstacle whatever to taking Phocylides' advice.

But excessive care of the body, over and above physical training, is pretty well the biggest obstacle of all. It's troublesome in managing a household, in military service, and even in a sedentary public office.

Yet the most important of all, surely, is that it makes any kind of learning,   c
thought, or private meditation difficult, for it's always imagining some

---

46. Phocylides of Miletus was a mid-sixth-century elegiac and hexameter poet best known for his epigrams.

headaches or dizziness and accusing philosophy of causing them. Hence, wherever this kind of virtue is practiced and examined, excessive care of the body hinders it, for it makes a person think he's ill and be all the time concerned about his body.

It probably does.

Therefore, won't we say that Asclepius knew this, and that he taught medicine for those whose bodies are healthy in their natures and habits *d* but have some specific disease? His medicine is for these people with these habits. He cured them of their disease with drugs or surgery and then ordered them to live their usual life so as not to harm their city's affairs. But for those whose bodies were riddled with disease, he didn't attempt to prescribe a regimen, drawing off a little here and pouring in a little there, in order to make their life a prolonged misery and enable them to produce offspring in all probability like themselves. He *e* didn't think that he should treat someone who couldn't live a normal life, since such a person would be of no profit either to himself or to the city.

The Asclepius you're talking about was quite a statesman.

Clearly. And don't you see that because he was a statesman his sons turned out to be good men at Troy, practicing medicine as I say they did? *408* Don't you remember that they "sucked out the blood and applied gentle potions" to the wound Pandarus inflicted on Menelaus, but without prescribing what he should eat or drink after that, any more than they did for Eurypylus?[47] They considered their drugs to be sufficient to cure men who were healthy and living an orderly life before being wounded, even *b* if they happened to drink wine mixed with barley and cheese right after receiving their wounds. But they didn't consider the lives of those who were by nature sick and licentious to be profitable either to themselves or to anyone else. Medicine isn't intended for such people and they shouldn't be treated, not even if they're richer than Midas.

The sons of Asclepius you're talking about were indeed very sophisticated.

Appropriately so. But Pindar and the tragedians don't agree with us. They say that Asclepius was the son of Apollo, that he was bribed with gold to heal a rich man, who was already dying, and that he was killed by lightning for doing so. But, in view of what we said before, we won't *c* believe this. We'll say that if Asclepius was the son of a god, he was not a money-grubber, and that if he was a money-grubber, he was not the son of a god.

That's right. But what do you say about the following, Socrates? Don't

47. *Iliad* 4.218–19. In our text Machaon is acting alone.

we need to have good doctors in our city? And the best will surely be those who have handled the greatest number of sick and of healthy people. In the same way, the best judges[48] will be those who have associated with   *d* people whose natures are of every kind.

I agree that the doctors and judges must be good. But do you know the kind I consider to be so?

If you'll tell me.

I'll try. But you ask about things that aren't alike in the same question.

In what way?

The cleverest doctors are those who, in addition to learning their craft, have had contact with the greatest number of very sick bodies from childhood on, have themselves experienced every illness, and aren't very healthy by nature, for they don't treat bodies with their bodies, I suppose—   *e* if they did, we wouldn't allow their bodies to be or become bad. Rather they treat the body with their souls, and it isn't possible for the soul to treat anything well, if it is or has been bad itself.

That's right.

As for the judge, he *does* rule other souls with his own soul. And it isn't   *409* possible for a soul to be nurtured among vicious souls from childhood, to associate with them, to indulge in every kind of injustice, and come through it able to judge other people's injustices from its own case, as it can diseases of the body. Rather, if it's to be fine and good, and a sound judge of just things, it must itself remain pure and have no experience of bad character while it's young. That's the reason, indeed, that decent people appear simple and easily deceived by unjust ones when they are young. It's because they have no models in themselves of the evil experiences of   *b* the vicious to guide their judgments.

That's certainly so.

Therefore, a good judge must not be a young person but an old one, who has learned late in life what injustice is like and who has become aware of it not as something at home in his own soul, but as something alien and present in others, someone who, after a long time, has recognized that injustice is bad by nature, not from his own experience of it, but through knowledge.   *c*

Such a judge would be the most noble one of all.

And he'd be good, too, which was what you asked, for someone who has a good soul is good. The clever and suspicious person, on the other

---

48. The Greek word is *dikastēs*, a member of a jury. Athenian juries decided both the question of guilt and the penalty, however. Hence they combined the functions that we divide between the jury and the judge. Since Plato is obviously thinking of the act of judging here, "judge" is a less misleading translation than "juror."

hand, who has committed many injustices himself and thinks himself a wise villain, appears clever in the company of those like himself, because he's on his guard and is guided by the models within himself. But when he meets with good older people, he's seen to be stupid, distrustful at the wrong time, and ignorant of what a sound character is, since he has no

d   model of this within himself. But since he meets vicious people more often than good ones, he seems to be clever rather than unlearned, both to himself and to others.

That's completely true.

Then we mustn't look for the good judge among people like that but among the sort we described earlier. A vicious person would never know either himself or a virtuous one, whereas a naturally virtuous person, when educated, will in time acquire knowledge of both virtue and vice. And it is someone like that who becomes wise, in my view, and not the bad

e   person.

I agree with you.

Then won't you legislate in our city for the kind of medicine we mentioned and for this kind of judging, so that together they'll look after those

410 who are naturally well endowed in body and soul? But as for the ones whose bodies are naturally unhealthy or whose souls are incurably evil, won't they let the former die of their own accord and put the latter to death?

That seems to be best both for the ones who suffer such treatment and for the city.

However, *our* young people, since they practice that simple sort of music and poetry that we said produces moderation, will plainly be wary of coming to need a judge.

That's right.

And won't a person who's educated in music and poetry pursue physical

b   training in the same way, and choose to make no use of medicine except when unavoidable?

I believe so.

He'll work at physical exercises in order to arouse the spirited part of his nature, rather than to acquire the physical strength for which other athletes diet and labor.

That's absolutely right.

Then, Glaucon, did those who established education in music and poetry and in physical training do so with the aim that people attribute to

c   them, which is to take care of the body with the latter and the soul with the former, or with some other aim?

What other aim do you mean?

It looks as though they established both chiefly for the sake of the soul.

How so?

Haven't you noticed the effect that lifelong physical training, unaccompanied by any training in music and poetry, has on the mind, or the effect of the opposite, music and poetry without physical training?

What effects are you talking about?

Savagery and toughness in the one case and softness and overcultivation   *d*
in the other.

I get the point. You mean that those who devote themselves exclusively to physical training turn out to be more savage than they should, while those who devote themselves to music and poetry turn out to be softer than is good for them?

Moreover, the source of the savageness is the spirited part of one's nature. Rightly nurtured, it becomes courageous, but if it's overstrained, it's likely to become hard and harsh.

So it seems.

And isn't it the philosophic part of one's nature that provides the cultivation? If it is relaxed too far, it becomes softer than it should, but if   *e*
properly nurtured, it is cultivated and orderly.

So it is.

Now, we say that our guardians must have both these natures.

They must indeed.

And mustn't the two be harmonized with each other?

Of course.

And if this harmony is achieved, the soul is both moderate and courageous?   *411*

Certainly.

But if it is inharmonious, it is cowardly and savage?

Yes, indeed.

Therefore, when someone gives music an opportunity to charm his soul with the flute and to pour those sweet, soft, and plaintive tunes we mentioned through his ear, as through a funnel, when he spends his whole life humming them and delighting in them, then, at first, whatever spirit he has is softened, just as iron is tempered, and from being hard and useless, it is made useful. But if he keeps at it unrelentingly and is beguiled by the music, after a time his spirit is melted and dissolved until it vanishes,   *b*
and the very sinews of his soul are cut out and he becomes "a feeble warrior."[49]

That's right.

And if he had a spiritless nature from the first, this process is soon completed. But if he had a spirited nature, his spirit becomes weak and

49. *Iliad* 17.588.

unstable, flaring up at trifles and extinguished as easily. The result is that such people become quick-tempered, prone to anger, and filled with
c   discontent, rather than spirited.

That's certainly true.

What about someone who works hard at physical training and eats well but never touches music or philosophy? Isn't he in good physical condition at first, full of resolution and spirit? And doesn't he become more courageous than he was before?

Certainly.

d   But what happens if he does nothing else and never associates with the Muse? Doesn't whatever love of learning he might have had in his soul soon become enfeebled, deaf, and blind, because he never tastes any learning or investigation or partakes of any discussion or any of the rest of music and poetry, to nurture or arouse it?

It does seem to be that way.

I believe that someone like that becomes a hater of reason and of music. He no longer makes any use of persuasion but bulls his way through every situation by force and savagery like a wild animal, living in ignorance and
e   stupidity without either rhythm or grace.

That's most certainly how he'll live.

It seems, then, that a god has given music and physical training to human beings not, except incidentally, for the body and the soul but for the spirited and wisdom-loving parts of the soul itself, in order that these might be in harmony with one another, each being stretched and relaxed
412 to the appropriate degree.

It seems so.

Then the person who achieves the finest blend of music and physical training and impresses it on his soul in the most measured way is the one we'd most correctly call completely harmonious and trained in music, much more so than the one who merely harmonizes the strings of his instrument.

That's certainly so, Socrates.

Then, won't we always need this sort of person as an overseer in our city, Glaucon, if indeed its constitution is to be preserved?
b   It seems that we'll need someone like that most of all.

These, then, are the patterns for education and upbringing. Should we enumerate the dances of these people, or their hunts, chases with hounds, athletic contests, and horse races? Surely, they're no longer hard to discover, since it's pretty clear that they must follow the patterns we've already established.

Perhaps so.

All right, then what's the next thing we have to determine? Isn't it which of these same people will rule and which be ruled?

Of course.   *c*

Now, isn't it obvious that the rulers must be older and the ruled younger?

Yes, it is.

And mustn't the rulers also be the best of them?

That, too.

And aren't the best farmers the ones who are best at farming?

Yes.

Then, as the rulers must be the best of the guardians, mustn't they be the ones who are best at guarding the city?

Yes.

Then, in the first place, mustn't they be knowledgeable and capable, and mustn't they care for the city?

That's right.   *d*

Now, one cares most for what one loves.

Necessarily.

And someone loves something most of all when he believes that the same things are advantageous to it as to himself and supposes that if it does well, he'll do well, and that if it does badly, then he'll do badly too.

That's right.

Then we must choose from among our guardians those men who, upon examination, seem most of all to believe throughout their lives that they must eagerly pursue what is advantageous to the city and be wholly   *e* unwilling to do the opposite.

Such people would be suitable for the job at any rate.

I think we must observe them at all ages to see whether they are guardians of this conviction and make sure that neither compulsion nor magic spells will get them to discard or forget their belief that they must do what is best for the city.

What do you mean by discarding?

I'll tell you. I think the discarding of a belief is either voluntary or involuntary—voluntary when one learns that the belief is false, involuntary in the case of all true beliefs.   *413*

I understand voluntary discarding but not involuntary.

What's that? Don't you know that people are voluntarily deprived of bad things, but involuntarily deprived of good ones? And isn't being deceived about the truth a bad thing, while possessing the truth is good? Or don't you think that to believe the things that are is to possess the truth?

That's right, and I do think that people are involuntarily deprived of true opinions.

But can't they also be so deprived by theft, magic spells, and compulsion?   *b*

Now, I don't understand again.

I'm afraid I must be talking like a tragic poet! By "the victims of theft"

I mean those who are persuaded to change their minds or those who forget, because time, in the latter case, and argument, in the former, takes away their opinions without their realizing it. Do you understand now?

Yes.

By "the compelled" I mean those whom pain or suffering causes to change their mind.

I understand that, and you're right.

The "victims of magic," I think you'd agree, are those who change their
c   mind because they are under the spell of pleasure or fear.

It seems to me that everything that deceives does so by casting a spell.

Then, as I said just now, we must find out who are the best guardians of their conviction that they must always do what they believe to be best for the city. We must keep them under observation from childhood and set them tasks that are most likely to make them forget such a conviction
d   or be deceived out of it, and we must select whoever keeps on remembering it and isn't easily deceived, and reject the others. Do you agree?

Yes.

And we must subject them to labors, pains, and contests in which we can watch for these traits.

That's right.

Then we must also set up a competition for the third way in which people are deprived of their convictions, namely, magic. Like those who lead colts into noise and tumult to see if they're afraid, we must expose our young people to fears and pleasures, testing them more thoroughly
e   than gold is tested by fire. If someone is hard to put under a spell, is apparently gracious in everything, is a good guardian of himself and the music and poetry he has learned, and if he always shows himself to be rhythmical and harmonious, then he is the best person both for himself and for the city. Anyone who is tested in this way as a child, youth, and
414 adult, and always comes out of it untainted, is to be made a ruler as well as a guardian; he is to be honored in life and to receive after his death the most prized tombs and memorials. But anyone who fails to prove himself in this way is to be rejected. It seems to me, Glaucon, that rulers and guardians must be selected and appointed in some such way as this, though we've provided only a general pattern and not the exact details.

It's also seems to me that they must be selected in this sort of way.
b   Then, isn't it truly most correct to call these people complete guardians, since they will guard against external enemies and internal friends, so that the one will lack the power and the other the desire to harm the city? The young people we've hitherto called guardians we'll now call *auxiliaries* and supporters of the guardians' convictions.

I agree.

How, then, could we devise one of those useful falsehoods we were talking about a while ago,[50] one noble falsehood that would, in the best case, persuade even the rulers, but if that's not possible, then the others   *c* in the city?

What sort of falsehood?

Nothing new, but a Phoenician story which describes something that has happened in many places. At least, that's what the poets say, and they've persuaded many people to believe it too. It hasn't happened among us, and I don't even know if it could. It would certainly take a lot of persuasion to get people to believe it.

You seem hesitant to tell the story.

When you hear it, you'll realize that I have every reason to hesitate.

Speak, and don't be afraid.

I'll tell it, then, though I don't know where I'll get the audacity or even   *d* what words I'll use. I'll first try to persuade the rulers and the soldiers and then the rest of the city that the upbringing and the education we gave them, and the experiences that went with them, were a sort of dream, that in fact they themselves, their weapons, and the other craftsmen's tools were at that time really being fashioned and nurtured inside the earth,   *e* and that when the work was completed, the earth, who is their mother, delivered all of them up into the world. Therefore, if anyone attacks the land in which they live, they must plan on its behalf and defend it as their mother and nurse and think of the other citizens as their earthborn brothers.

It isn't for nothing that you were so shy about telling your falsehood.

Appropriately so. Nevertheless, listen to the rest of the story. "All of   *415* you in the city are brothers," we'll say to them in telling our story, "but the god who made you mixed some gold into those who are adequately equipped to rule, because they are most valuable. He put silver in those who are auxiliaries and iron and bronze in the farmers and other craftsmen. For the most part you will produce children like yourselves, but, because you are all related, a silver child will occasionally be born from a golden   *b* parent, and vice versa, and all the others from each other. So the first and most important command from the god to the rulers is that there is nothing that they must guard better or watch more carefully than the mixture of metals in the souls of the next generation. If an offspring of theirs should be found to have a mixture of iron or bronze, they must not pity him in any way, but give him the rank appropriate to his nature and drive him   *c* out to join the craftsmen and farmers. But if an offspring of these people is found to have a mixture of gold or silver, they will honor him and take

50. See 382a ff.

him up to join the guardians or the auxiliaries, for there is an oracle which
says that the city will be ruined if it ever has an iron or a bronze guardian."
So, do you have any device that will make our citizens believe this story?

d   I can't see any way to make them believe it themselves, but perhaps
there is one in the case of their sons and later generations and all the other
people who come after them.

I understand pretty much what you mean, but even that would help to
make them care more for the city and each other. However, let's leave
this matter wherever tradition takes it. And let's now arm our earthborn
and lead them forth with their rulers in charge. And as they march, let
them look for the best place in the city to have their camp, a site from

e   which they can most easily control those within, if anyone is unwilling to
obey the laws, or repel any outside enemy who comes like a wolf upon the
flock. And when they have established their camp and made the requisite
sacrifices, they must see to their sleeping quarters. What do you say?

I agree.

And won't these quarters protect them adequately both in winter and
summer?

Of course, for it seems to me that you mean their housing.

Yes, but housing for soldiers, not for money-makers.

416   How do you mean to distinguish these from one another?

I'll try to tell you. The most terrible and most shameful thing of all is
for a shepherd to rear dogs as auxiliaries to help him with his flocks in
such a way that, through licentiousness, hunger, or some other bad trait
of character, they do evil to the sheep and become like wolves instead of
dogs.

That's certainly a terrible thing.

b   Isn't it necessary, therefore, to guard in every way against our auxiliaries
doing anything like that to the citizens because they are stronger, thereby
becoming savage masters instead of kindly allies?

It is necessary.

And wouldn't a really good education endow them with the greatest
caution in this regard?

But surely they have had an education like that.

Perhaps we shouldn't assert this dogmatically, Glaucon. What we can
assert is what we were saying just now, that they must have the right
education, whatever it is, if they are to have what will most make them

c   gentle to each other and to those they are guarding.

That's right.

Now, someone with some understanding might say that, besides this
education, they must also have the kind of housing and other property
that will neither prevent them from being the best guardians nor encourage

d   them to do evil to the other citizens.

That's true.

Consider, then, whether or not they should live in some such way as this, if they're to be the kind of men we described. First, none of them should possess any private property beyond what is wholly necessary. Second, none of them should have a house or storeroom that isn't open for all to enter at will. Third, whatever sustenance moderate and courageous warrior-athletes require in order to have neither shortfall nor surplus in   *e* a given year they'll receive by taxation on the other citizens as a salary for their guardianship. Fourth, they'll have common messes and live together like soldiers in a camp. We'll tell them that they always have gold and silver of a divine sort in their souls as a gift from the gods and so have no further need of human gold. Indeed, we'll tell them that it's impious for them to defile this divine possession by any admixture of such gold, because many impious deeds have been done that involve the currency used by ordinary people, while their own is pure. Hence, for them alone *417* among the city's population, it is unlawful to touch or handle gold or silver. They mustn't be under the same roof as it, wear it as jewelry, or drink from gold or silver goblets. In this way they'd save both themselves and the city. But if they acquire private land, houses, and currency themselves, they'll be household managers and farmers instead of guardians—hostile masters of the other citizens instead of their allies. They'll spend their   *b* whole lives hating and being hated, plotting and being plotted against, more afraid of internal than of external enemies, and they'll hasten both themselves and the whole city to almost immediate ruin. For all these reasons, let's say that the guardians must be provided with housing and the rest in this way, and establish this as a law. Or don't you agree?

I certainly do, Glaucon said.

BOOK IV

Given the austere life-style afforded to the guardians in the kallipolis, the question Adeimantus raises about their happiness at the beginning of this book is a natural one. Everyone is supposed to be happy in the kallipolis (420b, 519e), yet the guardians, who have the most power, do not seem to have been made happy at all. Socrates' response (420b–421c) is complex and should be read together with 465e ff. The goal of the kallipolis, he says, is not to make any one group in the city outstandingly happy at the expense of others, as Thrasymachus claimed, but to make everyone as happy as his nature allows (421c). This will be accomplished, he argues, if everyone in it practices the craft for which his natural aptitude is highest, whether it is producing, guarding, or ruling (434a–c).

Hence the guardians must above all protect their system of elementary education, for this provides the training in civic virtue without which no system of laws, no constitution, can hope to achieve anything worthwhile (423c–427a). But though Socrates has proposed many innovations in religious education as part of his reform of music and poetry and physical training, he is more conservative when it comes to religious practice. The laws concerning that, he says, are to be left up to "the traditional lawgiver," namely, the Delphian Apollo (427b–c).

The kallipolis is pronounced established (427d). Since it is completely good (427e), it must have all the virtues of a city (see 352d–354a), namely, wisdom, courage, moderation, and justice. Therefore the search for the justice in it is guaranteed not to be futile.

By the time that search has concluded (434d), wisdom, courage, moderation, and justice have each been identified with distinct structural features of the kallipolis, but those identifications will not be secure until the very same structural features are shown to be identical to those virtues in the individual soul (434d–435a).

This leads to the argument for the division of the soul into three parts—appetitive, spirited, rational—corresponding to the three major classes in the kallipolis—producers, guardians, rulers (435c–441c). Once this argument is complete, it remains to find the virtues in the soul and to show that they are the same structural features of it as of the kallipolis (441c–444e).

The final question raised in Book IV is the central one of the Republic, namely, whether it is more profitable to be just or unjust (445a). Glaucon is ready to

answer it at this point (445a–b) but Socrates is not (445b), for, in his view, the
question cannot be clearly answered until much more work has been done on
virtue and vice (445b–e).

And Adeimantus interrupted: How would you defend yourself, Socrates,
he said, if someone told you that you aren't making these men very happy   *419*
and that it's their own fault? The city really belongs to them, yet they
derive no good from it. Others own land, build fine big houses, acquire
furnishings to go along with them, make their own private sacrifices to the
gods, entertain guests, and also, of course, possess what you were talking
about just now, gold and silver and all the things that are thought to belong
to people who are blessedly happy. But one might well say that your
guardians are simply settled in the city like mercenaries and that all they
do is watch over it.   *420*

Yes, I said, and what's more, they work simply for their keep and get
no extra wages as the others do. Hence, if they want to take a private trip
away from the city, they won't be able to; they'll have nothing to give to
their mistresses, nothing to spend in whatever other ways they wish, as
people do who are considered happy. You've omitted these and a host of
other, similar facts from your charge.

Well, let them be added to the charge as well.

Then, are you asking how we should defend ourselves?   *b*

Yes.

I think we'll discover what to say if we follow the same path as before.
We'll say that it wouldn't be surprising if these people were happiest just
as they are, but that, in establishing our city, we aren't aiming to make any
one group outstandingly happy but to make the whole city so, as far as
possible. We thought that we'd find justice most easily in such a city and
injustice, by contrast, in the one that is governed worst and that, by
observing both cities, we'd be able to judge the question we've been
inquiring into for so long. We take ourselves, then, to be fashioning the   *c*
happy city, not picking out a few happy people and putting them in it, but
making the whole city happy. (We'll look at the opposite city soon.[1])

Suppose, then, that someone came up to us while we were painting a
statue and objected that, because we had painted the eyes (which are the
most beautiful part) black rather than purple, we had not applied the most
beautiful colors to the most beautiful parts of the statue. We'd think it
reasonable to offer the following defense: "You mustn't expect us to paint
the eyes so beautifully that they no longer appear to be eyes at all, and the *d*

---

1. This discussion begins at 445c, but is interrupted and doesn't begin again until
Book VIII.

same with the other parts. Rather you must look to see whether by dealing with each part appropriately, we are making the whole statue beautiful." Similarly, you mustn't force us to give our guardians the kind of happiness that would make them something other than guardians. We know how to
e   clothe the farmers in purple robes, festoon them with gold jewelry, and tell them to work the land whenever they please. We know how to settle our potters on couches by the fire, feasting and passing the wine around, with their wheel beside them for whenever they want to make pots. And we can make all the others happy in the same way, so that the whole city is happy. Don't urge us to do this, however, for if we do, a farmer wouldn't
421 be a farmer, nor a potter a potter, and none of the others would keep to the patterns of work that give rise to a city. Now, if cobblers become inferior and corrupt and claim to be what they are not, that won't do much harm to the city. Hence, as far as they and the others like them are concerned, our argument carries less weight. But if the guardians of our laws and city are merely believed to be guardians but are not, you surely see that they'll destroy the city utterly, just as they alone have the opportunity to govern it well and make it happy.

If we are making true guardians, then, who are least likely to do evil to the city, and if the one who brought the charge is talking about farmers
b   and banqueters who are happy as they would be at a festival rather than in a city, then he isn't talking about a city at all, but about something else. With this in mind, we should consider whether in setting up our guardians we are aiming to give them the greatest happiness, or whether—since our aim is to see that the city as a whole has the greatest happiness—we must compel and persuade the auxiliaries and guardians to follow our other
c   policy and be the best possible craftsmen at their own work, and the same with all the others. In this way, with the whole city developing and being governed well, we must leave it to nature to provide each group with its share of happiness.

I think you put that very well, he said.

Will you also think that I'm putting things well when I make the next point, which is closely akin to this one?

Which one exactly?

Consider whether or not the following things corrupt the other workers,
d   so that they become bad.

What things?

Wealth and poverty.

How do they corrupt the other workers?

Like this. Do you think that a potter who has become wealthy will still be willing to pay attention to his craft?

Not at all.

Won't he become more idle and careless than he was?

Much more.

Then won't he become a worse potter?

Far worse.

And surely if poverty prevents him from having tools or any of the other things he needs for his craft, he'll produce poorer work and will teach his sons, or anyone else he teaches, to be worse craftsmen.   *e*

Of course.

So poverty and wealth make a craftsman and his products worse.

Apparently.

It seems, then, that we've found other things that our guardians must guard against in every way, to prevent them from slipping into the city unnoticed.

What are they?

Both wealth and poverty. The former makes for luxury, idleness, and   *422* revolution; the latter for slavishness, bad work, and revolution as well.

That's certainly true. But consider this, Socrates: If our city hasn't got any money, how will it be able to fight a war, especially if it has to fight against a great and wealthy city?

Obviously, it will be harder to fight one such city and easier to fight   *b* two.

How do you mean?

First of all, if our city has to fight a city of the sort you mention, won't it be a case of warrior-athletes fighting against rich men?

Yes, as far as that goes.

Well, then, Adeimantus, don't you think that one boxer who has had the best possible training could easily fight two rich and fat nonboxers?

Maybe not at the same time.

Not even by escaping from them and then turning and hitting the one who caught up with him first, and doing this repeatedly in stifling heat and sun? Wouldn't he, in his condition, be able to handle even more than   *c* two such people?

That certainly wouldn't be surprising.

And don't you think that the rich have more knowledge and experience of boxing than of how to fight a war?

I do.

Then in all likelihood our athletes will easily be able to fight twice or three times their own numbers in a war.

I agree, for I think what you say is right.

What if they sent envoys to another city and told them the following truth: "We have no use for gold or silver, and it isn't lawful for us to   *d* possess them, so join us in this war, and you can take the property of those

who oppose us for yourselves." Do you think that anyone hearing this
would choose to fight hard, lean dogs, rather than to join them in fighting
fat and tender sheep?

No, I don't. But if the wealth of all the cities came to be gathered in a
e single one, watch out that it doesn't endanger your nonwealthy city.

You're happily innocent if you think that anything other than the kind
of city we are founding deserves to be called *a city*.

What do you mean?

We'll have to find a greater title for the others because each of them is
a great many cities, not *a* city, as they say in the game.[2] At any rate, each
of them consists of two cities at war with one another, that of the poor
423 and that of the rich, and each of these contains a great many. If you
approach them as one city, you'll be making a big mistake. But if you
approach them as many and offer to give to the one city the money, power,
and indeed the very inhabitants of the other, you'll always find many allies
and few enemies. And as long as your own city is moderately governed in
the way that we've just arranged, it will, even if it has only a thousand men
to fight for it, be the greatest. Not in reputation; I don't mean that, but
the greatest in fact. Indeed, you won't find a city as great as this one among
either Greeks or barbarians, although many that are many times its size
b may seem to be as great. Do you disagree?

No, I certainly don't.

Then this would also be the best limit for our guardians to put on the
size of the city. And they should mark off enough land for a city that size
and let the rest go.

What limit is that?

I suppose the following one. As long as it is willing to remain *one* city,
it may continue to grow, but it cannot grow beyond that point.
c That is a good limit.

Then, we'll give our guardians this further order, namely, to guard in
every way against the city's being either small or great in reputation instead
of being sufficient in size and one in number.

At any rate, that order will be fairly easy for them to follow.

And the one we mentioned earlier is even easier, when we said that, if
an offspring of the guardians is inferior, he must be sent off to join the
other citizens and that, if the others have an able offspring, he must join
d the guardians. This was meant to make clear that each of the other citizens

---

2. The reference is obscure; it may be to a saying or proverb or to a game like
checkers called *poleis* or cities, in which the set of pieces on each side, or perhaps any
subset of them, were called cities, while the individual members of the sets were called
dogs.

is to be directed to what he is naturally suited for, so that, doing the one work that is his own, he will become not many but one, and the whole city will itself be naturally one not many.

That *is* easier than the other.

These orders we give them, Adeimantus, are neither as numerous nor as important as one might think. Indeed, they are all insignificant, provided, as the saying goes, that they guard the one great thing, though I'd rather call it sufficient than great.   *e*

What's that?

Their education and upbringing, for if by being well educated they become reasonable men, they will easily see these things for themselves, as well as all the other things we are omitting, for example, that marriage, the having of wives, and the procreation of children must be governed as far as possible by the old proverb: Friends possess everything in common. *424*

That would be best.

And surely, once our city gets a good start, it will go on growing in a cycle. Good education and upbringing, when they are preserved, produce good natures, and useful natures, who are in turn well educated, grow up even better than their predecessors, both in their offspring and in other respects, just like other animals.   *b*

That's likely.

To put it briefly, those in charge must cling to education and see that it isn't corrupted without their noticing it, guarding it against everything. Above all, they must guard as carefully as they can against any innovation in music and poetry or in physical training that is counter to the established order.[3] And they should dread to hear anyone say:

> *People care most for the song*
> *That is newest from the singer's lips.*[4]

Someone might praise such a saying, thinking that the poet meant not new songs but new ways of singing. Such a thing shouldn't be praised,   *c* and the poet shouldn't be taken to have meant it, for the guardians must beware of changing to a new form of music, since it threatens the whole system. As Damon says, and I am convinced, the musical modes are never changed without change in the most important of a city's laws.

You can count me among the convinced as well, Adeimantus said.

Then it seems, I said, that it is in music and poetry that our guardians must build their bulwark.   *d*

At any rate, lawlessness easily creeps in there unnoticed.

3. See Book II n. 1.
4. *Odyssey* 1.351–2. Plato's text of Homer is slightly different from ours.

Yes, as if music and poetry were only play and did no harm at all.

It is harmless—except, of course, that when lawlessness has established itself there, it flows over little by little into characters and ways of life. Then, greatly increased, it steps out into private contracts, and from private contracts, Socrates, it makes its insolent way into the laws and government,

e until in the end it overthrows everything, public and private.

Well, is that the way it goes?

I think so.

Then, as we said at first, our children's games must from the very beginning be more law-abiding, for if their games become lawless, and the children follow suit, isn't it impossible for them to grow up into good

425 and law-abiding men?

It certainly is.

But when children play the right games from the beginning and absorb lawfulness from music and poetry, it follows them in everything and fosters their growth, correcting anything in the city that may have gone wrong before—in other words, the very opposite of what happens where the games are lawless.

That's true.

These people will also discover the seemingly insignificant conventions their predecessors have destroyed.

Which ones?

Things like this: When it is proper for the young to be silent in front

b of their elders, when they should make way for them or stand up in their presence, the care of parents, hair styles, the clothes and shoes to wear, deportment, and everything else of that sort. Don't you agree?

I do.

I think it's foolish to legislate about such things. Verbal or written decrees will never make them come about or last.

How could they?

At any rate, Adeimantus, it looks as though the start of someone's

c education determines what follows. Doesn't like always encourage like?

It does.

And the final outcome of education, I suppose we'd say, is a single newly finished person, who is either good or the opposite.

Of course.

That's why I wouldn't go on to try to legislate about such things.

And with good reason.

Then, by the gods, what about market business, such as the private contracts people make with one another in the marketplace, for example,

d or contracts with manual laborers, cases of insult or injury, the bringing of lawsuits, the establishing of juries, the payment and assessment of whatever dues are necessary in markets and harbors, the regulation of market, city, harbor, and the rest—should we bring ourselves to legislate about any of these?

It isn't appropriate to dictate to men who are fine and good. They'll easily find out for themselves whatever needs to be legislated about such things.   e

Yes, provided that a god grants that the laws we have already described are preserved.

If not, they'll spend their lives enacting a lot of other laws and then amending them, believing that in this way they'll attain the best.

You mean they'll live like those sick people who, through licentiousness, aren't willing to abandon their harmful way of life?

That's right.

And such people carry on in an altogether amusing fashion, don't they? Their medical treatment achieves nothing, except that their illness 426 becomes worse and more complicated, and they're always hoping that someone will recommend some new medicine to cure them.

That's exactly what happens to people like that.

And isn't it also amusing that they consider their worst enemy to be the person who tells them the truth, namely, that until they give up drunkenness, overeating, lechery, and idleness, no medicine, cautery, or surgery, no charms, amulets, or anything else of that kind will do them any good?   b

It isn't amusing at all, for it isn't amusing to treat someone harshly when he's telling the truth.

You don't seem to approve of such men.

I certainly don't, by god.

Then, you won't approve either if a whole city behaves in that way, as we said. Don't you think that cities that are badly governed behave exactly like this when they warn their citizens not to disturb the city's whole political establishment on pain of death? The person who is honored and   c considered clever and wise in important matters by such badly governed cities is the one who serves them most pleasantly, indulges them, flatters them, anticipates their wishes, and is clever at fulfilling them.

Cities certainly do seem to behave in that way, and I don't approve of it at all.

What about those who are willing and eager to serve such cities? Don't you admire their courage and readiness?   d

I do, except for those who are deceived by majority approval into believing that they are true statesmen.

What do you mean? Have you no sympathy for such men? Or do you think it's possible for someone who is ignorant of measurement not to believe it himself when many others who are similarly ignorant tell him that he is six feet tall?   e

No, I don't think that.

Then don't be too hard on them, for such people are surely the most amusing of all. They pass laws on the subjects we've just been enumerating and then amend them, and they always think they'll find a way to put a stop to cheating on contracts and the other things I mentioned, not realizing that they're really just cutting off a Hydra's head.[5]

427 Yet that's all they're doing.

I'd have thought, then, that the true lawgiver oughtn't to bother with that form of law or constitution, either in a badly governed city or in well-governed one—in the former, because it's useless and accomplishes nothing; in the latter, because anyone could discover some of these things, while the others follow automatically from the ways of life we established.

b What is now left for us to deal with under the heading of legislation?

For us nothing, but for the Delphic Apollo it remains to enact the greatest, finest, and first of laws.

What laws are those?

Those having to do with the establishing of temples, sacrifices, and other forms of service to gods, daimons, and heroes, the burial of the dead, and the services that ensure their favor. We have no knowledge of these things, and in establishing our city, if we have any understanding,

c we won't be persuaded to trust them to anyone other than the ancestral guide. And this god, sitting upon the rock at the center of the earth,[6] is without a doubt the ancestral guide on these matters for all people.

Nicely put. And that's what we must do.

d Well, son of Ariston, your city might now be said to be established. The next step is to get an adequate light somewhere and to call upon your brother as well as Polemarchus and the others, so as to look inside it and see where the justice and the injustice might be in it, what the difference between them is, and which of the two the person who is to be happy should possess, whether its possession is unnoticed by all the gods and human beings or not.

You're talking nonsense, Glaucon said. You promised to look for them yourself because you said it was impious for you not to come to the rescue

e of justice in every way you could.

That's true, and I must do what I promised, but you'll have to help.

We will.

I hope to find it in this way. I think our city, if indeed it has been correctly founded, is completely good.

---

5. The Hydra was a mythical monster. When one of its heads was cut off, two or three new heads grew in its place. Heracles had to slay the Hydra as one of his labors.

6. I.e. on the rock in the sanctuary at Delphi, which was believed to be the navel or center of the earth.

Necessarily so.

Clearly, then, it is wise, courageous, moderate, and just.

Clearly.

Then, if we find any of these in it, what's left over will be the ones we haven't found?

Of course.   *428*

Therefore, as with any other four things, if we were looking for any one of them in something and recognized it first, that would be enough for us, but if we recognized the other three first, this itself would be sufficient to enable us to recognize what we are looking for. Clearly it couldn't be anything other than what's left over.

That's right.

Therefore, since there are four virtues, mustn't we look for them in the same way?

Clearly.

Now, the first thing I think I can see clearly in the city is wisdom, and there seems to be something odd about it.   *b*

What's that?

I think that the city we described is really wise. And that's because it has good judgment, isn't it?

Yes.

Now, this very thing, good judgment, is clearly some kind of knowledge, for it's through knowledge, not ignorance, that people judge well.

Clearly.

But there are many kinds of knowledge in the city.

Of course.

Is it because of the knowledge possessed by its carpenters, then, that the city is to be called wise and sound in judgment?

Not at all. It's called skilled in carpentry because of that.   *c*

Then it isn't to be called wise because of the knowledge by which it arranges to have the best wooden implements.

No, indeed.

What about the knowledge of bronze items or the like?

It isn't because of any knowledge of that sort.

Nor because of the knowledge of how to raise a harvest from the earth, for it's called skilled in farming because of that.

I should think so.

Then, is there some knowledge possessed by some of the citizens in the city we just founded that doesn't judge about any particular matter but about the city as a whole and the maintenance of good relations, both internally and with other cities?   *d*

There is indeed.

What is this knowledge, and who has it?

It is guardianship, and it is possessed by those rulers we just now called complete guardians.

Then, what does this knowledge entitle you to say about the city?

That it has good judgment and is really wise.

Who do you think that there will be more of in our city, metal-workers
e or these true guardians?

There will be far more metal-workers.

Indeed, of all those who are called by a certain name because they have some kind of knowledge, aren't the guardians the least numerous?

By far.

Then, a whole city established according to nature would be wise because of the smallest class and part in it, namely, the governing or ruling one. And to this class, which seems to be by nature the smallest, belongs
429 a share of the knowledge that alone among all the other kinds of knowledge is to be called wisdom.

That's completely true.

Then we've found one of the four virtues, as well as its place in the city, though I don't know how we found it.

Our way of finding it seems good enough to me.

And surely courage and the part of the city it's in, the part on account of which the city is called courageous, aren't difficult to see.

How is that?

b Who, in calling the city cowardly or courageous, would look anywhere other than to the part of it that fights and does battle on its behalf?

No one would look anywhere else.

At any rate, I don't think that the courage or cowardice of its other citizens would cause the city itself to be called either courageous or cowardly.

No, it wouldn't.

The city is courageous, then, because of a part of itself that has the power to preserve through everything its belief about what things are to
c be feared, namely, that they are the things and kinds of things that the lawgiver declared to be such in the course of educating it. Or don't you call that courage?

I don't completely understand what you mean. Please, say it again.

I mean that courage is a kind of preservation.

What sort of preservation?

That preservation of the belief that has been inculcated by the law through education about what things and sorts of things are to be feared. And by preserving this belief "through everything," I mean preserving it
d and not abandoning it because of pains, pleasures, desires, or fears. If you like, I'll compare it to something I think it resembles.

I'd like that.

You know that dyers, who want to dye wool purple, first pick out from the many colors of wool the one that is naturally white, then they carefully prepare this in various ways, so that it will absorb the color as well as possible, and only at that point do they apply the purple dye. When something is dyed in this way, the color is fast—no amount of washing,   *e* whether with soap or without it, can remove it. But you also know what happens to material if it hasn't been dyed in this way, but instead is dyed purple or some other color without careful preparation.

I know that it looks washed out and ridiculous.

Then, you should understand that, as far as we could, we were doing something similar when we selected our soldiers and educated them in music and physical training. What we were contriving was nothing other *430* than this: That because they had the proper nature and upbringing, they would absorb the laws in the finest possible way, just like a dye, so that their belief about what they should fear and all the rest would become so fast that even such extremely effective detergents as pleasure, pain, fear, and desire wouldn't wash it out—and pleasure is much more potent than any powder, washing soda, or soap. This power to preserve through   *b* everything the correct and law-inculcated belief about what is to be feared and what isn't is what I call courage, unless, of course, you say otherwise.

I have nothing different to say, for I assume that you don't consider the correct belief about these same things, which you find in animals and slaves, and which is not the result of education, to be inculcated by law, and that you don't call it courage but something else.

That's absolutely true.   *c*

Then I accept your account of courage.

Accept it instead as my account of *civic* courage, and you will be right. We'll discuss courage more fully some other time, if you like. At present, our inquiry concerns not it but justice. And what we've said is sufficient for that purpose.

You're quite right.

There are now two things left for us to find in the city, namely, modera-tion[7] and—the goal of our entire inquiry—justice.   *d*

That's right.

Is there a way we could find justice so as not to have to bother with moderation any further?

I don't know any, and I wouldn't want justice to appear first if that

---

7. The Greek term is *sōphrosunē*. It has a very wide meaning: self-control, good sense, reasonableness, temperence, and (in some contexts) chastity. Someone who keeps his head under pressure or temptation possesses *sōphrosunē*.

means that we won't investigate moderation. So if you want to please me, look for the latter first.

e   I'm certainly willing. It would be wrong not to be.

Look, then.

We will. Seen from here, it is more like a kind of consonance and harmony than the previous ones.

In what way?

Moderation is surely a kind of order, the mastery of certain kinds of pleasures and desires. People indicate as much when they use the phrase "self-control" and other similar phrases. I don't know just what they mean by them, but they are, so to speak, like tracks or clues that moderation has left behind in language. Isn't that so?

Absolutely.

Yet isn't the expression "self-control" ridiculous? The stronger self that does the controlling is the same as the weaker self that gets controlled, so

431 that only one person is referred to in all such expressions.

Of course.

Nonetheless, the expression is apparently trying to indicate that, in the soul of that very person, there is a better part and a worse one and that, whenever the naturally better part is in control of the worse, this is expressed by saying that the person is self-controlled or master of himself. At any rate, one praises someone by calling him self-controlled. But when, on the other hand, the smaller and better part is overpowered by the larger, because of bad upbringing or bad company, this is called being

b self-defeated or licentious and is a reproach.

Appropriately so.

Take a look at our new city, and you'll find one of these in it. You'll say that it is rightly called self-controlled, if indeed something in which the better rules the worse is properly called moderate and self-controlled.

I am looking, and what you say is true.

Now, one finds all kinds of diverse desires, pleasures, and pains, mostly

c in children, women, household slaves, and in those of the inferior majority who are called free.

That's right.

But you meet with the desires that are simple, measured, and directed by calculation in accordance with understanding and correct belief only in the few people who are born with the best natures and receive the best education.

That's true.

Then, don't you see that in your city, too, the desires of the inferior

d many are controlled by the wisdom and desires of the superior few?

I do.

Therefore, if any city is said to be in control of itself and of its pleasures and desires, it is this one.

Absolutely.

And isn't it, therefore, also moderate because of all this?

It is.

And, further, if indeed the ruler and the ruled in any city share the same belief about who should rule, it is in this one. Or don't you agree?   *e*

I agree entirely.

And when the citizens agree in this way, in which of them do you say moderation is located? In the ruler or the ruled?

I suppose in both.

Then, you see how right we were to divine that moderation resembles a kind of harmony?

How so?

Because, unlike courage and wisdom, each of which resides in one part, making the city brave and wise respectively, moderation spreads throughout the whole. It makes the weakest, the strongest, and those in *432* between—whether in regard to reason, physical strength, numbers, wealth, or anything else—all sing the same song together. And this unanimity, this agreement between the naturally worse and the naturally better as to which of the two is to rule both in the city and in each one, is rightly called moderation.

I agree completely.   *b*

All right. We've now found, at least from the point of view of our present beliefs, three out of the four virtues in our city. So what kind of virtue is left, then, that makes the city share even further in virtue? Surely, it's clear that it is justice.

That is clear.

Then, Glaucon, we must station ourselves like hunters surrounding a wood and focus our understanding, so that justice doesn't escape us and vanish into obscurity, for obviously it's around here somewhere. So look and try eagerly to catch sight of it, and if you happen to see it before I do,   *c* you can tell me about it.

I wish I could, but you'll make better use of me if you take me to be a follower who can see things when you point them out to him.

Follow, then, and join me in a prayer.

I'll do that, just so long as you lead.

I certainly will, though the place seems to be impenetrable and full of shadows. It is certainly dark and hard to search though. But all the same, we must go on.

Indeed we must.   *d*

And then I caught sight of something. Ah ha! Glaucon, it looks as though there's a track here, so it seems that our quarry won't altogether escape us.

That's good news.

Either that, or we've just been stupid.

In what way?

Because what we are looking for seems to have been rolling around at our feet from the very beginning, and we didn't see it, which was ridiculous of us. Just as people sometimes search for the very thing they are holding
e in their hands, so we didn't look in the right direction but gazed off into the distance, and that's probably why we didn't notice it.

What do you mean?

I mean that, though we've been talking and hearing about it for a long time, I think we didn't understand what we were saying or that, in a way, we were talking about justice.

That's a long prelude for someone who wants to hear the answer.

433   Then listen and see whether there's anything in what I say. Justice, I think, is exactly what we said must be established throughout the city when we were founding it—either that or some form of it. We stated, and often repeated, if you remember, that everyone must practice one of the occupations in the city for which he is naturally best suited.

Yes, we did keep saying that.

Moreover, we've heard many people say and have often said ourselves that justice is doing one's own work and not meddling with what isn't
b   one's own.

Yes, we have.

Then, it turns out that this doing one's own work—provided that it comes to be in a certain way—is justice. And do you know what I take as evidence of this?

No, tell me.

I think that this is what was left over in the city when moderation, courage, and wisdom have been found. It is the power that makes it possible for them to grow in the city and that preserves them when they've
c   grown for as long as it remains there itself. And of course we said that justice would be what was left over when we had found the other three.

Yes, that must be so.

And surely, if we had to decide which of the four will make the city good by its presence, it would be a hard decision. Is it the agreement in belief between the rulers and the ruled? Or the preservation among the soldiers of the law-inspired belief about what is to be feared and what isn't? Or the
d   wisdom and guardianship of the rulers? Or is it, above all, the fact that every child, woman, slave, freeman, craftsman, ruler, and ruled each does his own work and doesn't meddle with what is other people's?

How could this fail to be a hard decision?

It seems, then, that the power that consists in everyone's doing his own work rivals wisdom, moderation, and courage in its contribution to the virtue of the city.   *e*

It certainly does.

And wouldn't you call this rival to the others in its contribution to the city's virtue justice?

Absolutely.

Look at it this way if you want to be convinced. Won't you order your rulers to act as judges in the city's courts?

Of course.

And won't their sole aim in delivering judgments be that no citizen should have what belongs to another or be deprived of what is his own?

They'll have no aim but that.

Because that is just?

Yes.

Therefore, from this point of view also, the having and doing of one's own would be accepted as justice.   *434*

That's right.

Consider, then, and see whether you agree with me about this. If a carpenter attempts to do the work of a cobbler, or a cobbler that of a carpenter, or they exchange their tools or honors with one another, or if the same person tries to do both jobs, and all other such exchanges are made, do you think that does any great harm to the city?

Not much.

But I suppose that when someone, who is by nature a craftsman or some other kind of money-maker, is puffed up by wealth, or by having a majority of votes, or by his own strength, or by some other such thing, and   *b* attempts to enter the class of soldiers, or one of the unworthy soldiers tries to enter that of the judges and guardians, and these exchange their tools and honors, or when the same person tries to do all these things at once, then I think you'll agree that these exchanges and this sort of meddling bring the city to ruin.

Absolutely.

Meddling and exchange between these three classes, then, is the greatest harm that can happen to the city and would rightly be called the worst thing someone could do to it.   *c*

Exactly.

And wouldn't you say that the worst thing that someone could do to his city is injustice?

Of course.

Then, that exchange and meddling is injustice. Or to put it the other

way around: For the money-making, auxiliary, and guardian classes each
to do its own work in the city, is the opposite. That's justice, isn't it, and
makes the city just?

d   I agree. Justice is that and nothing else.

Let's not take that as secure just yet, but if we find that the same form,
when it comes to be in each individual person, is accepted as justice there
as well, we can assent to it. What else can we say? But if that isn't what
we find, we must look for something else to be justice. For the moment,
however, let's complete the present inquiry. We thought that, if we first
tried to observe justice in some larger thing that possessed it, this would
make it easier to observe in a single individual.[8] We agreed that this larger
thing is a city, and so we established the best city we could, knowing well
e   that justice would be in one that was good. So, let's apply what has come
to light in the city to an individual, and if it is accepted there, all will be
well. But if something different is found in the individual, then we must
go back and test that on the city. And if we do this, and compare them
435 side by side, we might well make justice light up as if we were rubbing
fire-sticks together. And, when it has come to light, we can get a secure
grip on it for ourselves.

You're following the road we set, and we must do as you say.

Well, then, are things called by the same name, whether they are bigger
or smaller than one another, like or unlike with respect to that to which
that name applies?

Alike.

Then a just man won't differ at all from a just city in respect to the form
b   of justice; rather he'll be like the city.

He will.

But a city was thought to be just when each of the three natural classes
within it did its own work, and it was thought to be moderate, courageous,
and wise because of certain other conditions and states of theirs.

That's true.

Then, if an individual has these same three parts in his soul, we will
expect him to be correctly called by the same names as the city if he has
c   the same conditions in them.

Necessarily so.

Then once again we've come upon an easy question, namely, does the
soul have these three parts in it or not?

It doesn't look easy to me. Perhaps, Socrates, there's some truth in the
old saying that everything fine is difficult.

Apparently so. But you should know, Glaucon, that, in my opinion, we

8. See 368c–d.

will never get a precise answer using our present methods of argument—
although there is another longer and fuller road that does lead to such an   *d*
answer. But perhaps we can get an answer that's up to the standard of our
previous statements and inquiries.

Isn't that satisfactory? It would be enough for me at present.

In that case, it will be fully enough for me too.

Then don't weary, but go on with the inquiry.

Well, then, we are surely compelled to agree that each of us has within
himself the same parts and characteristics as the city? Where else would   *e*
they come from? It would be ridiculous for anyone to think that spiritedness
didn't come to be in cities from such individuals as the Thracians, Scythi-
ans, and others who live to the north of us who are held to possess spirit,
or that the same isn't true of the love of learning, which is mostly associated
with our part of the world, or of the love of money, which one might say   *436*
is conspicuously displayed by the Phoenicians and Egyptians.

It would.

That's the way it is, anyway, and it isn't hard to understand.

Certainly not.

But this *is* hard. Do we do these things with the same part of ourselves,
or do we do them with three different parts? Do we learn with one part,
get angry with another, and with some third part desire the pleasures of
food, drink, sex, and the others that are closely akin to them? Or, when
we set out after something, do we act with the whole of our soul, in each
case? This is what's hard to determine in a way that's up to the standards   *b*
of our argument.

I think so too.

Well, then, let's try to determine in that way whether these parts are
the same or different.

How?

It is obvious that the same thing will not be willing to do or undergo
opposites in the same part of itself, in relation to the same thing, at the
same time. So, if we ever find this happening in the soul, we'll know that
we aren't dealing with one thing but many.   *c*

All right.

Then consider what I'm about to say.

Say on.

Is it possible for the same thing to stand still and move at the same time
in the same part of itself?

Not at all.

Let's make our agreement more precise in order to avoid disputes later
on. If someone said that a person who is standing still but moving his
hands and head is moving and standing still at the same time, we wouldn't

consider, I think, that he ought to put it like that. What he ought to say is that one part of the person is standing still and another part is moving.

d   Isn't that so?

It is.

And if our interlocutor became even more amusing and was sophisticated enough to say that whole spinning tops stand still and move at the same time when the peg is fixed in the same place and they revolve, and that the same is true of anything else moving in a circular motion on the same spot, we wouldn't agree, because it isn't with respect to the same parts of themselves that such things both stand still and move. We'd say

e   that they have an axis and a circumference and that with respect to the axis they stand still, since they don't wobble to either side, while with respect to the circumference they move in a circle. But if they do wobble to the left or right, front or back, while they are spinning, we'd say that they aren't standing still in any way.

And we'd be right.

No such statement will disturb us, then, or make us believe that the same thing can be, do, or undergo opposites, at the same time, in the same

437 respect, and in relation to the same thing.

They won't make me believe it, at least.

Nevertheless, in order to avoid going through all these objections one by one and taking a long time to prove them all untrue, let's assume that our hypothesis is correct and carry on. But we agree that if it should ever be shown to be incorrect, all the consequences we've drawn from it will also be invalidated.

We should agree to that.

b   Then wouldn't you consider all the following, whether they are doings or undergoings, as pairs of opposites: Assent and dissent, wanting to have something and rejecting it, taking something and pushing it away?

Yes, they are opposites.

What about these? Wouldn't you include thirst, hunger, the appetites

c   as a whole, and wishing and willing somewhere in the class we mentioned? Wouldn't you say that the soul of someone who has an appetite for a thing wants what he has an appetite for and takes to himself what it is his will to have, and that insofar as he wishes something to be given to him, his soul, since it desires this to come about, nods assent to it as if in answer to a question?

I would.

What about not willing, not wishing, and not having an appetite? Aren't these among the very opposites—cases in which the soul pushes and drives things away?

d   Of course.

Then won't we say that there is a class of things called appetites and that the clearest examples are hunger and thirst?

We will.

One of these is for food and the other for drink?

Yes.

Now, insofar as it is thirst, is it an appetite in the soul for more than that for which we say that it is the appetite? For example, is thirst thirst for hot drink or cold, or much drink or little, or, in a word, for drink of a certain sort? Or isn't it rather that, where heat is present as well as thirst, it causes the appetite to be for something cold as well, and where cold for   *e* something hot, and where there is much thirst because of the presence of muchness, it will cause the desire to be for much, and where little for little? But thirst itself will never be for anything other than what it is in its nature to be for, namely, drink itself, and hunger for food.

That's the way it is, each appetite itself is only for its natural object, while the appetite for something of a certain sort depends on additions.

Therefore, let no one catch us unprepared or disturb us by claiming *438* that no one has an appetite for drink but rather good drink, nor food but good food, on the grounds that everyone after all has appetite for good things, so that if thirst is an appetite, it will be an appetite for good drink or whatever, and similarly with the others.[9]

All the same, the person who says that has a point.

But it seems to me that, in the case of all things that are related to something, those that are of a particular sort are related to a particular sort of thing, while those that are merely themselves are related to a thing   *b* that is merely itself.

I don't understand.

Don't you understand that the greater is such as to be greater than something?

Of course.

Than the less?

Yes.

And the much greater than the much less, isn't that so?

Yes.

And the once greater to the once less? And the going-to-be greater than the going-to-be less?

Certainly.

And isn't the same true of the more and the fewer, the double and the

9. Plato is here laying the foundations for his rejection of the principle, espoused by Socrates in many earlier dialogues, that weakness of will is impossible. See *Introduction* p. x.

c half, heavier and lighter, faster and slower, the hot and the cold, and all
other such things?

Of course.

And what about the various kinds of knowledge? Doesn't the same
apply? Knowledge itself is knowledge of what can be learned itself (or
whatever it is that knowledge is of), while a particular sort of knowledge
is of a particular sort of thing. For example, when knowledge of building

d houses came to be, didn't it differ from the other kinds of knowledge, and
so was called knowledge of building?

Of course.

And wasn't that because it was a different sort of knowledge from all
the others?

Yes.

And wasn't it because it was of a particular sort of thing that it itself
became a particular sort of knowledge? And isn't this true of all crafts and
kinds of knowledge?

It is.

Well, then, this is what I was trying to say—if you understand it now—
when I said that of all things that are related to something, those that are
merely themselves are related to things that are merely themselves, while
those that are of a particular sort are related to things of a particular sort.

e However, I don't mean that the sorts in question have to be the same for
them both. For example, knowledge of health or disease isn't healthy or
diseased, and knowledge of good and bad doesn't itself become good or
bad. I mean that, when knowledge became, not knowledge of the thing
itself that knowledge is of, but knowledge of something of a particular
sort, the result was that it itself became a particular sort of knowledge,
and this caused it to be no longer called knowledge without qualification,
but—with the addition of the relevant sort—medical knowledge or
whatever.

I understand, and I think that that's the way it is.

Then as for thirst, wouldn't you include it among things that are related
439 to something? Surely thirst is related to . . .

I know it's related to drink.

Therefore a particular sort of thirst is for a particular sort of drink. But
thirst itself isn't for much or little, good or bad, or, in a word, for drink
of a particular sort. Rather, thirst itself is in its nature only for drink itself.

Absolutely.

Hence the soul of the thirsty person, insofar as he's thirsty, doesn't wish

b anything else but to drink, and it wants this and is impelled towards it.

Clearly.

Therefore, if something draws it back when it is thirsting, wouldn't that

be something different in it from whatever thirsts and drives it like a beast
to drink? It can't be, we say, that the same thing, with the same part of
itself, in relation to the same, at the same time, does opposite things.

No, it can't.

In the same way, I suppose, it's wrong to say of the archer that his hands
at the same time push the bow away and draw it towards him. We ought
to say that one hand pushes it away and the other draws it towards him.

Absolutely.   c

Now, would we assert that sometimes there are thirsty people who don't
wish to drink?

Certainly, it happens often to many different people.

What, then, should one say about them? Isn't it that there is something
in their soul, bidding them to drink, and something different, forbidding
them to do so, that overrules the thing that bids?

I think so.

Doesn't that which forbids in such cases come into play—if it comes
into play at all—as a result of rational calculation, while what drives and
drags them to drink is a result of feelings and diseases?   d

Apparently.

Hence it isn't unreasonable for us to claim that they are two, and
different from one another. We'll call the part of the soul with which it
calculates the rational part and the part with which it lusts, hungers, thirsts,
and gets excited by other appetites the irrational appetitive part, companion
of certain indulgences and pleasures.

Yes. Indeed, that's a reasonable thing to think.   e

Then, let these two parts be distinguished in the soul. Now, is the
spirited part by which we get angry a third part or is it of the same nature
as either of the other two?

Perhaps it's like the appetitive part.

But I've heard something relevant to this, and I believe it. Leontius, the
son of Aglaion, was going up from the Piraeus along the outside of the
North Wall when he saw some corpses lying at the executioner's feet. He
had an appetite to look at them but at the same time he was disgusted and
turned away. For a time he struggled with himself and covered his face,
but, finally, overpowered by the appetite, he pushed his eyes wide open 440
and rushed towards the corpses, saying, "Look for yourselves, you evil
wretches, take your fill of the beautiful sight!"[10]

I've heard that story myself.

---

10. Leontius' desire to look at the corpses is sexual in nature, for a fragment of
contemporary comedy tells us that Leontius was known for his love of boys as pale as
corpses.

It certainly proves that anger sometimes makes war against the appetites, as one thing against another.

Besides, don't we often notice in other cases that when appetite forces someone contrary to rational calculation, he reproaches himself and gets
b   angry with that in him that's doing the forcing, so that of the two factions that are fighting a civil war, so to speak, spirit allies itself with reason? But I don't think you can say that you've ever seen spirit, either in yourself or anyone else, ally itself with an appetite to do what reason has decided must not be done.

No, by god, I haven't.

What happens when a person thinks that he has done something unjust?
c   Isn't it true that the nobler he is, the less he resents it if he suffers hunger, cold, or the like at the hands of someone whom he believes to be inflicting this on him justly, and won't his spirit, as I say, refuse to be aroused?

That's true.

But what happens if, instead, he believes that someone has been unjust to him? Isn't the spirit within him boiling and angry, fighting for what he believes to be just? Won't it endure hunger, cold, and the like and keep
d   on till it is victorious, not ceasing from noble actions until it either wins, dies, or calms down, called to heel by the reason within him, like a dog by a shepherd?

Spirit is certainly like that. And, of course, we made the auxiliaries in our city like dogs obedient to the rulers, who are themselves like shepherds of a city.

You well understand what I'm trying to say. But also reflect on this further point.
e   What?

The position of the spirited part seems to be the opposite of what we thought before. Then we thought of it as something appetitive, but now we say that it is far from being that, for in the civil war in the soul it aligns itself far more with the rational part.

Absolutely.

Then is it also different from the rational part, or is it some form of it, so that there are two parts in the soul—the rational and the appetitive— instead of three? Or rather, just as there were three classes in the city that
441 held it together, the money-making, the auxiliary, and the deliberative, is the spirited part a third thing in the soul that is by nature the helper of the rational part, provided that it hasn't been corrupted by a bad upbringing?

It must be a third.

Yes, provided that we can show it is different from the rational part, as we saw earlier it was from the appetitive one.

It isn't difficult to show that it is different. Even in small children, one can see that they are full of spirit right from birth, while as far as rational calculation is concerned, some never seem to get a share of it, while the majority do so quite late.   *b*

That's really well put. And in animals too one can see that what you say is true. Besides, our earlier quotation from Homer bears it out, where he says,

He struck his chest and spoke to his heart.[11]

For here Homer clearly represents the part that has calculated about better and worse as different from the part that is angry without calculation.   *c*

That's exactly right.

Well, then, we've now made our difficult way through a sea of argument. We are pretty much agreed that the same number and the same kinds of classes as are in the city are also in the soul of each individual.

That's true.

Therefore, it necessarily follows that the individual is wise in the same way and in the same part of himself as the city.

That's right.

And isn't the individual courageous in the same way and in the same part of himself as the city? And isn't everything else that has to do with   *d* virtue the same in both?

Necessarily.

Moreover, Glaucon, I suppose we'll say that a man is just in the same way as a city.

That too is entirely necessary.

And we surely haven't forgotten that the city was just because each of the three classes in it was doing its own work.

I don't think we could forget that.

Then we must also remember that each one of us in whom each part is doing its own work will himself be just and do his own.   *e*

Of course, we must.

Therefore, isn't it appropriate for the rational part to rule, since it is really wise and exercises foresight on behalf of the whole soul, and for the spirited part to obey it and be its ally?

It certainly is.

And isn't it, as we were saying, a mixture of music and poetry, on the one hand, and physical training, on the other, that makes the two parts harmonious, stretching and nurturing the rational part with fine words

11. See 390d.

and learning, relaxing the other part through soothing stories, and making
442 it gentle by means of harmony and rhythm?

That's precisely it.

And these two, having been nurtured in this way, and having truly
learned their own roles and been educated in them, will govern the
appetitive part, which is the largest part in each person's soul and is by
nature most insatiable for money. They'll watch over it to see that it isn't
filled with the so-called pleasures of the body and that it doesn't become
so big and strong that it no longer does its own work but attempts to
b   enslave and rule over the classes it isn't fitted to rule, thereby overturning
everyone's whole life.

That's right.

Then, wouldn't these two parts also do the finest job of guarding the
whole soul and body against external enemies—reason by planning, spirit
by fighting, following its leader, and carrying out the leader's decisions
through its courage?

Yes, that's true.

And it is because of the spirited part, I suppose, that we call a single
c   individual courageous, namely, when it preserves through pains and pleasures the declarations of reason about what is to be feared and what isn't.

That's right.

And we'll call him wise because of that small part of himself that rules
in him and makes those declarations and has within it the knowledge of
what is advantageous for each part and for the whole soul, which is the
community of all three parts.

Absolutely.

And isn't he moderate because of the friendly and harmonious relations
between these same parts, namely, when the ruler and the ruled believe
in common that the rational part should rule and don't engage in civil war
d   against it?

Moderation is surely nothing other than that, both in the city and in the
individual.

And, of course, a person will be just because of what we've so often
mentioned, and in that way.

Necessarily.

Well, then, is the justice in us at all indistinct? Does it seem to be
something different from what we found in the city?

It doesn't seem so to me.

If there are still any doubts in our soul about this, we could dispel them
e   altogether by appealing to ordinary cases.

Which ones?

For example, if we had to come to an agreement about whether someone

similar in nature and training to our city had embezzled a deposit of gold
or silver that he had accepted, who do you think would consider him to
have done it rather than someone who isn't like him?   *443*

No one.

And would he have anything to do with temple robberies, thefts, betray-
als of friends in private life or of cities in public life?

No, nothing.

And he'd be in no way untrustworthy in keeping an oath or other
agreement.

How could he be?

And adultery, disrespect for parents, and neglect of the gods would be
more in keeping with every other kind of character than his.

With every one.

And isn't the cause of all this that every part within him does its own
work, whether it's ruling or being ruled?   *b*

Yes, that and nothing else.

Then, are you still looking for justice to be something other than this
power, the one that produces men and cities of the sort we've described?

No, I certainly am not.

Then the dream we had has been completely fulfilled—our suspicion
that, with the help of some god, we had hit upon the origin and pattern
of justice right at the beginning in founding our city.[12]   *c*

Absolutely.

Indeed, Glaucon, the principle that it is right for someone who is by
nature a cobbler to practice cobblery and nothing else, for the carpenter
to practice carpentry, and the same for the others is a sort of image of
justice—that's why it's beneficial.

Apparently.

And in truth justice is, it seems, something of this sort. However, it isn't
concerned with someone's doing his own externally, but with what is inside
him, with what is truly himself and his own. One who is just does not   *d*
allow any part of himself to do the work of another part or allow the various
classes within him to meddle with each other. He regulates well what is
really his own and rules himself. He puts himself in order, is his own
friend, and harmonizes the three parts of himself like three limiting notes
in a musical scale—high, low, and middle. He binds together those parts
and any others there may be in between, and from having been many
things he becomes entirely one, moderate and harmonious. Only then   *e*
does he act. And when he does anything, whether acquiring wealth, taking
care of his body, engaging in politics, or in private contracts—in all of

12. See 432c–433b.

these, he believes that the action is just and fine that preserves this inner harmony and helps achieve it, and calls it so, and regards as wisdom the knowledge that oversees such actions. And he believes that the action that
444 destroys this harmony is unjust, and calls it so, and regards the belief that oversees it as ignorance.

That's absolutely true, Socrates.

Well, then, if we claim to have found the just man, the just city, and what the justice is that is in them, I don't suppose that we'll seem to be telling a complete falsehood.

No, we certainly won't.

Shall we claim it, then?

We shall.

So be it. Now, I suppose we must look for injustice.

Clearly.

b   Surely, it must be a kind of civil war between the three parts, a meddling and doing of another's work, a rebellion by some part against the whole soul in order to rule it inappropriately. The rebellious part is by nature suited to be a slave, while the other part is not a slave but belongs to the ruling class. We'll say something like that, I suppose, and that the turmoil and straying of these parts are injustice, licentiousness, cowardice, ignorance, and, in a word, the whole of vice.

That's what they are.

So, if justice and injustice are really clear enough to us, then acting
c   justly, acting unjustly, and doing injustice are also clear.

How so?

Because just and unjust actions are no different for the soul than healthy and unhealthy things are for the body.

In what way?

Healthy things produce health, unhealthy ones disease.

Yes.

And don't just actions produce justice in the soul and unjust ones
d   injustice?

Necessarily.

To produce health is to establish the components of the body in a natural relation of control and being controlled, one by another, while to produce disease is to establish a relation of ruling and being ruled contrary to nature.

That's right.

Then, isn't to produce justice to establish the parts of the soul in a natural relation of control, one by another, while to produce injustice is to establish a relation of ruling and being ruled contrary to nature?

Precisely.

Virtue seems, then, to be a kind of health, fine condition, and well-being of the soul, while vice is disease, shameful condition, and weakness.   *e*

That's true.

And don't fine ways of living lead one to the possession of virtue, shameful ones to vice?

Necessarily.

So it now remains, it seems, to enquire whether it is more profitable to act justly, live in a fine way, and be just, whether one is known to be so   *445* or not, or to act unjustly and be unjust, provided that one doesn't pay the penalty and become better as a result of punishment.

But, Socrates, this inquiry looks ridiculous to me now that justice and injustice have been shown to be as we have described. Even if one has every kind of food and drink, lots of money, and every sort of power to rule, life is thought to be not worth living when the body's nature is ruined. So even if someone can do whatever he wishes, except what will free him   *b* from vice and injustice and make him acquire justice and virtue, how can it be worth living when his soul—the very thing by which he lives—is ruined and in turmoil?

Yes, it is ridiculous. Nevertheless, now that we've come far enough to be able to see most clearly that this is so, we mustn't give up.

That's absolutely the last thing we must do.

Then come here, so that you can see how many forms of vice there are,   *c* anyhow that I consider worthy of examination.

I'm following you, just tell me.

Well, from the vantage point we've reached in our argument, it seems to me that there is one form of virtue and an unlimited number of forms of vice, four of which are worth mentioning.

How do you mean?

It seems likely that there are as many types of soul as there are specific types of political constitution.

How many is that?

Five forms of constitution and five of souls.   *d*

What are they?

One is the constitution we've been describing. And it has two names. If one outstanding man emerges among the rulers, it's called a kingship; if more than one, it's called an aristocracy.

That's true.

Therefore, I say that this is one form of constitution. Whether one man emerges or many, none of the significant laws of the city would be changed, if they followed the upbringing and education we described.   *e*

Probably not.

BOOK V

Book V continues the discussion of virtue and vice in souls and cities that was begun at the end of Book IV. But it is immediately interrupted by Polemarchus and the other interlocutors, all of whom want Socrates to explain the remark he made in passing at 423e–424a about the guardians possessing their wives and children in common. Socrates' lengthy response to their request occupies the majority of the book (451c–471c). In it he makes the revolutionary proposal that children should be brought up by the city rather than by their biological parents, and that men and women with the same natural ability should receive the same education and training and do the same kind of work. Hence there will be female guardians and rulers in the kallipolis, as well as male ones. Many of Socrates' remarks suggest that these proposals apply to everyone in the kallipolis, not just to the guardians (e.g. 455e), but there are other indications (e.g. 450c) that they apply only to the guardians alone. It must be admitted that Plato has not been as explicit and clear on this matter as we might wish.

Glaucon agrees that a city of the sort Socrates has described would be the best one, but he wonders whether or not it could ever really come about (471c–e). After some important clarification of the nature of the task (472a–473c), Socrates undertakes to show that it could. The smallest change that would transform an already existing city into the kallipolis is if its kings or rulers become philosophers or if philosophers become its kings or rulers (473c–e). This proposal, Socrates thinks, is likely to produce even more outrage than those about women and children (473c), but he thinks that outrage will subside when he explains what true philosophers are really like (474b–c).

The remainder of Book V is occupied by the beginning of Socrates' portrait of these philosophers, which consists of a complex argument intended to show that only they can have access to forms and that without such access knowledge is impossible (474c–480a).

This is the kind of city and constitution, then, that I call good and correct,
449 and so too is this kind of man. And if indeed this is the correct kind, all the others—whether as city governments or as organizations of the individual soul—are bad and mistaken. Their badness is of four kinds.

What are they? he said.

I was going to enumerate them and explain how I thought they developed out of one another,[1] but Polemarchus, who was sitting a little further away than Adeimantus, extended his hand and took hold of the latter's cloak by   *b* the shoulder from above. He drew Adeimantus towards him, while he himself leaned forward and said something to him. We overheard nothing of what he said except the words "Shall we let it go, or what?"

We certainly won't let it go, Adeimantus said, now speaking aloud.

And I asked: What is it that you won't let go?

You, he said.

For what reason in particular?   *c*

We think that you're slacking off and that you've cheated us out of a whole important section of the discussion in order to avoid having to deal with it. You thought we wouldn't notice when you said—as though it were something trivial—that, as regards wives and children, anyone could see that the possessions of friends should be held in common.[2]

But isn't that right, Adeimantus?

Yes it is. But this "right," like the other things we've discussed, requires an explanation—in this case, an explanation of the manner in which they are to be held in common, for there may be many ways of doing this. So don't omit telling us about the particular one you mean. We've been   *d* waiting for some time, indeed, for you to tell us about the production of children—how they'll be produced and, once born, how they'll be brought up—and about the whole subject of having wives and children in common. We think that this makes a considerable difference—indeed all the difference—to whether a constitution is correct or not. So now, since you are beginning to describe another constitution before having adequately discussed these things, we are resolved, as you overheard, not to let you off until you explain all this as fully as the rest.   *450*

Include me, Glaucon said, as a partner in this resolution.

In fact, Socrates, Thrasymachus added, you can take this as the resolution of all of us.

What a thing you've done, I said, in stopping me! What an argument you've started up again from the very beginning, as it were, about the constitution! I was delighted to think that it had already been described and was content to have these things accepted as they were stated before. You don't realize what a swarm of arguments you've stirred up by calling me to account now. I saw the swarm and passed the topic by in order to   *b* save us a lot of trouble.

---

1. This task is taken up in Book VIII.
2. See 423e–424a.

Well, said Thrasymachus, are we here to search for gold[3] or to listen to an argument?

The latter, I said, but within reason.

It's within reason, Socrates, Glaucon said, for people with any understanding to listen to an argument of this kind their whole life long. So don't mind about us, and don't get tired yourself. Rather, tell us at length what your thoughts are on the topic we inquired about, namely, what the
c   common possession of wives and children will amount to for the guardians and how the children will be brought up while they're still small, for the time between birth and the beginning of education seems to be the most difficult period of all. So try to tell us what the manner of this upbringing must be.

It isn't an easy subject to explain, for it raises even more incredulity than the topics we've discussed so far. People may not believe that what we say is possible or that, even if it could be brought about, it would be for the best. It's for this reason that I hesitated to bring it up, namely, that
d   our argument might seem to be no more than wishful thinking.

Then don't hesitate, for your audience isn't inconsiderate, incredulous, or hostile.

Are you trying to encourage me by saying that?

I am.

Well, you're doing the opposite. Your encouragement would be fine, if I could be sure I was speaking with knowledge, for one can feel both secure and confident when one knows the truth about the dearest and most important things and speaks about them among those who are
e   themselves wise and dear friends. But to speak, as I'm doing, at a time when one is unsure of oneself and searching for the truth, is a frightening
451 and insecure thing to do. I'm not afraid of being laughed at—that would be childish indeed. But I am afraid that, if I slip from the truth, just where it's most important not to, I'll not only fall myself but drag my friends down as well. So I bow to Adrasteia[4] for what I'm going to say, for I suspect that it's a lesser crime to kill someone involuntarily than to mislead people about fine, good, and just institutions. Since it's better to run this risk among enemies than among friends, you've well and truly encouraged
b   me!

---

3. Literally: to refine gold. A proverbial expression applied to those who neglect the task at hand for some more fascinating but less profitable pursuit. Thrasymachus seems to be reminding Socrates of his own words at 336e.

4. Adrasteia was a kind of Nemesis, a punisher of pride and proud words. The "bow to Adrasteia" is therefore a kind of apology for the kind of act or statement that might otherwise spur her to take action.

Glaucon laughed and said: Well, Socrates, if we suffer from any false note you strike in the argument, we'll release you and absolve you of any guilt as in a homicide case: your hands are clean, and you have not deceived us. So take courage and speak.

I will, for the law says that someone who kills involuntarily is free of guilt when he's absolved by the injured party.[5] So it's surely reasonable to think the same is true in my case as well.

With that as your defense, speak.

Then I'll have to go back to what should perhaps have been said in   c sequence, although it may be that this way of doing things is in fact right and that after the completion of the male drama, so to speak, we should then go through the female one[6]—especially as you insist on it so urgently.

For men born and educated as we've described there is, in my opinion, no right way to acquire and use women and children other than by following the road on which we started them. We attempted, in the argument, to set up the men as guardians of the herd.[7]

Yes.

Then let's give them a birth and rearing consistent with that and see   d whether it suits us or not.

How?

As follows: Do we think that the wives of our guardian watchdogs should guard what the males guard, hunt with them, and do everything else in common with them? Or should we keep the women at home, as incapable of doing this, since they must bear and rear the puppies, while the males work and have the entire care of the flock?

Everything should be in common, except that the females are weaker   e and the males stronger.

And is it possible to use any animals for the same things if you don't give them the same upbringing and education?

No, it isn't.

Therefore, if we use the women for the same things as the men, they must also be taught the same things.

Yes.   *452*

---

5. See Plato, *Laws* 869e.

6. This may be an allusion to the mimes of Sophron of Syracuse (c. 470–400 B.C.), which were classified as male mimes and female mimes, because males were represented in the former, females in the latter.

7. It is useful to contrast Plato's views on women with those of his contemporaries in Athens. The most reliable brief discussion of the latter is John Gould, "Law, Custom and Myth: Aspects of the Social Position of Women in Classical Athens," *Journal of Hellenic Studies* 100 (1980): 38–59.

Now, we gave the men music and poetry and physical training.

Yes.

Then we must give these two crafts, as well as those having to do with warfare, to the women also to use in the same way as the men use them.

That seems to follow from what you say.

But perhaps much of what we are saying, since it is contrary to custom, would incite ridicule if it were carried out in practice as we've described.

It certainly would.

What is the most ridiculous thing that you see in it? Isn't it obviously the women exercising naked in the palestras[8] with the men? And not just the young women, but the older ones too—like old men in gymnasiums
b who, even though their bodies are wrinkled and not pleasant to look at, still love to do physical training.

Yes, that would look really ridiculous as things stand at present.

But surely, now that we've started to speak about this, we mustn't fear the various jokes that wits will make about this kind of change in music and poetry, physical training, and—last but not least—in bearing arms
c and riding horses.

You're right.

And now that we've begun to speak about this, we must move on to the tougher part of the law, begging these people not to be silly (though that is their own work!) but to take the matter seriously. They should remember that it wasn't very long ago that the Greeks themselves thought it shameful and ridiculous (as the majority of the barbarians still do) for even men to be seen naked and that when the Cretans and then the Lacedaemonians began the gymnasiums, the wits of those times could also have ridiculed
d it all. Or don't you think so?

I do.

But I think that, after it was found in practice to be better to strip than to cover up all those parts, then what was ridiculous to the eyes faded away in the face of what argument showed to be the best. This makes it clear that it's foolish to think that anything besides the bad is ridiculous or to try to raise a laugh at the sight of anything besides what's stupid or
e bad or (putting it the other way around) it's foolish to take seriously any standard of what is fine and beautiful other than the good.

That's absolutely certain.

However, mustn't we first agree about whether our proposals are possible or not? And mustn't we give to anyone who wishes the opportunity to question us—whether in jest or in earnest—about whether female human
453 nature *can* share all the tasks of that of the male, or none of them, or some

8. A palestra is a wrestling school and training ground.

but not others, and to ask in which class the waging of war belongs? Wouldn't this, as the best beginning, also be likely to result in the best conclusion?

Of course.

Shall we give the argument against ourselves, then, on behalf of those who share these reservations, so that their side of the question doesn't fall by default?

There's no reason not to.   *b*

Then let's say this on their behalf: "Socrates and Glaucon, there's no need for others to argue with you, for you yourselves, when you began to found your city, agreed that each must do his own work in accordance with his nature."

And I think we certainly did agree to that.

"Can you deny that a woman is by nature very different from a man?"

Of course not.

"And isn't it appropriate to assign different work to each in accordance with its nature?"

Certainly.   *c*

"How is it, then, that you aren't mistaken and contradicting yourselves when you say that men and women must do the same things, when their natures are so completely separate and distinct?"

Do you have any defense against that attack?

It isn't easy to think of one on the spur of the moment, so I'll ask you to explain the argument on our side as well, whatever it is.

This and many other such things, Glaucon, which I foresaw earlier, were what I was afraid of, so that I hesitated to tackle the law concerning the possession and upbringing of women and children.   *d*

By god, it doesn't seem to be an easy topic.

It isn't. But the fact is that whether someone falls into a small diving pool or into the middle of the biggest ocean, he must swim all the same.

He certainly must.

Then we must swim too, and try to save ourselves from the sea of argument, hoping that a dolphin will pick us up or that we'll be rescued by some other desperate means.[9]

It seems so.   *e*

Come, then. Let's see if we can find a way out. We've agreed that different natures must follow different ways of life and that the natures of men and women are different. But now we say that those different natures must follow the same way of life. Isn't that the accusation brought against us?

9. See Herodotus, *Histories* 1.23–24 for the story of Arion's rescue by the dolphin.

That's it exactly.

454   Ah! Glaucon, great is the power of the craft of disputation.
Why is that?
Because many fall into it against their wills. They think they are having
not a quarrel but a conversation, because they are unable to examine what
has been said by dividing it up according to forms. Hence, they pursue
mere verbal contradictions of what has been said and have a quarrel rather
than a conversation.
That does happen to lots of people, but it isn't happening to us at the
moment, is it?

b   It most certainly is, for it looks to me, at any rate, as though we are
falling into disputation against our will.
How?
We're bravely, but in a quarrelsome and merely verbal fashion, pursuing
the principle that natures that aren't the same must follow different ways
of life. But when we assigned different ways of life to different natures
and the same ones to the same, we didn't at all examine the form of natural
difference and sameness we had in mind or in what regard we were
distinguishing them.
No, we didn't look into that.

c   Therefore, we might just as well, it seems, ask ourselves whether the
natures of bald and long-haired men are the same or opposite. And, when
we agree that they are opposite, then, if the bald ones are cobblers, we
ought to forbid the long-haired ones to be cobblers, and if the long-haired
ones are cobblers, we ought to forbid this to the bald ones.
That would indeed be ridiculous.
And aren't we in this ridiculous position because at that time we did
not introduce every form of difference and sameness in nature, but focused
on the one form of sameness and difference that was relevant to the
particular ways of life themselves? We meant, for example, that a male

d   and female doctor have souls of the same nature. Or don't you think so?
I do.
But a doctor and a carpenter have different ones?
Completely different, surely.
Therefore, if the male sex is seen to be different from the female with
regard to a particular craft or way of life, we'll say that the relevant one
must be assigned to it. But if it's apparent that they differ only in this
respect, that the females bear children while the males beget them, we'll
say that there has been no kind of proof that women are different from

e   men with respect to what we're talking about, and we'll continue to believe
that our guardians and their wives must have the same way of life.
And rightly so.
Next, we'll tell anyone who holds the opposite view to instruct us in

this: With regard to what craft or way of life involved in the constitution
of the city are the natures of men and women not the same but different?   *455*
    That's a fair question, at any rate.
    And perhaps he'd say, just as you did a moment ago, that it isn't easy
to give an immediate answer, but with enough consideration it should not
be difficult.
    Yes, he might say that.
    Shall we ask the one who raises this objection to follow us and see
whether we can show him that no way of life concerned with the management of the city is peculiar to women?   *b*
    Of course.
    "Come, now," we'll say to him, "give us an answer: Is this what you
meant by one person being naturally well suited for something and another
being naturally unsuited? That the one learned it easily, the other with
difficulty; that the one, after only a brief period of instruction, was able to
find out things for himself, while the other, after much instruction, couldn't
even remember what he'd learned; that the body of the one adequately
served his thought, while the body of the other opposed his. Are there any
other things besides these by which you distinguished those who are   *c*
naturally well suited for anything from those who are not?"
    No one will claim that there are any others.
    Do you know of anything practiced by human beings in which the male
sex isn't superior to the female in all these ways? Or must we make a long
story of it by mentioning weaving, baking cakes, and cooking vegetables,
in which the female sex is believed to excel and in which it is most
ridiculous of all for it to be inferior?   *d*
    It's true that one sex is much superior to the other in pretty well
everything, although many women are better than many men in many
things. But on the whole it is as you say.
    Then there is no way of life concerned with the management of the city
that belongs to a woman because she's a woman or to a man because he's
a man, but the various natures are distributed in the same way in both
creatures. Women share by nature in every way of life just as men do, but
in all of them women are weaker than men.   *e*
    Certainly.
    Then shall we assign all of them to men and none to women?
    How can we?
    We'll say, I suppose, that one woman is a doctor, another not, and that
one is musical by nature, another not.
    Of course.
    And, therefore, won't one be athletic or warlike, while another is unwar-
like and no lover of physical training?   *456*
    I suppose so.

Further, isn't one woman philosophical or a lover of wisdom, while another hates wisdom? And isn't one spirited and another spiritless?

That too.

So one woman may have a guardian nature and another not, for wasn't it qualities of this sort that we looked for in the natures of the men we selected as guardians?

Certainly.

Therefore, men and women are by nature the same with respect to guarding the city, except to the extent that one is weaker and the other stronger.

Apparently.

b   Then women of this sort must be chosen along with men of the same sort to live with them and share their guardianship, seeing that they are adequate for the task and akin to the men in nature.

Certainly.

And mustn't we assign the same way of life to the same natures?

We must.

We've come round, then, to what we said before and have agreed that it isn't against nature to assign an education in music, poetry, and physical training to the wives of the guardians.

Absolutely.

c   Then we're not legislating impossibilities or indulging in mere wishful thinking. The law we established is in accord with nature. It's rather the way things are at present that seems to be against nature.

So it seems.

Now, weren't we trying to determine whether our proposals were both possible and optimal?

Yes, we were.

And haven't we now agreed that they're possible?

Yes.

Then mustn't we next reach agreement about whether or not they're optimal?

Clearly.

Should we have one kind of education to produce women guardians, then, and another to produce men, especially as they have the same natures

d   to begin with?

No.

Then, what do you think about this?

What?

About one man being better and another worse. Or do you think they're all alike?

Certainly not.

In the city we're establishing, who do you think will prove to be better men, the guardians, who receive the education we've described, or the cobblers, who are educated in cobblery?

Your question is ridiculous.

I understand. Indeed, aren't the guardians the best of the citizens?   *e*

By far.

And what about the female guardians? Aren't they the best of the women?

They're by far the best.

Is there anything better for a city than having the best possible men and women as its citizens?

There isn't.

And isn't it music and poetry and physical training, lending their support in the way we described, that bring this about?   *457*

Of course.

Then the law we've established isn't only possible; it is also optimal for a city?

Yes.

Then the guardian women must strip for physical training, since they'll wear virtue or excellence instead of clothes. They must share in war and the other guardians' duties in the city and do nothing else. But the lighter parts must be assigned to them because of the weakness of their sex. And the man who laughs at naked women doing physical training for the sake of what is best is "plucking the unripe fruit"[10] of laughter and doesn't   *b* know, it seems, what he's laughing at or what he's doing, for it is and always will be the finest saying that the beneficial is beautiful, while the harmful is ugly.

Absolutely.

Can we say, then, that we've escaped one wave of criticism in our discussion of the law about women, that we haven't been altogether swept away by laying it down that male and female guardians must share their entire way of life, and that our argument is consistent when it states that   *c* this is both possible and beneficial?

And it's certainly no small wave that you've escaped.

You won't think that it's so big when you get a look at the next one.

Tell me about it, and I'll decide.

I suppose that the following law goes along with the last one and the others that preceded it.

Which one?

That all these women are to belong in common to all the men, that

10. Plato is here adapting a phrase of Pindar, "plucking the unripe fruit of wisdom."

none are to live privately with any man, and that the children, too, are to
d be possessed in common, so that no parent will know his own offspring
or any child his parent.

This wave is far bigger than the other, for there's doubt both about its
possibility and about whether or not it's beneficial.

I don't think that its being beneficial would be disputed or that it would
be denied that the common possession of women and children would be
the greatest good, if indeed it is possible. But I think that there would be
a lot of disagreement about whether or not it is possible.

e There could very well be dispute about both.

You mean that I'll have to face a coalition of arguments. I thought I'd
escape one of them, if you believed that the proposal was beneficial, and
that I'd have only the one about whether or not it's possible left to deal
with.

But you didn't escape unobserved, so you have to give an argument for
both.

Well, then, I'll have to accept my punishment. But do me this favor.
Let me, as if on a holiday, do what lazy people do who feast on their own
458 thoughts of food when out for a solitary walk. Instead of finding out how
something they desire might actually come about, these people pass that
over, so as to avoid tiring deliberations about what's possible and what
isn't. They assume that what they desire is available and proceed to arrange
the rest, taking pleasure in thinking through everything they'll do when
b they have what they want, thereby making their lazy souls even lazier. I'm
getting soft myself at the moment, so I want to delay consideration of the
feasibility of our proposal until later. With your permission, I'll assume
that it's feasible and examine how the rulers will arrange these matters
when they come to pass. And I'll try to show that nothing could be more
beneficial to the city and its guardians than those arrangements. These
are the things I'll examine with you first, and I'll deal with the other
question later, but only if you'll permit me to do it this way.

You have my permission, so carry on with your examination.

I suppose that our rulers and auxiliaries—if indeed they're worthy of
c the names—will be willing to command and to obey respectively. In some
cases, the rulers will themselves be obeying our laws, and in others,
namely, the ones we leave to their discretion, they'll give directions that
are in the spirit of our laws.

Probably so.

Then you, as their lawgiver, will select women just as you did men, with
natures as similar to theirs as possible, and hand them over to the men.
And since they have common dwellings and meals, rather than private
d ones, and live together and mix together both in physical training and in
the rest of their upbringing, they will, I suppose, be driven by innate

necessity to have sex with one another. Or don't you think we're talking about necessities here?

The necessities aren't geometrical but erotic, and they're probably better than the others at persuading and compelling the majority of people.

That's right. But the next point, Glaucon, is that promiscuity is impious in a city of happy people, and the rulers won't allow it.   *e*

No, for it isn't right.

Then it's clear that our next task must be to make marriage as sacred as possible. And the sacred marriages will be those that are most beneficial.

Absolutely.

How, then, will they be most beneficial? Tell me this, Glaucon: I see that you have hunting dogs and quite a flock of noble fighting birds at   *459* home. Have you noticed anything about their mating and breeding?

Like what?

In the first place, although they're all noble, aren't there some that are the best and prove themselves to be so?

There are.

Do you breed them all alike, or do you try to breed from the best as much as possible?

I try to breed from the best.

And do you breed from the youngest or the oldest or from those in their   *b* prime?

From those in their prime.

And do you think that if they weren't bred in this way, your stock of birds and dogs would get much worse?

I do.

What about horses and other animals? Are things any different with them?

It would be strange if they were.

Dear me! If this also holds true of human beings, our need for excellent rulers is indeed extreme.

It does hold of them. But what of it?   *c*

Because our rulers will then have to use a lot of drugs. And while an inferior doctor is adequate for people who are willing to follow a regimen and don't need drugs, when drugs are needed, we know that a bolder doctor is required.

That's true. But what exactly do you have in mind?

I mean that it looks as though our rulers will have to make considerable use of falsehood and deception for the benefit of those they rule. And we said that all such falsehoods are useful as a form of drug.[11]   *d*

And we were right.

---

11. See 382c ff. and 414b ff.

Well, it seems we were right, especially where marriages and the producing of children are concerned.

How so?

It follows from our previous agreements, first, that the best men must have sex with the best women as frequently as possible, while the opposite is true of the most inferior men and women, and, second, that if our herd is to be of the highest possible quality, the former's offspring must be
e   reared but not the latter's. And this must all be brought about without being noticed by anyone except the rulers, so that our herd of guardians remains as free from dissension as possible.

That's absolutely right.

Therefore certain festivals and sacrifices will be established by law at which we'll bring the brides and grooms together, and we'll direct our poets to compose appropriate hymns for the marriages that take place.
460 We'll leave the number of marriages for the rulers to decide, but their aim will be to keep the number of males as stable as they can, taking into account war, disease, and similar factors, so that the city will, as far as possible, become neither too big nor too small.

That's right.

Then there'll have to be some sophisticated lotteries introduced, so that at each marriage the inferior people we mentioned will blame luck rather than the rulers when they aren't chosen.

There will.

And among other prizes and rewards the young men who are good in
b   war or other things must be given permission to have sex with the women more often, since this will also be a good pretext for having them father as many of the children as possible.

That's right.

And then, as the children are born, they'll be taken over by the officials appointed for the purpose, who may be either men or women or both, since our offices are open to both sexes.

Yes.

I think they'll take the children of good parents to the nurses in charge
c   of the rearing pen situated in a separate part of the city, but the children of inferior parents, or any child of the others that is born defective, they'll hide in a secret and unknown place, as is appropriate.[12]

It is, if indeed the guardian breed is to remain pure.

And won't the nurses also see to it that the mothers are brought to the

---

12. There can be no doubt that Plato is recommending infanticide by exposure for these babies, a practice which was quite common in ancient Greece as a method of birth control.

rearing pen when their breasts have milk, taking every precaution to insure that no mother knows her own child and providing wet nurses if the mother's milk is insufficient? And won't they take care that the mothers *d* suckle the children for only a reasonable amount of time and that the care of sleepless children and all other such troublesome duties are taken over by the wet nurses and other attendants?

You're making it very easy for the wives of the guardians to have children.

And that's only proper. So let's take up the next thing we proposed. We said that the children's parents should be in their prime.

True.

Do you share the view that a woman's prime lasts about twenty years and a man's about thirty? *e*

Which years are those?

A woman is to bear children for the city from the age of twenty to the age of forty, a man from the time that he passes his peak as a runner until he reaches fifty-five.

At any rate, that's the physical and mental prime for both. *461*

Then, if a man who is younger or older than that engages in reproduction for the community, we'll say that his offense is neither pious nor just, for the child he begets for the city, if it remains hidden, will be born in darkness, through a dangerous weakness of will, and without the benefit of the sacrifices and prayers offered at every marriage festival, in which the priests and priestesses, together with the entire city, ask that the children of good and beneficial parents may always prove themselves still better and more beneficial. *b*

That's right.

The same law will apply if a man still of begetting years has a child with a woman of child-bearing age without the sanction of the rulers. We'll say that he brings to the city an illegitimate, unauthorized, and unhallowed child.

That's absolutely right.

However, I think that when women and men have passed the age of having children, we'll leave them free to have sex with whomever they wish, with these exceptions: For a man—his daughter, his mother, his daughter's children, and his mother's ancestors; for a woman—her son *c* and his descendants, her father and his ancestors. Having received these instructions, they should be very careful not to let a single fetus see the light of day, but if one is conceived and forces its way to the light, they must deal with it in the knowledge that no nurture is available for it.

That's certainly sensible. But how will they recognize their fathers and daughters and the others you mentioned? *d*

They have no way of knowing. But a man will call all the children born in the tenth or seventh month after he became a bridegroom his sons, if they're male, and his daughters, if they're female, and they'll call him father. He'll call their children his grandchildren, and they'll call the group to which he belongs grandfathers and grandmothers. And those who were born at the same time as their mothers and fathers were having children

e   they'll call their brothers and sisters. Thus, as we were saying, the relevant groups will avoid sexual relations with each other. But the law will allow brothers and sisters to have sex with one another if the lottery works out that way and the Pythia[13] approves.

That's absolutely right.

This, then, Glaucon, is how the guardians of your city have their wives and children in common. We must now confirm that this arrangement is both consistent with the rest of the constitution and by far the best. Or how else are we to proceed?

462   In just that way.

Then isn't the first step towards agreement to ask ourselves what we say is the greatest good in designing the city—the good at which the legislator aims in making the laws—and what is the greatest evil? And isn't the next step to examine whether the system we've just described fits into the tracks of the good and not into those of the bad?

Absolutely.

Is there any greater evil we can mention for a city than that which tears it apart and makes it many instead of one? Or any greater good than that

b   which binds it together and makes it one?

There isn't.

And when, as far as possible, all the citizens rejoice and are pained by the same successes and failures, doesn't this sharing of pleasures and pains bind the city together?

It most certainly does.

But when some suffer greatly, while others rejoice greatly, at the same things happening to the city or its people, doesn't this privatization of

c   pleasures and pains dissolve the city?

Of course.

And isn't that what happens whenever such words as "mine" and "not mine" aren't used in unison? And similarly with "someone else's"?

Precisely.

Then, is the best-governed city the one in which most people say "mine" and "not mine" about the same things in the same way?

It is indeed.

13. The priestess of Apollo at Delphi.

What about the city that is most like a single person? For example, when one of us hurts his finger, the entire organism that binds body and soul together into a single system under the ruling part within it is aware of this, and the whole feels the pain together with the part that suffers. That's why we say that the man has a pain in his finger. And the same can be   *d* said about any part of a man, with regard either to the pain it suffers or to the pleasure it experiences when it finds relief.

Certainly. And, as for your question, the city with the best government *is* most like such a person.

Then, whenever anything good or bad happens to a single one of its citizens, such a city above all others will say that the affected part is its own and will share in the pleasure or pain as a whole.   *e*

If it has good laws, that must be so.

It's time now to return to our own city, to look there for the features we've agreed on, and to determine whether it or some other city possesses them to the greatest degree.

Then that's what we must do.

What about those other cities? Aren't there rulers and people in them, as well as in ours?   *463*

There are.

Besides fellow citizens, what do the people call the rulers in those other cities?

In many they call them despots, but in democracies they are called just this—rulers.[14]

What about the people in our city? Besides fellow citizens, what do they call their rulers?

Preservers[15] and auxiliaries.   *b*

And what do they in turn call the people?

Providers of upkeep and wages.

What do the rulers call the people in other cities?

Slaves.

And what do the rulers call each other?

Co-rulers.

And ours?

Co-guardians.

Can you tell me whether a ruler in those other cities could address some of his co-rulers as his kinsmen and others as outsiders?

14. The Athenian democracy had nine *archontes*, or rulers, in Plato's time. These included the chief magistrates, the chief military leader, and an important authority in religious matters.

15. See 429c.

Yes, many could.

And doesn't he consider his kinsman to be his own, and doesn't he

c   address him as such, while he considers the outsider not to be his own?
He does.

What about your guardians? Could any of them consider a co-guardian
as an outsider or address him as such?

There's no way he could, for when he meets any one of them, he'll hold
that he's meeting a brother or sister, a father or mother, a son or daughter,
or some ancestor or descendant of theirs.

You put that very well. But tell me this: Will your laws require them
simply to use these kinship names or also to do all the things that go along

d   with the names? Must they show to their "fathers" the respect, solicitude,
and obedience we show to our parents by law? Won't they fare worse at
the hands of gods and humans, as people whose actions are neither pious
nor just, if they do otherwise? Will these be the oracular sayings they hear
from all the citizens from their childhood on, or will they hear something
else about their fathers—or the ones they're told are their fathers—and
other relatives?

The former. It would be absurd if they only mouthed kinship names

e   without doing the things that go along with them.

Therefore, in our city more than in any other, they'll speak in unison
the words we mentioned a moment ago. When any one of them is doing
well or badly, they'll say that "mine" is doing well or that "mine" is doing
badly.

That's absolutely true.

464   Now, didn't we say that the having and expressing of this conviction is
closely followed by the having of pleasures and pains in common?

Yes, and we were right.

Then won't our citizens, more than any others, have the same thing in
common, the one they call "mine"? And, having that in common, won't
they, more than any others, have common pleasures and pains?

Of course.

And, in addition to the other institutions, the cause of this is the having
of wives and children in common by the guardians?

That more than anything else is the cause.

But we agreed that the having of pains and pleasures in common is the
greatest good for a city, and we characterized a well-governed city in terms

b   of the body's reaction to pain or pleasure in any one of its parts.

And we were right to agree.

Then, the cause of the greatest good for our city has been shown to be
the having of wives and children in common by the auxiliaries.

It has.

And, of course, this is consistent with what we said before, for we said somewhere that, if they're going to be guardians, they mustn't have private houses, property, or possessions, but must receive their upkeep from the other citizens as a wage for their guardianship and enjoy it in common.[16]   c

That's right.

Then isn't it true, just as I claimed, that what we are saying now, taken together with what we said before, makes even better guardians out of them and prevents them from tearing the city apart by not calling the same thing "mine"? If different people apply the term to different things, one would drag into his own house whatever he could separate from the others, and another would drag things into a different house to a different wife and children, and this would make for private pleasures and pains at   d
private things. But our people, on the other hand, will think of the same things as their own, aim at the same goal, and, as far as possible, feel pleasure and pain in unison.

Precisely.

And what about lawsuits and mutual accusations? Won't they pretty well disappear from among them, because they have everything in common except their own bodies? Hence they'll be spared all the dissension that arises between people because of the possession of money, children, and families.   e

They'll necessarily be spared it.

Nor could any lawsuits for insult or injury justly occur among them, for we'll declare that it's a fine and just thing for people to defend themselves against others of the same age, since this will compel them to stay in good physical shape.

That's right.

This law is also correct for another reason: If a spirited person vents *465* his anger in this way, it will be less likely to lead him into more serious disputes.

Certainly.

But an older person will be authorized to rule and punish all the younger ones.

Clearly.

And surely it's also obvious that a younger person won't strike or do any sort of violence to an older one or fail to show him respect in other ways, unless the rulers command it, for there are two guardians sufficient to prevent him from doing such things—shame and fear. Shame will prevent him from laying a hand on his parents, and so will the fear that

16. See 416d ff.

b the others would come to the aid of the victim, some as his sons, some as
his brothers, and some as his fathers.

That's the effect they'll have.

Then, in all cases, won't the laws induce men to live at peace with one
another?

Very much so.

And if there's no discord among the guardians, there's no danger that
the rest of the city will break into civil war, either with them or among
themselves.

Certainly not.

I hesitate to mention, since they're so unseemly, the pettiest of the evils
the guardians would therefore escape: The poor man's flattery of the rich,
c the perplexities and sufferings involved in bringing up children and in
making the money necessary to feed the household, getting into debt,
paying it off, and in some way or other providing enough money to hand
over to their wives and household slaves to manage. All of the various
troubles men endure in these matters are obvious, ignoble, and not worth
discussing.

d They're obvious even to the blind.

They'll be free of all these, and they'll live a life more blessedly happy
than that of the victors in the Olympian games.

How?

The Olympian victors are considered happy on account of only a small
part of what is available to our guardians, for the guardians' victory is even
greater, and their upkeep from public funds more complete. The victory
they gain is the preservation of the whole city, and the crown of victory
that they and their children receive is their upkeep and all the necessities
of life. They receive rewards from their own city while they live, and at
e their death they're given a worthy burial.

Those are very good things.

Do you remember that, earlier in our discussion, someone—I forget
who—shocked us by saying that we hadn't made our guardians happy,
that it was possible for them to have everything that belongs to the citizens,
466 yet they had nothing? We said, I think, that if this happened to come up
at some point, we'd look into it then, but that our concern at the time was
to make our guardians true guardians and the city the happiest we could,
rather than looking to any one group within it and moulding it for happiness.[17]

I remember.

Well, then, if the life of our auxiliaries is apparently much finer and

17. See 419a ff.

better than that of Olympian victors, is there any need to compare it to
the lives of cobblers, farmers, or other craftsmen?   *b*

Not in my opinion.

Then it's surely right to repeat here what I said then: If a guardian
seeks happiness in such a way that he's no longer a guardian and isn't
satisfied with a life that's moderate, stable, and—as we say—best, but a
silly, adolescent idea of happiness seizes him and incites him to use his
power to take everything in the city for himself, he'll come to know the *c*
true wisdom of Hesiod's saying that somehow "the half is worth more
than the whole."[18]

If he takes my advice, he'll keep to his own life-style.

You agree, then, that the women and men should associate with one
another in education, in things having to do with children, and in guarding
the other citizens in the way we've described; that both when they remain
in the city and when they go to war, they must guard together and hunt
together like dogs and share in everything as far as possible; and that by *d*
doing so they'll be doing what's best and not something contrary either to
woman's nature as compared with man's or to the natural association of
men and women with one another.

I agree.

Then doesn't it remain for us to determine whether it's possible to
bring about this association among human beings, as it is among animals,
and to say just how it might be done?

You took the words right out of my mouth.

As far as war is concerned, I think it's clear how they will wage it.   *e*

How so?

Men and women will campaign together. They'll take the sturdy children with them, so that, like the children of other craftsmen, they can see
what they'll have to do when they grow up. But in addition to observing,
they can serve and assist in everything to do with the war and help their
mothers and fathers. Haven't you noticed in the other crafts how the *467*
children of potters, for example, assist and observe for a long time before
actually making any pots?

I have indeed.

And should these craftsmen take more care in training their children
by appropriate experience and observation than the guardians?

Of course not; that would be completely ridiculous.

Besides, every animal fights better in the presence of its young.   *b*

That's so. But, Socrates, there's a considerable danger that in a defeat—
and such things are likely to happen in a war—they'll lose their children's

18. *Works and Days* 40.

lives as well as their own, making it impossible for the rest of the city to recover.

What you say is true. But do you think that the first thing we should provide for is the avoidance of all danger?

Not at all.

Well, then, if people will probably have to face some danger, shouldn't it be the sort that will make them better if they come through it successfully?

Obviously.

And do you think that whether or not men who are going to be warriors observe warfare when they're still boys makes such a small difference that
c   it isn't worth the danger of having them do it?

No, it does make a difference to what you're talking about.

On the assumption, then, that the children are to be observers of war, if we can contrive some way to keep them secure, everything will be fine, won't it?

Yes.

Well, then, in the first place, their fathers won't be ignorant, will they, about which campaigns are dangerous and which are not, but rather as
d   knowledgeable about this as any human beings can be?

Probably so.

Then they'll take the children to some campaigns and not to others?

Correct.

And they'll put officers in charge of them whose age and experience qualifies them to be leaders and tutors?

Appropriately so.

But, as we say, the unexpected often occurs.

Indeed.

With this in mind, we must provide the children with wings when they're small, so that they can fly away and escape.
e   What do you mean?

We must mount them on horses as early as possible—not on spirited or aggressive horses, but on very fast and manageable ones—and when they've learned to ride, they must be taken to observe a war. In this way, they'll get the best look at their own work and, if the need arises, make the securest possible escape to safety, following their older guides.

I think you're right.
468   What about warfare itself? What attitude should your soldiers have to each other and to the enemy? Are my views about this right or not?

First, tell me what they are.

If one of them leaves his post or throws away his shield or does anything else of that sort through cowardice, shouldn't he be reduced to being a craftsman or farmer?

Certainly.

And shouldn't anyone who is captured alive be left to his captors as a gift to do with as they wish?

Absolutely.   *b*

But don't you think that anyone who distinguishes himself and earns high esteem should, while still on the campaign, first be crowned with wreaths by each of the adolescents and children who accompany the expedition?

I do.

And what about shaken by the right hand?

That too.

But I suppose that you wouldn't go this far?

Namely?

That he should kiss and be kissed by each of them.

That most of all. And I'd add this to the law: As long as the campaign lasts, no one he wants to kiss shall be allowed to refuse, for then, if one of them happens to be in love with another, whether male or female, he'll   *c* be all the more eager to win the rewards of valor.

Excellent. And we've already stated that, since he's a good person, more marriages will be available to him, and he'll be selected for such things more frequently than the others, so that he'll beget as many children as possible.

Yes, we did say that.

Indeed, according to Homer too, it is just to honor in such ways those young people who are good, for he says that Ajax, when he distinguished himself in battle, "was rewarded with the long cut off the backbone."[19]   *d* And that's an appropriate honor for a courageous young man, since it will both honor him and increase his strength.

That's absolutely right.

Then we'll follow Homer in these matters at least. And insofar as good people have shown themselves to be good, we'll honor them at sacrifices and all such occasions with hymns, "seats of honor, meats, and well-filled cups of wine,"[20] and in all the other ways we mentioned, so that, in addition to honoring good men and women, we'll continue to train them.   *e*

That's excellent.

All right. And as for those who died on the campaign, won't we say, first of all, that, if their deaths were distinguished, they belong to the golden race?

That above all.

And won't we believe with Hesiod that, whenever any of that race die, they become

19. *Iliad* 7.321.
20. *Iliad* 8.162.

469   *Sacred daimons living upon the earth,*
          Noble spirits, protectors against evil, guardians of articulate mortals?[21]

We'll certainly believe that.

Then we'll inquire from the god[22] what kind of distinguished funeral we should give to daimonic and godlike people, and we'll follow his instructions.

Of course.

And for the remainder of time, we'll care for their graves and worship at them as we would at those of daimons. And we'll follow the same rites
b   for anyone whom we judge to have lived an outstandingly good life, whether he died of old age or in some other way.

That is only just.

Now, what about enemies? How will our soldiers deal with them?

In what respect?

First, enslavement. Do you think it is just for Greeks to enslave Greek cities, or, as far as they can, should they not even allow other cities to do so, and make a habit of sparing the Greek race, as a precaution against
c   being enslaved by the barbarians?

It's altogether and in every way best to spare the Greek race.

Then isn't it also best for the guardians not to acquire a Greek slave and to advise the other Greeks not to do so either?

Absolutely. In that way they'd be more likely to turn against the barbarians and keep their hands off one another.

What about despoiling the dead? Is it a good thing to strip the dead of anything besides their armor after a victory? Or don't cowards make this
d   an excuse for not facing the enemy—as if they were doing something of vital importance in bending over a corpse? And haven't many armies been lost because of such plundering?

Indeed, they have.

Don't you think it's slavish and money-loving to strip a corpse? Isn't it small-minded and womanish to regard the body as your enemy, when the enemy himself has flitted away, leaving behind only the instrument with which he fought? Or do you think such behavior any different from that
e   of dogs who get angry with the stone that hits them and leave the thrower alone?

It's no different at all.

Then may our soldiers strip corpses or refuse the enemy permission to pick up their dead?

21. *Works and Days* 122. On daimons, see 382e n.23.
22. Apollo. See 427b.

No, by god, they certainly may not.

Moreover, we won't take enemy arms to the temples as offerings, and if we care about the goodwill of other Greeks, we especially won't do this with *their* arms. Rather we'd be afraid of polluting[23] the temples if we brought them such things from our own people, unless, of course, the god tells us otherwise.   *470*

That's absolutely right.

What about ravaging the land of the Greeks and burning their houses? Will your soldiers do things of this sort to their enemies?

I'd like to hear *your* opinion about that.

Well, I think they should do neither of these things but destroy the year's harvest only. Do you want me to tell you why?   *b*

Of course.

It seems to me that as we have two names, "war" and "civil war," so there are two things and the names apply to two kinds of disagreements arising in them. The two things I'm referring to are what is one's own and akin, on the one hand, and what's foreign and strange, on the other. The name "civil war" applies to hostilities with one's own, while "war" applies to hostilities with strangers.

That's certainly to the point.

Then see whether this is also to the point: I say that the Greek race is its own and akin, while the barbarians are strange and foreign.   *c*

That's right.

Then when Greeks do battle with barbarians or barbarians with Greeks, we'll say that they're natural enemies and that such hostilities are to be called war. But when Greeks fight with Greeks, we'll say that they are natural friends and that in such circumstances Greece is sick and divided into factions and that such hostilities are to be called civil war.   *d*

I, at any rate, agree to think of it that way.

Now, notice that, wherever something of the sort that's currently called civil war occurs and a city is divided, if either party ravages the land of the others and burns their houses, it's thought that this is abominable and that neither party loves their city, since otherwise they'd never have ravaged their very nurse and mother.[24] However, it *is* thought appropriate for the victors to carry off the harvest of the vanquished. Nonetheless, their attitude of mind should be that of people who'll one day be reconciled and who won't always be at war.   *e*

This way of thinking is far more civilized than the other.

---

23. Greek views on pollution, which is now a foreign concept to us, are discussed in R. Parker, *Miasma* (Oxford: Clarendon Press, 1983).

24. See 414e.

What about the city you're founding? It is Greek, isn't it?

It has to be.

Then, won't your citizens be good and civilized?

Indeed they will.

Then, won't they love Greece? Won't they consider Greece as their own and share the religion of the other Greeks?

Yes, indeed.

Then won't they consider their differences with Greeks—people who
471 are their own—not as war but as civil war?

Of course.

And won't they quarrel like people who know that one day they'll be reconciled?

Certainly.

Then they'll moderate their foes in a friendly spirit, not punish them with enslavement and destruction, for they're moderators, not enemies.

That's right.

And being Greeks, they won't ravage Greece or burn her houses, nor will they agree that in any of her cities all the inhabitants—men, women, and children—are their enemies, but that whatever differences arise are caused by the few enemies that any city inevitably contains. Because of this, because the majority are friendly, they won't ravage the country or
b   destroy the houses, and they'll continue their quarrel only to the point at which those who caused it are forced to pay the penalty by those who were its innocent victims.

I agree that this is the way our citizens must treat their enemies, and they must treat barbarians the way Greeks currently treat each other.

Then shall we also impose this law on the guardians: Neither ravage
c   the country nor burn the houses?

Consider it imposed. And let's also assume that this law and its predecessors are all fine. But I think, Socrates, that if we let you go on speaking about this subject, you'll never remember the one you set aside in order to say all this, namely, whether it's possible for this constitution to come into being and in what way it could be brought about. I agree that, if it existed, all the things we've mentioned would be good for the city in which they occurred. And I'll add some that you've left out. The guardians would be excellent fighters against an enemy because they'd be least likely to desert each other, since they know each other as brothers, fathers, and
d   sons, and call each other by those names. Moreover, if their women joined their campaigns, either in the same ranks or positioned in the rear to frighten the enemy and in case their help should ever be needed, I know that this would make them quite unbeatable. And I also see all the good things that they'd have at home that you've omitted. Take it that I agree

that all these things would happen, as well as innumerable others, if this   *e*
kind of constitution came into being, and say no more on that subject. But
rather let's now try to convince ourselves that it is possible and how it is
possible, and let the rest go.

This is a sudden attack that you've made on my argument, and you   *472*
show no sympathy for my delay. Perhaps you don't realize that, just as I've
barely escaped from the first two waves of objections, you're bringing the
third—the biggest and most difficult one—down upon me. When you see
and hear it, you'll surely be completely sympathetic, and recognize that it
was, after all, appropriate for me to hesitate and be afraid to state and look
into so paradoxical a view.

The more you speak like that, the less we'll let you off from telling us
how it's possible for this constitution to come into being. So speak instead
of wasting time.   *b*

Well, then, we must first remember that we got to this point while trying
to discover what justice and injustice are like.

We must. But what of it?

Nothing. But if we discover what justice is like, will we also maintain
that the just man is in no way different from the just itself, so that he is
like justice in every respect? Or will we be satisfied if he comes as close
to it as possible and participates in it far more than anyone else?   *c*

We'll be satisfied with that.

Then it was in order to have a model that we were trying to discover
what justice itself is like and what the completely just man would be like,
if he came into being, and what kind of man he'd be if he did, and likewise
with regard to injustice and the most unjust man. We thought that, by
looking at how their relationship to happiness and its opposite seemed to
us, we'd also be compelled to agree about ourselves as well, that the one
who was most like them would have a portion of happiness most like theirs.   *d*
But we weren't trying to discover these things in order to prove that it's
possible for them to come into being.

That's true.

Do you think that someone is a worse painter if, having painted a model
of what the finest and most beautiful human being would be like and
having rendered every detail of his picture adequately, he could not prove
that such a man could come into being?

No, by god, I don't.

Then what about our own case? Didn't we say that we were making a
theoretical model of a good city?[25]   *e*

Certainly.

25. See 369a–c.

So do you think that our discussion will be any less reasonable if we can't prove that it's possible to found a city that's the same as the one in our theory?

Not at all.

Then that's the truth of the matter. But if, in order to please you, I must also be willing to show how and under what conditions it would most be possible to found such a city, then you should agree to make the same concessions to me, in turn, for the purposes of this demonstration.

Which ones?

Is it possible to do anything in practice the same as in theory? Or is it in the nature of practice to grasp truth less well than theory does, even if 473 some people don't think so? Will you first agree to this or not?

I agree.

Then don't compel me to show that what we've described in theory can come into being exactly as we've described it. Rather, if we're able to discover how a city could come to be governed in a way that most closely approximates our description, let's say that we've shown what you ordered us to show, namely, that it's possible for our city to come to be. Or wouldn't b you be satisfied with that? I would be satisfied with it.

So would I.

Then next, it seems, we should try to discover and point out what's now badly done in cities that keeps them from being governed in that way and what's the smallest change that would enable our city to reach our sort of constitution—one change, if possible, or if not one, two, and if not two, then the fewest in number and the least extensive.

c   That's absolutely right.

There is one change we could point to that, in my opinion, would accomplish this. It's certainly neither small nor easy, but it is possible.

What is it?

Well, I've now come to what we likened to the greatest wave. But I shall say what I have to say, even if the wave is a wave of laughter that will simply drown me in ridicule and contempt. So listen to what I'm going to say.

Say on.

Until philosophers rule as kings or those who are now called kings and leading men genuinely and adequately philosophize, that is, until political d   power and philosophy entirely coincide, while the many natures who at present pursue either one exclusively are forcibly prevented from doing so, cities will have no rest from evils, Glaucon, nor, I think, will the human race. And, until this happens, the constitution we've been describ-e   ing in theory will never be born to the fullest extent possible or see the light of the sun. It's because I saw how very paradoxical this statement would be that I hesitated to make it for so long, for it's hard to face up to the fact that there can be no happiness, either public or private, in any other city.

Socrates, after hurling a speech and statement like that at us, you must expect that a great many people (and not undistinguished ones either) will cast off their cloaks and, stripped for action, snatch any available weapon, and make a determined rush at you, ready to do terrible things. So, unless *474* you can hold them off by argument and escape, you really will pay the penalty of general derision.

Well, you are the one that brought this on me.

And I was right to do it. However, I won't betray you, but rather defend you in any way I can—by goodwill, by urging you on, and perhaps by being able to give you more appropriate answers than someone else. So, with the promise of this assistance, try to show the unbelievers that things are as you say they are.   *b*

I must try it, then, especially since you agree to be so great an ally. If we're to escape from the people you mention, I think we need to define for them who the philosophers are that we dare to say must rule. And once that's clear, we should be able to defend ourselves by showing that the people we mean are fitted by nature both to engage in philosophy and to rule in a city, while the rest are naturally fitted to leave philosophy alone   *c* and follow their leader.

This would be a good time to give that definition.

Come, then, follow me, and we'll see whether or not there's some way to set it out adequately.

Lead on.

Do you need to be reminded or do you remember that, if it's rightly said that someone loves something, then he mustn't love one part of it and not another, but he must love all of it?[26]

I think you'll have to remind me, for I don't understand it at all.   *d*

That would be an appropriate response, Glaucon, for somebody else to make. But it isn't appropriate for an erotically inclined man to forget that all boys in the bloom of youth pique the interest of a lover of boys and arouse him and that all seem worthy of his care and pleasure. Or isn't that the way you people behave to fine and beautiful boys? You praise a snub-nosed one as cute, a hook-nosed one you say is regal, one in between is well proportioned, dark ones look manly, and pale ones are children of the gods. And as for a honey-colored boy, do you think that this very term   *e* is anything but the euphemistic coinage of a lover who found it easy to

---

26. Socrates here seems to be applying the principle he introduced at 438a–b. See 475c.

tolerate sallowness, provided it was accompanied by the bloom of youth?
475 In a word, you find all kinds of terms and excuses so as not to reject
anyone whose flower is in bloom.

If you insist on taking me as your example of what erotically inclined
men do, then, for the sake of the argument, I agree.

Further, don't you see wine-lovers behave in the same way? Don't they
love every kind of wine and find any excuse to enjoy it?

Certainly.

And I think you see honor-lovers, if they can't be generals, be captains,
and, if they can't be honored by people of importance and dignity, they
put up with being honored by insignificant and inferior ones, for they
b   desire the whole of honor.

Exactly.

Then do you agree to this or not? When we say that someone desires
something, do we mean that he desires everything of that kind or that he
desires one part of it but not another?

We mean he desires everything.

Then won't we also say that the philosopher doesn't desire one part of
wisdom rather than another, but desires the whole thing?

Yes, that's true.

And as for the one who's choosy about what he learns, especially if he's
young and can't yet give an account of what is useful and what isn't, we
c   won't say that he is a lover of learning or a philosopher, for we wouldn't
say that someone who's choosy about his food is hungry or has an appetite
for food or is a lover of food—instead, we'd say that he is a bad eater.

And we'd be right to say it.

But the one who readily and willingly tries all kinds of learning, who
turns gladly to learning and is insatiable for it, is rightly called a philosopher, isn't he?

d   Then many strange people will be philosophers, for the lovers of sights
seem to be included, since they take pleasure in learning things. And the
lovers of sounds are very strange people to include as philosophers, for
they would never willingly attend a serious discussion or spend their time
that way, yet they run around to all the Dionysiac festivals, omitting none,
whether in cities or villages, as if their ears were under contract to listen
to every chorus. Are we to say that these people—and those who learn
e   similar things or petty crafts—are philosophers?

No, but they are *like* philosophers.

And who are the true philosophers?

Those who love the sight of truth.

That's right, but what exactly do you mean by it?

It would not be easy to explain to someone else, but I think that you
will agree to this.

To what?

Since the beautiful is the opposite of the ugly, they are two.

Of course.   476

And since they are two, each is one?

I grant that also.

And the same account is true of the just and the unjust, the good and the bad, and all the forms.[27] Each of them is itself one, but because they manifest themselves everywhere in association with actions, bodies, and one another, each of them appears to be many.

That's right.

So, I draw this distinction: On one side are those you just now called lovers of sights, lovers of crafts, and practical people; on the other side are those we are arguing about and whom one would alone call philosophers.   b

How do you mean?

The lovers of sights and sounds like beautiful sounds, colors, shapes, and everything fashioned out of them,[28] but their thought is unable to see and embrace the nature of the beautiful itself.

That's for sure.

In fact, there are very few people who would be able to reach the beautiful itself and see it by itself. Isn't that so?

Certainly.   c

What about someone who believes in beautiful things,[29] but doesn't believe in the beautiful itself and isn't able to follow anyone who could lead him to the knowledge of it? Don't you think he is living in a dream rather than a wakened state? Isn't this dreaming: whether asleep or awake, to think that a likeness is not a likeness but rather the thing itself that it is like?

I certainly think that someone who does that is dreaming.

But someone who, to take the opposite case, believes in the beautiful itself, can see both it and the things that participate in it and doesn't believe that the participants are it or that it itself is the participants—is he   d living in a dream or is he awake?

He's very much awake.

So we'd be right to call his thought knowledge, since he knows, but we should call the other person's thought opinion, since he opines?

Right.

---

27. See 596a ff.

28. A poem is fashioned out of sounds and a painting out of colors and shapes. See 600e–601b.

29. Socrates may be referring here either to particular things that are beautiful or to the various beauties in them, which are properties or universals. The same is true later when Socrates speaks of "the many just things," "the many doubles," and the rest.

What if the person who has opinion but not knowledge is angry with us and disputes the truth of what we are saying? Is there some way to console
e   him and persuade him gently, while hiding from him that he isn't in his right mind?[30]

There must be.

Consider, then, what we'll say to him. Won't we question him like this? First, we'll tell him that nobody begrudges him any knowledge he may have and that we'd be delighted to discover that he knows something. Then we'll say: "Tell us, does the person who knows know something or nothing?" You answer for him.

He knows something.

Something that is or something that is not?[31]

477   Something that is, for how could something that is not be known?

Then we have an adequate grasp of this: No matter how many ways we examine it, what is completely is completely knowable and what is in no way is in every way unknowable?

A most adequate one.

Good. Now, if anything is such as to be and also not to be, won't it be intermediate between what purely is and what in no way is?

Yes, it's intermediate.

Then, as knowledge is set over what is, while ignorance is of necessity set over what is not, mustn't we find an intermediate between knowledge and ignorance to be set over what is intermediate between what is and
b   what is not, if there is such a thing?

Certainly.

Do we say that opinion is something?

Of course.

A different power from knowledge or the same?

A different one.

Opinion, then, is set over one thing, and knowledge over another, according to the power of each.

---

30. It is important to note that the argument that follows is intended to convince the lovers of sights and crafts that they have opinion rather than knowledge. Since these people are defined as being unable to countenance forms, the argument cannot achieve its purpose if it simply presupposes that there are forms or draws on the theory of forms, for the lovers of sight and crafts will not be convinced by an argument which appeals to something they are unable to accept.

31. Because of the ambiguity of the verb *einai* ("to be"), Socrates could be asking any or all of the following questions: (1) "Something that exists or something that does not exist?" (existential "is"); (2) "Something that is beautiful (say) or something that is not beautiful?" (predicative "is"); (3) "Something that is true or something that is not true?" (veridical "is").

Right.

Now, isn't knowledge by its nature set over what is, to know it as it is? But first maybe we'd better be a bit more explicit.

How so?

Powers are a class of the things that are that enable us—or anything   c
else for that matter—to do whatever we are capable of doing. Sight, for example, and hearing are among the powers, if you understand the kind of thing I'm referring to.

I do.

Here's what I think about them. A power has neither color nor shape nor any feature of the sort that many other things have and that I use to distinguish those things from one another. In the case of a power, I use only what it is set over and what it does, and by reference to these I call   d
each the power it is: What is set over the same things and does the same I call the same power; what is set over something different and does something different I call a different one. Do you agree?

I do.

Then let's back up. Is knowledge a power, or what class would you put it in?

It's a power, the strongest of them all.

And what about opinion, is it a power or some other kind of thing?   e

It's a power as well, for it is what enables us to opine.

A moment ago you agreed that knowledge and opinion aren't the same.

How could a person with any understanding think that a fallible power is the same as an infallible one?

Right. Then we agree that opinion is clearly different from knowledge. *478*

It is different.

Hence each of them is by nature set over something different and does something different?

Necessarily.

Knowledge is set over what is, to know it as it is?

Yes.

And opinion opines?

Yes.

Does it opine the very thing that knowledge knows, so that the knowable and the opinable are the same, or is this impossible?

It's impossible, given what we agreed, for if a different power is set over something different, and opinion and knowledge are different powers, then the knowable and the opinable cannot be the same.   b

Then, if what is is knowable, the opinable must be something other than what is?

It must.

Do we, then, opine what is not? Or is it impossible to opine what is not? Think about this. Doesn't someone who opines set his opinion over something? Or is it possible to opine, yet to opine nothing?

It's impossible.

But someone who opines opines some one thing?

Yes.

Surely the most accurate word for that which is not isn't 'one thing' but
c   'nothing'?

Certainly.

But we had to set ignorance over what is not and knowledge over what is?

That's right.

So someone opines neither what is nor what is not?

How could it be otherwise?

Then opinion is neither ignorance nor knowledge?

So it seems.

Then does it go beyond either of these? Is it clearer than knowledge or darker than ignorance?

No, neither.

Is opinion, then, darker than knowledge but clearer than ignorance?

It is.
d   Then it lies between them?

Yes.

So opinion is intermediate between those two?

Absolutely.

Now, we said that, if something could be shown, as it were, to be and not to be at the same time, it would be intermediate between what purely is and what in every way is not, and that neither knowledge nor ignorance would be set over it, but something intermediate between ignorance and knowledge?

Correct.

And now the thing we call opinion has emerged as being intermediate between them?

It has.

Apparently, then, it only remains for us to find what participates in both
e   being and not being and cannot correctly be called purely one or the other, in order that, if there is such a thing, we can rightly call it the opinable, thereby setting the extremes over the extremes and the intermediate over the intermediate. Isn't that so?

It is.

Now that these points have been established, I want to address a
479 question to our friend who doesn't believe in the beautiful itself or any

form of the beautiful itself that remains always the same in all respects but who does believe in the many beautiful things—the lover of sights who wouldn't allow anyone to say that the beautiful itself is one or that the just is one or any of the rest: "My dear fellow," we'll say, "of all the many beautiful things, is there one that will not also appear ugly? Or is there one of those just things that will not also appear unjust? Or one of those pious things that will not also appear impious?"

There isn't one, for it is necessary that they appear to be beautiful in a way and also to be ugly in a way, and the same with the other things you   *b* asked about.

What about the many doubles? Do they appear any the less halves than doubles?

Not one.

So, with the many bigs and smalls and lights and heavies, is any one of them any more the thing someone says it is than its opposite?

No, each of them always participates in both opposites.

Is any one of the manys what someone says it is, then, any more than it is not what he says it is?

No, they are like the ambiguities one is entertained with at dinner parties or like the children's riddle about the eunuch who threw something at a bat—the one about what he threw at it and what it was in,[32] for they   *c* are ambiguous, and one cannot understand them as fixedly being or fixedly not being or as both or as neither.

Then do you know how to deal with them? Or can you find a more appropriate place to put them than intermediate between being and not being? Surely, they can't *be* more than what is or *not be* more than what is not, for apparently nothing is darker than what is not or clearer than what is.   *d*

Very true.

We've now discovered, it seems, that according to the many conventions of the majority of people about beauty and the others, they[33] are rolling around as intermediates between what is not and what purely is.[34]

We have.

---

32. The riddle seems to have been: A man who is not a man saw and did not see a bird that was not a bird in a tree (*xulon*) that was not a tree; he hit (*ballō*) and did not hit it with a stone that was not a stone. The answer is that a eunuch with bad eyesight saw a bat on a rafter, threw a pumice stone at it and missed. "He saw a bird" is ambiguous between "he saw what was actually a bird" and "he saw what he took to be a bird," *xulon* means both "tree" and "rafter" or "roof tree," and *ballō* means both "to throw" and "to hit." The rest is obvious.

33. I.e. the many beautiful things, etc.

34. See 484c–d, 493a ff.

And we agreed earlier that anything of that kind would have to be called the opinable, not the knowable—the wandering intermediate grasped by the intermediate power.

We did.

As for those who study the many beautiful things but do not see the
e   beautiful itself and are incapable of following another who leads them to it, who see many just things but not the just itself, and so with everything— these people, we shall say, opine everything but have no knowledge of anything they opine.

Necessarily.

What about the ones who in each case study the things themselves that are always the same in every respect? Won't we say that they know and don't opine?

That's necessary too.

Shall we say, then, that these people love and embrace the things that
480 knowledge is set over, as the others do the things that opinion is set over? Remember we said that the latter saw and loved beautiful sounds and colors and the like but wouldn't allow the beautiful itself to be anything?

We remember, all right.

We won't be in error, then, if we call such people lovers of opinion rather than philosophers or lovers of wisdom and knowledge? Will they be angry with us if we call them that?

Not if they take my advice, for it isn't right to be angry with those who speak the truth.

As for those who in each case embrace the thing itself, we must call them philosophers, not lovers of opinion?

Most definitely.

BOOK VI

Only the philosophers have knowledge, and that alone is sufficient to qualify them to be the rulers, provided that they aren't inferior to the nonphilosophers in virtue (484d). So Socrates tries to show that they are in fact supremely virtuous (485a–487a). Adeimantus accepts his arguments, but points out that the majority of people will simply go on believing that philosophers are unsuited to rule, because they know from experience that most philosophers are vicious, while the few decent ones are useless (487a–d). Socrates surprisingly agrees with the majority about this. The people the majority take to be philosophers are either vicious or useless (487d–496e), but that is because the few decent ones, who possess a true philosophical nature, are not raised under the right sort of constitution (497a–b). If the majority ever saw a philosopher who had been raised in that way, they too would agree that he should rule their city (500e–501a).

The guardians, in the most exact sense of the term, must be philosophers (503b), then, and they must have all the traits already mentioned, but they must also be tested to see whether or not they can master the most important subjects (503e). These are the subjects that enable someone to come to know the good itself, i.e. the form of the good (504e–505b). Socrates cannot explain directly what the good itself is, but he describes "what is apparently an offspring of the good and most like it" (506b–e). This description is the famous Sun analogy (507a–509c). It is completed by the Line analogy, which occupies the remainder of the book (509d–511e). These analogies dramatically portray Plato's views on knowledge and reality, which, together with his earlier description of the state of philosophy in the actual world, are expressed in some of the most brilliant and passionate writing in all of philosophy.

And so, Glaucon, I said, after a somewhat lengthy and difficult discussion, both the philosophers and the nonphilosophers have revealed who they are. 484

It probably wouldn't have been easy, he said, to have them do it in a shorter one.

Apparently not. But for my part, I think that the matter would have been better illuminated if we had only it to discuss and not all the other things that remain to be treated in order to discover the difference between the just life and the unjust one. b

What's our next topic?

What else but the one that's next in order? Since those who are able to grasp what is always the same in all respects are philosophers, while those who are not able to do so and who wander among the many things that vary in every sort of way are not philosophers, which of the two should be the leaders in a city?

What would be a sensible answer to that?

We should establish as guardians those who are clearly capable of
c guarding the laws and the ways of life of the city.

That's right.

And isn't it clear that the guardian who is to keep watch over everything should be keen-sighted rather than blind?

Of course it's clear.

Do you think, then, that there's any difference between the blind and those who are really deprived of the knowledge of each thing that is? The latter have no clear model in their souls, and so they cannot—in the manner of painters—look to what is most true, make constant reference
d to it, and study it as exactly as possible. Hence they cannot establish here on earth conventions about what is fine or just or good, when they need to be established, or guard and preserve them, once they have been established.

No, by god, there isn't much difference between them.

Should we, then, make these blind people our guardians or rather those who know each thing that is and who are not inferior to the others, either in experience or in any other part of virtue?

It would be absurd to choose anyone but philosophers, if indeed they're not inferior in these ways, for the respect in which they are superior is pretty well the most important one.

Then shouldn't we explain how it is possible for someone to have both
485 these sorts of qualities?

Certainly.

Then, as we said at the beginning of this discussion, it is necessary to understand the nature of philosophers first,[1] for I think that, if we can reach adequate agreement about that, we'll also agree that the same people *can* have both qualities and that no one but they should be leaders in cities.

How so?

Let's agree that philosophic natures always love the sort of learning that makes clear to them some feature of the being that always is and does not
b wander around between coming to be and decaying.

And further, let's agree that, like the honor-lovers and erotically inclined

---

1. See 474b–c.

men we described before,[2] they love all such learning and are not willing
to give up any part of it, whether large or small, more valuable or less so.

That's right.

Consider next whether the people we're describing must also have this
in their nature?   *c*

What?

They must be without falsehood—they must refuse to accept what is
false, hate it, and have a love for the truth.

That's a reasonable addition, at any rate.

It's not only reasonable, it's entirely necessary, for it's necessary for a
man who is erotically inclined by nature to love everything akin to or
belonging to the boy he loves.

That's right.

And could you find anything that belongs more to wisdom than truth
does?

Of course not.

Then is it possible for the same nature to be a philosopher—a lover of
wisdom—and a lover of falsehood?   *d*

Not at all.

Then someone who loves learning must above all strive for every kind
of truth from childhood on.

Absolutely.

Now, we surely know that, when someone's desires incline strongly for
one thing, they are thereby weakened for others, just like a stream that
has been partly diverted into another channel.

Of course.

Then, when someone's desires flow towards learning and everything of
that sort, he'd be concerned, I suppose, with the pleasures of the soul
itself by itself, and he'd abandon those pleasures that come through the
body—if indeed he is a true philosopher and not merely a counterfeit one.

That's completely necessary.   *e*

Then surely such a person is moderate and not at all a money-lover.
It's appropriate for others to take seriously the things for which money
and large expenditures are needed, but not for him.

That's right.

And of course there's also this to consider when you are judging whether *486*
a nature is philosophic or not.

What's that?

If it is at all slavish, you should not overlook that fact, for pettiness is
altogether incompatible with a soul that is always reaching out to grasp
everything both divine and human as a whole.

2. See 474c–475c.

That's completely true.

And will a thinker high-minded enough to study all time and all being consider human life to be something important?

He couldn't possibly.

b   Then will he consider death to be a terrible thing?

He least of all.

Then it seems a cowardly and slavish nature will take no part in true philosophy.

Not in my opinion.

And is there any way that an orderly person, who isn't money-loving, slavish, a boaster, or a coward, could become unreliable or unjust?

There isn't.

Moreover, when you are looking to see whether a soul is philosophic or not, you'll look to see whether it is just and gentle, from youth on, or savage and hard to associate with.

Certainly.

c   And here's something I think you won't leave out.

What?

Whether he's a slow learner or a fast one. Or do you ever expect anyone to love something when it pains him to do it and when much effort brings only small return?

No, it couldn't happen.

And what if he could retain nothing of what he learned, because he was full of forgetfulness? Could he fail to be empty of knowledge?

How could he?

Then don't you think that, if he's laboring in vain, he'd inevitably come to hate both himself and that activity in the end?

Of course.

Then let's never include a forgetful soul among those who are suffi-
d   ciently philosophical for our purposes, but look for one with a good memory.

Absolutely.

Now, we'd certainly say that the unmusical and graceless element in a person's nature draws him to lack of due measure.

Of course.

And do you think that truth is akin to what lacks due measure or to what is measured?

To what is measured.

Then, in addition to those other things, let's look for someone whose thought is by nature measured and graceful and is easily led to the form of each thing that is.

Of course.

Well, then, don't you think the properties we've enumerated are compat-

ible with one another and that each is necessary to a soul that is to have
an adequate and complete grasp of that which is?   *e*

They're all completely necessary.   *487*

Is there any objection you can find, then, to a way of life that no one
can adequately follow unless he's by nature good at remembering, quick
to learn, high-minded, graceful, and a friend and relative of truth, justice,
courage, and moderation?

Not even Momus³ could find one.

When such people have reached maturity in age and education, wouldn't
you entrust the city to them and to them alone?

And Adeimantus replied: No one would be able to contradict the things
you've said, Socrates, but on each occasion that you say them, your hearers
are affected in some such way as this. They think that, because they're   *b*
inexperienced in asking and answering questions, they're led astray a little
bit by the argument at every question and that, when these little bits are
added together at the end of the discussion, a big false step appears that
is the opposite of what they said at the outset. Just as inexperienced
checkers players are trapped by the experts in the end and can't make a
move, so they too are trapped in the end and have nothing to say in this   *c*
different kind of checkers, which is played not with disks but with words.
Yet the truth isn't affected by this outcome. I say this with a view to the
present case, for someone might well say now that he's unable to oppose
you as you ask each of your questions, yet he sees that of all those who
take up philosophy—not those who merely dabble in it while still young
in order to complete their upbringing and then drop it, but those who
continue in it for a longer time—the greatest number become cranks, not   *d*
to say completely vicious, while those who seem completely decent are
rendered useless to the city because of the way of life you recommend.

When I'd heard him out, I said: Do you think that what these people
say is false?

I don't know, but I'd be glad to hear what you think.

You'd hear that they seem to me to speak the truth.

How, then, can it be true to say that there will be no end to evils in our   *e*
cities until philosophers—people we agree to be useless—rule in them?

The question you ask needs to be answered by means of an image or
simile.

And you, of course, aren't used to speaking in similes!

So! Are you making fun of me now that you've landed me with a claim
that's so hard to establish? In any case, listen to my simile, and you'll
appreciate all the more how strained my images are. What the most decent *488*
people experience in relation to their city is so hard to bear that there's

---

3. Momus is a personification of blame or censure.

no other single experience like it. Hence to find an image of it and a defense for them, I must construct it from many sources, just as painters paint goat-stags by combining the features of different things. Imagine, then, that something like the following happens on a ship or on many ships. The shipowner is bigger and stronger than everyone else on board,

b but he's hard of hearing, a bit short-sighted, and his knowledge of seafaring is equally deficient. The sailors are quarreling with one another about steering the ship, each of them thinking that he should be the captain, even though he's never learned the art of navigation, cannot point to anyone who taught it to him, or to a time when he learned it. Indeed, they claim that it isn't teachable and are ready to cut to pieces anyone who says that it is. They're always crowding around the shipowner, begging him

c and doing everything possible to get him to turn the rudder over to them. And sometimes, if they don't succeed in persuading him, they execute the ones who do succeed or throw them overboard, and then, having stupefied their noble shipowner with drugs, wine, or in some other way, they rule the ship, using up what's in it and sailing in the way that people like that are prone to do. Moreover, they call the person who is clever at persuading

d or forcing the shipowner to let them rule a "navigator," a "captain," and "one who knows ships," and dismiss anyone else as useless. They don't understand that a true captain must pay attention to the seasons of the year, the sky, the stars, the winds, and all that pertains to his craft, if he's really to be the ruler of a ship. And they don't believe there is any craft that would enable him to determine where he should steer the ship to,

e independently of whether the others want to go there or not, or any possibility of mastering this alleged craft or of practicing it at the same time as the craft of navigation. Don't you think that the true captain will be called a real stargazer, a babbler, and a good-for-nothing by those who

489 sail in ships governed in that way, in which such things happen?

I certainly do.

I don't think that you need to examine the simile in detail to see that the ships resemble cities and their attitude to the true philosophers, but you already understand what I mean.

Indeed, I do.

Then first tell this simile to anyone who wonders why philosophers aren't honored in the cities, and try to persuade him that there would be

b far more cause for wonder if they were honored.

I will tell him.

Next tell him that what he says is true, that the best among the philosophers are useless to the majority. Tell him not to blame those decent people for this but the ones who don't make use of them. It isn't natural for the captain to beg the sailors to be ruled by him nor for the wise to knock at the doors of the rich—the man who came up with that wisecrack made a mistake.[4] The natural thing is for the sick person, rich or poor, to knock at the doctor's door, and for anyone who needs to be ruled to knock at the door of the one who can rule him. It isn't for the ruler, if he's truly any use, to beg the others to accept his rule. Tell him that he'll make no mistake in likening those who rule in our cities at present to the sailors we mentioned just now, and those who are called useless stargazers to the true captains.

That's absolutely right.

Therefore, it isn't easy for the best ways of life to be highly esteemed by people who, as in these circumstances, follow the opposite ways. By far the greatest and most serious slander on philosophy, however, results from those who profess to follow the philosophic way of life. I mean those of whom the prosecutor of philosophy declared that the greatest number are completely vicious and the most decent useless. And I admitted that what he said was true, didn't I?

Yes.

And haven't we explained why the decent ones are useless?

Yes, indeed.

Then, do you next want us to discuss why it's inevitable that the greater number are vicious and to try to show, if we can, that philosophy isn't responsible for this either?

Certainly.

Then, let's begin our dialogue by reminding ourselves of the point at which we began to discuss the nature that someone must have if he is to become a fine and good person. First of all, if you remember, he had to be guided by the truth and always pursue it in every way, or else he'd really be a boaster, with no share at all in true philosophy.

That's what was said.

And isn't this view completely contrary to the opinions currently held about him?

It certainly is.

Then, won't it be reasonable for us to plead in his defense that it is the nature of the real lover of learning to struggle toward what is, not to remain with any of the many things that are believed to be, that, as he moves on, he neither loses nor lessens his erotic love until he grasps the being[5] of each nature itself with the part of his soul that is fitted to grasp it, because of its kinship with it,[6] and that, once getting near what really is and having

---

4. Aristotle, *Rhetoric* 1391a7–12, says that it was Simonides who, when asked whether it was better to be rich or wise, replied: "Rich—because the wise spend their time at the doors of the rich."

5. See 507b for an explanation of what "the being" (*ho estin*) of something is.

6. See 611e–612a, *Phaedo* 79d, *Timaeus* 90a–c.

intercourse with it and having begotten understanding and truth, he knows, truly lives, is nourished, and—at that point, but not before—is relieved from the pains of giving birth?

That is the most reasonable defense possible.

Well, then, will such a person have any part in the love of falsehood, or will he entirely hate it?

c   He'll hate it.

And if truth led the way, we'd never say, I suppose, that a chorus of evils could ever follow in its train.

How could it?

But rather a healthy and just character, with moderation following it.

That's right.

What need is there, then, to marshal all over again from the beginning the members of the philosophic nature's chorus in their inevitable array? Remember that courage, high-mindedness, ease in learning, and a good memory all belong to it. Then you objected, saying that anyone would be

d   compelled to agree with what we said, but that, if he abandoned the argument and looked at the very people the argument is about, he'd say that some of them were useless, while the majority had every kind of vice. So we examined the reason for this slander and have now arrived at the point of explaining why the majority of them are bad. And it's for this reason that we've again taken up the nature of the true philosophers and defined what it necessarily has to be.

e   That's true.

We must now look at the ways in which this nature is corrupted, how it's destroyed in many people, while a small number (the ones that are called useless rather than bad) escape. After that, we must look in turn at the natures of the souls that imitate the philosophic nature and establish them-

491 selves in its way of life, so as to see what the people are like who thereby arrive at a way of life they are unworthy of and that is beyond them and who, because they often strike false notes, bring upon philosophy the reputation that you said it has with everyone everywhere.

In what ways are they corrupted?

I'll try to enumerate them for you if I can. I suppose that everyone would agree that only a few natures possess all the qualities that we just now said were essential to becoming a complete philosopher and that seldom occur

b   naturally among human beings. Or don't you think so?

I certainly do.

Consider, then, the many important ways in which these few can be corrupted.

What are they?

What will surprise you most, when you hear it, is that each of the things we praised in that nature tends to corrupt the soul that has it and to drag it away from philosophy. I mean courage, moderation, and the other things we mentioned.

That does sound strange.

Furthermore, all the things that are said to be good also corrupt it and   c
drag it away—beauty, health, physical strength, relatives who are powerful in the city, and all that goes with these. You understand what I have in mind?

I do, and I'd be glad to learn even more about it.

If you correctly grasp the general point I'm after, it will be clear to you, and what I've said before won't seem so strange.

What do you want me to do?

We know that the more vigorous any seed, developing plant, or animal   d
is, the more it is deficient in the things that are appropriate for it to have when it is deprived of suitable food, season, or location.

For the bad is more opposed to the good than is the merely not good.

Of course.

Then it's reasonable to say that the best nature fares worse, when unsuitably nurtured, than an ordinary one.

It is.

Then won't we say the same thing about souls too, Adeimantus, that those with the best natures become outstandingly bad when they receive a   e
bad upbringing? Or do you think that great injustices and pure wickedness originate in an ordinary nature rather than in a vigorous one that has been corrupted by its upbringing? Or that a weak nature is ever the cause of either great good or great evil?

No, you're right.

Now, I think that the philosophic nature as we defined it will inevitably grow to possess every virtue if it happens to receive appropriate instruction,   492
but if it is sown, planted, and grown in an inappropriate environment, it will develop in quite the opposite way, unless some god happens to come to its rescue. Or do you agree with the general opinion that certain young people are actually corrupted by sophists—that there are certain sophists with significant influence on the young who corrupt them through private teaching? Isn't it rather the very people who say this who are the greatest sophists of all, since they educate most completely, turning young and old, men and women, into precisely the kind of people they want them to be?   b

When do they do that?

When many of them are sitting together in assemblies, courts, theaters, army camps, or in some other public gathering of the crowd, they object very loudly and excessively to some of the things that are said or done and approve others in the same way, shouting and clapping, so that the very rocks and surroundings echo the din of their praise or blame and double   c
it. In circumstances like that, what is the effect, as they say, on a young

person's heart? What private training can hold out and not be swept away
by that kind of praise or blame and be carried by the flood wherever it
goes, so that he'll say that the same things are beautiful or ugly as the
crowd does, follow the same way of life as they do, and be the same sort
of person as they are?

d   He will be under great compulsion to do so, Socrates.

And yet we haven't mentioned the greatest compulsion of all.

What's that?

It's what these educators and sophists impose by their actions if their
words fail to persuade. Or don't you know that they punish anyone who
isn't persuaded, with disenfranchisement, fines, or death?

They most certainly do.

What other sophist, then, or what private conversations do you think
will prevail in opposition to these?

e   I don't suppose that any will.

No, indeed, it would be very foolish even to try to oppose them, for
there isn't now, hasn't been in the past, nor ever will be in the future
anyone with a character so unusual that he has been educated to virtue in
spite of the contrary education he received from the mob—I mean, a
human character; the divine, as the saying goes, is an exception to the
rule. You should realize that if anyone is saved and becomes what he
ought to be under our present constitutions, he has been saved—you
493 might rightly say—by a divine dispensation.

I agree.

Well, then, you should also agree to this.

What?

Not one of those paid private teachers, whom the people call sophists
and consider to be their rivals in craft,[7] teaches anything other than the
convictions that the majority express when they are gathered together.
Indeed, these are precisely what the sophists call wisdom. It's as if someone
were learning the moods and appetites of a huge, strong beast that he's
b   rearing—how to approach and handle it, when it is most difficult to deal
with or most gentle and what makes it so, what sounds it utters in either
condition, and what sounds soothe or anger it. Having learned all this
through tending the beast over a period of time, he calls this knack wisdom,
gathers his information together as if it were a craft,[8] and starts to teach
it. In truth, he knows nothing about which of these convictions is fine or
shameful, good or bad, just or unjust, but he applies all these names in
c   accordance with how the beast reacts—calling what it enjoys good and

---

7. The craft in question is presumably that of teaching virtue.

8. See 332c n. 10. The distinction between a craft (*technē*) and a knack (*tribē, empeiria*)
is explained in the *Gorgias* 462b ff.

what angers it bad. He has no other account to give of these terms. And he calls what he is compelled to do just and fine, for he hasn't seen and cannot show anyone else how much compulsion and goodness really differ. Don't you think, by god, that someone like that is a strange educator?

I do indeed.

Then does this person seem any different from the one who believes that it is wisdom to understand the moods and pleasures of a majority gathered from all quarters, whether they concern painting, music, or, for   *d* that matter, politics? If anyone approaches the majority to exhibit his poetry or some other piece of craftsmanship or his service to the city and gives them mastery over him to any degree beyond what's unavoidable, he'll be under Diomedean compulsion,[9] as it's called, to do the sort of thing of which they approve. But have you ever heard anyone presenting an argument that such things are truly good and beautiful that wasn't absolutely ridiculous?

No, and I don't expect ever to hear one.   *e*

Keeping all this in mind, recall the following question: Can the majority in any way tolerate or accept the reality of the beautiful itself, as opposed to the many beautiful things, or the reality of each thing itself, as opposed to the corresponding many?   *494*

Not in any way.

Then the majority cannot be philosophic.

They cannot.

Hence they inevitably disapprove of those who practice philosophy?

Inevitably.

And so do all those private individuals who associate with the majority and try to please them.

Clearly.

Then, because of all that, do you see any salvation for someone who is by nature a philosopher, to insure that he'll practice philosophy correctly to the end? Think about what we've said before. We agreed that ease in learning, a good memory, courage, and high-mindedness belong to the   *b* philosophic nature.

Yes.

And won't someone with a nature like that be first among the children in everything, especially if his body has a nature that matches that of his soul?

---

9. The origin of the phrase is uncertain but a likely source is in the following story. Odysseus attempted to kill Diomedes when the two were returning from Troy to the Greek camp, but failed. Diomedes punished him by tying his arms together and driving him home with blows from the flat of his sword. But, whatever the source, the phrase refers to inescapable compulsion.

How could he not be?

Then I suppose that, as he gets older, his family and fellow citizens will want to make use of him in connection with their own affairs.

Of course.

Therefore they'll pay court to him with their requests and honors, trying
c by their flattery to secure for themselves ahead of time the power that is going to be his.

That's what usually happens, at any rate.

What do you think someone like that will do in such circumstances, especially if he happens to be from a great city, in which he's rich, well-born, good-looking, and tall? Won't he be filled with impractical expectations and think himself capable of managing the affairs, not only of the Greeks, but of the barbarians as well? And as a result, won't he exalt himself to great heights and be brimming with pretension and pride
d that is empty and lacks understanding?[10]

He certainly will.

And if someone approaches a young man in that condition and gently tells him the truth, namely, that that there's no understanding in him, that he needs it, and that it can't be acquired unless he works like a slave to attain it, do you think that it will be easy for him to listen when he's in the midst of so many evils?

Far from it.

And even if a young man of that sort somehow sees the point and is guided and drawn to philosophy because of his noble nature and his
e kinship with reason, what do you think those people will do, if they believe that they're losing their use of him and his companionship? Is there anything they won't do or say to him to prevent him from being persuaded? Or anything they won't do or say about his persuader—whether plotting against him in private or publicly bringing him into court—to prevent him from such persuasion?

495 There certainly isn't.

Then, is there any chance that such a person will practice philosophy?

None at all.

Do you see, then, that we weren't wrong to say that, when someone with a philosophic nature is badly brought up, the very components of his nature—together with the other so-called goods, such as wealth and other similar advantages—are themselves in a way the cause of his falling away from the philosophic way of life?

I do, and what we said was right.

---

10. It is widely believed that Plato has Alcibiades in mind here and in what follows. See Plato, *Symposium* 215d–216d. Alcibiades' extraordinary career is described in Thucydides, Books 6–8.

These, then, are the many ways in which the best nature—which is already rare enough, as we said—is destroyed and corrupted, so that it cannot follow the best way of life. And it is among these men that we find *b* the ones who do the greatest evils to cities and individuals and also—if they happen to be swept that way by the current[11]—the greatest good, for a petty nature will never do anything great, either to an individual or a city.

That's very true.

When these men, for whom philosophy is most appropriate, fall away from her, they leave her desolate and unwed, and they themselves lead *c* lives that are inappropriate and untrue. Then others, who are unworthy of her, come to her as to an orphan deprived of the protection of kinsmen and disgrace her. These are the ones who are responsible for the re-proaches that you say are cast upon philosophy by those who revile her, namely, that some of those who consort with her are useless, while the majority deserve to suffer many bad things.

Yes, that is indeed what is said.

And it's a reasonable thing to say, for other little men—the ones who are most sophisticated at their own little crafts—seeing that this position, which is full of fine names and adornments, is vacated, leap gladly from those little crafts to philosophy, like prisoners escaping from jail who take *d* refuge in a temple. Despite her present poor state, philosophy is still more high-minded than these other crafts, so that many people with defective natures desire to possess her, even though their souls are cramped and spoiled by the mechanical nature of their work, in just the way that their bodies are mutilated by their crafts and labors. Isn't that inevitable? *e*

It certainly is.

Don't you think that a man of this sort looks exactly like a little bald-headed tinker who has come into some money and, having been just released from jail, has taken a bath, put on a new cloak, got himself up as a bridegroom, and is about to marry the boss's daughter because she is poor and abandoned?

They're exactly the same.   *496*

And what kind of children will that marriage produce? Won't they be illegitimate and inferior?

They have to be.

What about when men who are unworthy of education approach philos-ophy and consort with her unworthily? What kinds of thoughts and opin-ions are we to say they beget? Won't they truly be what are properly called sophisms, things that have nothing genuine about them or worthy of being called true wisdom?

---

11. See 485d.

That's absolutely right.

Then there remains, Adeimantus, only a very small group who consort with philosophy in a way that's worthy of her: A noble and well brought-up character, for example, kept down by exile, who remains with philosophy

b according to his nature because there is no one to corrupt him, or a great soul living in a small city, who disdains the city's affairs and looks beyond them. A very few might be drawn to philosophy from other crafts that they rightly despise because they have good natures. And some might be held back by the bridle that restrains our friend Theages[12]—for he's in every way qualified to be tempted away from philosophy, but his physical illness

c restrains him by keeping him out of politics. Finally, my own case is hardly worth mentioning—my daimonic sign[13]—because it has happened to no one before me, or to only a very few. Now, the members of this small group have tasted how sweet and blessed a possession philosophy is, and at the same time they've also seen the madness of the majority and realized, in a word, that hardly anyone acts sanely in public affairs and that there is no ally with whom they might go to the aid of justice and survive, that

d instead they'd perish before they could profit either their city or their friends and be useless both to themselves and to others, just like a man who has fallen among wild animals and is neither willing to join them in doing injustice nor sufficiently strong to oppose the general savagery alone. Taking all this into account, they lead a quiet life and do their own work. Thus, like someone who takes refuge under a little wall from a storm of dust or hail driven by the wind, the philosopher—seeing others filled with lawlessness—is satisfied if he can somehow lead his present life free from injustice and impious acts and depart from it with good hope, blameless

e and content.

497 Well, that's no small thing for him to have accomplished before departing.

But it isn't the greatest either, since he didn't chance upon a constitution that suits him. Under a suitable one, his own growth will be fuller, and he'll save the community as well as himself. It seems to me that we've now sensibly discussed the reasons why philosophy is slandered and why the slanderer is unjust—unless, of course, you have something to add.

I have nothing to add on that point. But which of our present constitutions do you think is suitable for philosophers?

b None of them. That's exactly my complaint: None of our present

---

12. Theages figures in a Platonic dialogue named after him, which discusses the relationship between politics and philosophy. However, this dialogue is judged by many scholars to be of doubtful authenticity.

13. See Plato, *Apology* 31c–32a, where Socrates explains that his *daimonion* has kept him out of politics.

constitutions is worthy of the philosophic nature, and, as a result, this
nature is perverted and altered, for, just as a foreign seed, sown in alien
ground, is likely to be overcome by the native species and to fade away
among them, so the philosophic nature fails to develop its full power and
declines into a different character. But if it were to find the best constitu-   c
tion, as it is itself the best, it would be clear that it is really divine and that
other natures and ways of life are merely human. Obviously you're going
to ask next what the best constitution is.

You're wrong there; I wasn't going to ask that, but whether it was the
constitution we described when we were founding our city or some other
one.

In the other respects, it is that one. But we said even then[14] that
there must always be some people in the city who have a theory of the
constitution, the same one that guided you, the lawgiver, when you made
the laws.   d

We did say that.

Yes, but we didn't emphasize it sufficiently, for fear of what your
objections have made plain, namely, that its proof would be long and
difficult. And indeed what remains is by no means easy to go through.

What's that?

How a city can engage in philosophy without being destroyed, for all
great things are prone to fall, and, as the saying goes, fine things are really
hard to achieve.[15]

Nevertheless, to complete our discussion, we'll have to get clear about   e
this.

If anything prevents us from doing it, it won't be lack of willingness but
lack of ability. At least you'll see how willing I am, for notice again how
enthusiastically and recklessly I say that the manner in which a city ought
to take up the philosophic way of life is the opposite of what it does at
present.

How?

At present, those who study philosophy do so as young men who have
just left childhood behind and have yet to take up household management
and money-making. But just when they reach the hardest part—I mean   498
the part that has to do with giving a rational account—they abandon it and
are regarded as fully trained in philosophy. In later life, they think they're
doing well if they are willing to be in an invited audience when others are
doing philosophy, for they think they should do this only as a sideline.
And, with a few exceptions, by the time they reach old age, their eagerness

14. See 412a–b, which gives a hint of this need.
15. See Plato, *Hippias Major* 304b ff.

for philosophy is quenched more thoroughly than the sun of Heraclitus,
b   which is never rekindled.[16]

What should they do?

Entirely the opposite. As youths and children, they should put their minds to youthful education and philosophy and take care of their bodies at a time when they are growing into manhood, so as to acquire a helper for philosophy. As they grow older and their souls begin to reach maturity, they should increase their mental exercises. Then, when their strength begins to fail and they have retired from politics and military service, they should graze freely in the pastures of philosophy and do nothing else—I
c   mean the ones who are to live happily and, in death, add a fitting destiny in that other place to the life they have lived.

You seem to be speaking with true enthusiasm, Socrates. But I'm sure that most of your hearers, beginning with Thrasymachus, will oppose you with even greater enthusiasm and not be at all convinced.

Don't slander Thrasymachus and me just as we've become friends—
d   not that we were enemies before. We won't relax our efforts until we either convince him and the others or, at any rate, do something that may benefit them in a later incarnation, when, reborn, they happen upon these arguments again.[17]

That's a short time you're talking about!

It's nothing compared to the whole of time. All the same, it's no wonder that the majority of people aren't convinced by our arguments, for they've never seen a *man* that fits our *plan* (and the rhymes of this sort they have heard are usually intended and not, like this one, the product of mere
e   chance).[18] That is to say, they've never seen a man or a number of men who themselves rhymed with virtue, were assimilated to it as far as possible,
499   and ruled in a city of the same type. Or do you think they have?

I don't think so at all.

Nor have they listened sufficiently to fine and free arguments that search out the truth in every way for the sake of knowledge but that keep away from the sophistications and eristic quibbles that, both in public trials and in private gatherings, aim at nothing except reputation and disputation.

No, they haven't.

---

16. Aristotle (*Meteorologica* 355a14) reports Heraclitus as believing that "the sun is new every day." Hence the sun not only sets or is quenched at night, it actually ceases to exist, being replaced by a totally new sun the next morning.

17. See 614b ff.

18. Plato is mocking the rhetoricians, who were overfond of rhyme. Hence his own words, *ou gar pōpote eidon genomenon to nun legomenon*, which mean "they've never seen anything come into being which matches our account," exhibit the phenomenon he is mocking.

It was because of this, because we foresaw these difficulties, that we were afraid. Nonetheless, we were compelled by the truth to say that no city, constitution, or individual man will ever become perfect until either   *b* some chance event compels those few philosophers who aren't vicious (the ones who are now called useless) to take charge of a city, whether they want to or not, and compels the city to obey them, or until a god inspires the present rulers and kings or their offspring with a true erotic love for true philosophy. Now, it cannot be reasonably maintained, in my view, that either of these things is impossible, but if it could, we'd be justly   *c* ridiculed for indulging in wishful thinking. Isn't that so?

It is.

Then, if in the limitless past, those who were foremost in philosophy were forced to take charge of a city or if this is happening now in some foreign place far beyond our ken or if it will happen in the future, we are prepared to maintain our argument that, at whatever time the muse of   *d* philosophy controls a city, the constitution we've described will also exist at that time, whether it is past, present, or future. Since it is not impossible for this to happen, we are not speaking of impossibilities. That it is *difficult* for it to happen, however, we agree ourselves.

That's my opinion, anyway.

But the majority don't share your opinion—is that what you are going to say?

They probably don't.

You should not make such wholesale charges against the majority, for they'll no doubt come to a different opinion, if instead of indulging your love of victory at their expense, you soothe them and try to remove their   *e* slanderous prejudice against the love of learning, by pointing out what you mean by a philosopher and by defining the philosophic nature and way of life, as we did just now, so that they'll realize that you don't mean the   *500* same people as they do. And if they once see it your way, even you will say that they'll have a different opinion from the one you just attributed to them and will answer differently. Or do you think that anyone who is gentle and without malice is harsh with someone who is neither irritable nor malicious? I'll anticipate your answer and say that a few people may have such a harsh character, but not the majority.

And, of course, I agree.

Then don't you also agree that the harshness the majority exhibit   *b* towards philosophy is caused by those outsiders who don't belong and who've burst in like a band of revellers, always abusing one another, indulging their love of quarrels, and arguing about human beings in a way that is wholly inappropriate to philosophy?

I do indeed.

No one whose thoughts are truly directed towards the things that are,

Adeimantus, has the leisure to look down at human affairs or to be filled
with envy and hatred by competing with people. Instead, as he looks at
and studies things that are organized and always the same, that neither do
injustice to one another nor suffer it, being all in a rational order, he
imitates them and tries to become as like them as he can. Or do you think
that someone can consort with things he admires without imitating them?

I do not. It's impossible.

Then the philosopher, by consorting with what is ordered and divine
and despite all the slanders around that say otherwise, himself becomes
as divine and ordered as a human being can.

That's absolutely true.

And if he should come to be compelled to put what he sees there into
people's characters, whether into a single person or into a populace,
instead of shaping only his own, do you think that he will be a poor
craftsman of moderation, justice, and the whole of popular virtue?

He least of all.

And when the majority realize that what we are saying about the philosopher is true, will they be harsh with him or mistrust us when we say that
the city will never find happiness until its outline is sketched by painters
who use the divine model?

They won't be harsh, if indeed they realize this. But what sort of sketch
do you mean?

They'd take the city and the characters of human beings as their sketching slate, but first they'd wipe it clean—which isn't at all an easy thing to
do. And you should know that this is the plain difference between them
and others, namely, that they refuse to take either an individual or a city
in hand or to write laws, unless they receive a clean slate or are allowed
to clean it themselves.

And they'd be right to refuse.

Then don't you think they'd next sketch the outline of the constitution?

Of course.

And I suppose that, as they work, they'd look often in each direction,
towards the natures of justice, beauty, moderation,[19] and the like, on the
one hand, and towards those they're trying to put into human beings, on
the other. And in this way they'd mix and blend the various ways of life
in the city until they produced a human image based on what Homer too
called "the divine form and image" when it occurred among human
beings.[20]

That's right.

19. I.e. the forms of justice, beauty, and moderation. See 476b, *Phaedo* 103b, *Parmenides* 132d, *Cratylus* 389a–390a.

20. See, for example, *Iliad* 1.131.

They'd erase one thing, I suppose, and draw in another until they'd made characters for human beings that the gods would love as much as possible.   c

At any rate, that would certainly result in the finest sketch.

Then is this at all persuasive to those you said were straining to attack us—that the person we were praising is really a painter of constitutions? They were angry because we entrusted the city to him: Are they any calmer, now that they've heard what we had to say?

They'll be much calmer, if they have any moderation.

Indeed, how could they possibly dispute it? Will they deny that philosophers are lovers of what is or of the truth?   d

That would be absurd.

Or that their nature as we've described it is close to the best?

They can't deny that either.

Or that such a nature, if it follows its own way of life, isn't as completely good and philosophic as any other? Or that the people we excluded are more so?

Certainly not.   e

Then will they still be angry when we say that, until philosophers take control of a city, there'll be no respite from evil for either city or citizens, and the constitution we've been describing in theory will never be completed in practice?

They'll probably be less angry.

Then if it's all right with you, let's not say that they'll simply be less angry but that they'll become altogether gentle and persuaded, so that they'll be shamed into agreeing with us, if nothing else.   502

It's all right with me.

Let's assume, therefore, that they've been convinced on this point. Will anyone dispute our view that the offspring of kings or rulers could be born with philosophic natures?

No one would do that.

Could anyone claim that, if such offspring are born, they'll inevitably be corrupted? We agree ourselves that it's hard for them to be saved from corruption, but could anyone claim that in the whole of time not one of them could be saved?   b

How could he?

But surely one such individual would be sufficient to bring to completion all the things that now seem so incredible, provided that his city obeys him.

One would be sufficient.

If a ruler established the laws and ways of life we've described, it is surely not impossible that the citizens would be willing to carry them out.

Not at all.

And would it be either astonishing or impossible that others should think as we do?

c   I don't suppose it would.

But I think our earlier discussion was sufficient to show that these arrangements are best, if only they are possible.

Indeed it was.

Then we can now conclude that this legislation is best, if only it is possible, and that, while it is hard for it to come about, it is not impossible.

We can.

Now that this difficulty has been disposed of, we must deal with what remains, namely, how the saviors of our constitution will come to be in the city, what subjects and ways of life will cause them to come into being,

d   and at what ages they'll take each of them up.

Indeed we must.

It wasn't very clever of me to omit from our earlier discussion the troublesome topics of acquiring wives, begetting children, and appointing rulers, just because I knew that the whole truth would provoke resentment and would be hard to bring about in practice, for as it turned out, I had to go through these matters anyway. The subject of women and children

e   has been adequately dealt with, but that of the rulers has to be taken up again from the beginning. We said, if you remember, that they must show themselves to be lovers of their city when tested by pleasure and pain and

503   that they must hold on to their resolve through labors, fears, and all other adversities. Anyone who was incapable of doing so was to be rejected, while anyone who came through unchanged—like gold tested in a fire— was to be made ruler and receive prizes both while he lived and after his death. These were the sort of things we were saying while our argument, afraid of stirring up the very problems that now confront us, veiled its face

b   and slipped by.

That's very true; I do remember it.

We hesitated to say the things we've now dared to say anyway. So let's now also dare to say that those who are to be made our guardians in the most exact sense of the term must be philosophers.

Let's do it.

Then you should understand that there will probably be only a few of them, for they have to have the nature we described, and its parts mostly grow in separation and are rarely found in the same person.

c   What do you mean?

You know that ease of learning, good memory, quick wits, smartness, youthful passion, high-mindedness, and all the other things that go along with these are rarely willing to grow together in a mind that will choose an orderly life that is quiet and completely stable, for the people who possess the former traits are carried by their quick wits wherever chance leads them and have no stability at all.

That's true.

On the other hand, people with stable characters, who don't change easily, who aren't easily frightened in battle, and whom one would employ because of their greater reliability, exhibit similar traits when it comes to *d* learning: They are as hard to move and teach as people whose brains have become numb, and they are filled with sleep and yawning whenever they have to learn anything.

That's so.

Yet we say that someone must have a fine and goodly share of both characters, or he won't receive the truest education, honors, or rule.

That's right.

Then, don't you think that such people will be rare?

Of course.

Therefore they must be tested in the labors, fears, and pleasures we *e* mentioned previously. But they must also be exercised in many other subjects—which we didn't mention but are adding now—to see whether they can tolerate the most important subjects or will shrink from them like the cowards who shrink from other tests.   *504*

It's appropriate to examine them like that. But what do you mean by the most important subjects?

Do you remember when we distinguished three parts in the soul, in order to help bring out what justice, moderation, courage, and wisdom each is?

If I didn't remember that, it wouldn't be just for me to hear the rest.

What about what preceded it?

What was that?

We said, I believe, that, in order to get the finest possible view of these *b* matters, we would need to take a longer road that would make them plain to anyone who took it but that it was possible to give demonstrations of what they are that would be up to the standard of the previous argument.[21] And you said that that would be satisfactory. So it seems to me that our discussion at that time fell short of exactness, but whether or not it satisfied you is for you to say.

I thought you gave us good measure and so, apparently, did the others.

Any measure of such things that falls short in any way of that which is *c* is not good measure, for nothing incomplete is the measure of anything, although people are sometimes of the opinion that an incomplete treatment is nonetheless adequate and makes further investigation unnecessary.

21. See 435d.

Indeed, laziness causes many people to think that.

It is a thought that a guardian of a city and its laws can well do without.

Probably so.

Well, then, he must take the longer road and put as much effort into learning as into physical training, for otherwise, as we were just saying, he
d   will never reach the goal of the most important subject and the most appropriate one for him to learn.

Aren't these virtues, then, the most important things? he asked. Is there anything even more important than justice and the other virtues we discussed?

There is something more important. However, even for the virtues themselves, it isn't enough to look at a mere sketch, as we did before, while neglecting the most complete account. It's ridiculous, isn't it, to strain every nerve to attain the utmost exactness and clarity about other things of little value and not to consider the most important things worthy
e   of the greatest exactness?

It certainly is. But do you think that anyone is going to let you off without asking you what this most important subject is and what it concerns?

No, indeed, and you can ask me too. You've certainly heard the answer often enough, but now either you aren't thinking or you intend to make trouble for me again by interrupting. And I suspect the latter, for you've
505 often heard it said that the form of the good is the most important thing to learn about and that it's by their relation to it that just things and the others become useful and beneficial. You knew very well that I was going to say this and, besides, that we have no adequate knowledge of it. And you also knew that, if we don't know it, even the fullest possible knowledge of other things is of no benefit to us, any more than if we acquire any possession without the good of it. Or do you think that it is any advantage
b   to have every kind of possession without the good of it? Or to know everything except the good, thereby knowing nothing fine or good?

No, by god, I don't.

Furthermore, you certainly know that the majority believe that pleasure is the good, while the more sophisticated believe that it is knowledge.

Indeed I do.

Those who believe this can't tell us what sort of knowledge it is, however, but in the end are forced to say that it is knowledge of the good.

And that's ridiculous.

c   Of course it is. They blame us for not knowing the good and then turn around and talk to us as if we did know it. They say that it is knowledge of the good—as if we understood what they're speaking about when they utter the word "good."

That's completely true.

What about those who define the good as pleasure? Are they any less

full of confusion than the others? Aren't even they forced to admit that
there are bad pleasures?

Most definitely.

So, I think, they have to agree that the same things are both good and
bad. Isn't that true?

Of course.   *d*

It's clear, then, isn't it, why there are many large controversies about
this?

How could it be otherwise?

And isn't this also clear? In the case of just and beautiful things, many
people are content with what are believed to be so, even if they aren't
really so, and they act, acquire, and form their own beliefs on that basis.
Nobody is satisfied to acquire things he merely believes to be good,
however, but everyone wants the things that really *are* good and disdains
those that are merely believed to be so.

That's right.

Every soul pursues the good and does whatever it does for its sake. It   *e*
divines that the good is something but it is perplexed and cannot adequately
grasp what it is or acquire the sort of stable beliefs it has about other
things, and so it misses the benefit, if any, that even those other things
may give. Will we allow the best people in the city, to whom we entrust
everything, to be so in the dark about something of this kind and of this *506*
importance?

That's the last thing we'd do.

I don't suppose, at least, that just and fine things will have acquired
much of a guardian in someone who doesn't even know in what way they
are good. And I divine that no one will have adequate knowledge of them
until he knows this.

You've divined well.

But won't our constitution be perfectly ordered, if a guardian who knows
these things is in charge of it?   *b*

Necessarily. But, Socrates, you must also tell us whether you consider
the good to be knowledge or pleasure or something else altogether.

What a man! It's been clear for some time that other people's opinions
about these matters wouldn't satisfy you.

Well, Socrates, it doesn't seem right to me for you to be willing to state
other people's convictions but not your own, especially when you've spent
so much time occupied with these matters.   *c*

What? Do you think it's right to talk about things one doesn't know as
if one does know them?

Not as if one knows them, he said, but one ought to be willing to state
one's opinions as such.

What? Haven't you noticed that opinions without knowledge are shameful and ugly things? The best of them are blind—or do you think that those who express a true opinion without understanding are any different from blind people who happen to travel the right road?

They're no different.

Do you want to look at shameful, blind, and crooked things, then, when *d* you might hear illuminating and fine ones from other people?

By god, Socrates, Glaucon said, don't desert us with the end almost in sight. We'll be satisfied if you discuss the good as you discussed justice, moderation, and the rest.

That, my friend, I said, would satisfy me too, but I'm afraid that I won't be up to it and that I'll disgrace myself and look ridiculous by trying. So let's abandon the quest for what the good itself is for the time being, for *e* even to arrive at my own view about it is too big a topic for the discussion we are now started on.[22] But I am willing to tell you about what is apparently an offspring of the good and most like it. Is that agreeable to you, or would you rather we let the whole matter drop?

It is. The story about the father remains a debt you'll pay another time.

507 I wish that I could pay the debt in full, and you receive it instead of just the interest. So here, then, is this child and offspring of the good. But be careful that I don't somehow deceive you unintentionally by giving you an illegitimate account of the child.[23]

We'll be as careful as possible, so speak on.

I will when we've come to an agreement and recalled some things that we've already said both here and many times elsewhere.

b Which ones?

We say that there are many beautiful things and many good things, and so on for each kind, and in this way we distinguish them in words.

We do.

And beauty itself and good itself and all the things that we thereby set down as many, reversing ourselves, we set down according to a single form of each, believing that there is but one, and call it "the being" of each.[24]

That's true.

And we say that the many beautiful things and the rest are visible but not intelligible, while the forms are intelligible but not visible.

That's completely true.

c With what part of ourselves do we see visible things?

---

22. See 531e ff.

23. Throughout, Socrates is punning on the word *tokos*, which means either a child or the interest on capital.

24. The "being" of something is sometimes taken to refer to what we call its essence. Socrates would then be saying that the essence of the fineness present in many things is the form of the fine.

With our sight.

And so audible things are heard by hearing, and with our other senses we perceive all the other perceptible things.

That's right.

Have you considered how lavish the maker of our senses was in making the power to see and be seen?

I can't say I have.

Well, consider it this way. Do hearing and sound need another kind of thing in order for the former to hear and the latter to be heard, a third thing in whose absence the one won't hear or the other be heard?   *d*

No, they need nothing else.

And if there are any others that need such a thing, there can't be many of them. Can you think of one?

I can't.

You don't realize that sight and the visible have such a need?

How so?

Sight may be present in the eyes, and the one who has it may try to use it, and colors may be present in things, but unless a third kind of thing is present, which is naturally adapted for this very purpose, you know that sight will see nothing, and the colors will remain unseen.   *e*

What kind of thing do you mean?

I mean what you call light.

You're right.

Then it isn't an insignificant kind of link that connects the sense of sight and the power to be seen—it is a more valuable link than any other *508* linked things have got, if indeed light is something valuable.

And, of course, it's very valuable.

Which of the gods in heaven would you name as the cause and controller of this, the one whose light causes our sight to see in the best way and the visible things to be seen?

The same one you and others would name. Obviously, the answer to your question is the sun.

And isn't sight by nature related to that god in this way?

Which way?

Sight isn't the sun, neither sight itself nor that in which it comes to be, namely, the eye.   *b*

No, it certainly isn't.

But I think that it is the most sunlike of the senses.

Very much so.

And it receives from the sun the power it has, just like an influx from an overflowing treasury.

Certainly.

The sun is not sight, but isn't it the cause of sight itself and seen by it?

That's right.

Let's say, then, that this is what I called the offspring of the good, which the good begot as its analogue. What the good itself is in the intelligible realm, in relation to understanding and intelligible things, the sun is in
c the visible realm, in relation to sight and visible things.

How? Explain a bit more.

You know that, when we turn our eyes to things whose colors are no longer in the light of day but in the gloom of night, the eyes are dimmed and seem nearly blind, as if clear vision were no longer in them.

Of course.

Yet whenever one turns them on things illuminated by the sun, they see
d clearly, and vision appears in those very same eyes?

Indeed.

Well, understand the soul in the same way: When it focuses on something illuminated by truth and what is, it understands, knows, and apparently possesses understanding, but when it focuses on what is mixed with obscurity, on what comes to be and passes away, it opines and is dimmed, changes its opinions this way and that, and seems bereft of understanding.

It does seem that way.

So that what gives truth to the things known and the power to know to
e the knower is the form of the good. And though it is the cause of knowledge and truth, it is also an object of knowledge. Both knowledge and truth are beautiful things, but the good is other and more beautiful than they. In the visible realm, light and sight are rightly considered sunlike, but it is
509 wrong to think that they are the sun, so here it is right to think of knowledge and truth as goodlike but wrong to think that either of them is the good—for the good is yet more prized.

This is an inconceivably beautiful thing you're talking about, if it provides both knowledge and truth and is superior to them in beauty. You surely don't think that a thing like that could be pleasure.

Hush! Let's examine its image in more detail as follows.
b How?

You'll be willing to say, I think, that the sun not only provides visible things with the power to be seen but also with coming to be, growth, and nourishment, although it is not itself coming to be.

How could it be?

Therefore, you should also say that not only do the objects of knowledge owe their being known to the good, but their being is also due to it, although the good is not being, but superior to it in rank and power.
c And Glaucon facetiously said: By Apollo, what a daimonic superiority!

It's your own fault; you forced me to tell you my opinion about it.

And I don't want you to stop either. So continue to explain its similarity to the sun, if you've omitted anything.

I'm certainly omitting a lot.

Well, don't, not even the smallest thing.

I think I'll have to omit a fair bit, but, as far as is possible at the moment, I won't omit anything voluntarily.

Don't.

Understand, then, that, as we said, there are these two things, one *d* sovereign of the intelligible kind and place, the other of the visible (I don't say "of heaven" so as not to seem to you to be playing the sophist with the name[25]). In any case, you have two kinds of thing, visible and intelligible.

Right.

It is like a line divided into two unequal sections.[26] Then divide each section—namely, that of the visible and that of the intelligible—in the same ratio as the line. In terms now of relative clarity and opacity, one subsection of the visible consists of images. And by images I mean, first, shadows, then reflections in water and in all close-packed, smooth, and *e* shiny materials, and everything of that sort, if you understand.   *510*

I do.

In the other subsection of the visible, put the originals of these images, namely, the animals around us, all the plants, and the whole class of manufactured things.

Consider them put.

25. The play may be on the similarity of sound between *ouranou* ("of heaven") and *horatou* ("of the visible"). But it is more likely that Socrates is referring the fact that *ouranou* seems to contain the word *nou*, the genitive case of *nous* ("understanding"), and relative of *noētou* ("of the intelligible"). Hence if he said that the sun was sovereign of heaven, he might be taken to suggest in sophistical fashion that it was sovereign of the intelligible and that there was no real difference between the good and the sun.

26. The line is illustrated below:

Understanding (*noêsis*)

Thought (*dianoia*)

Belief (*pistis*)

Imagination (*eikasia*)

Would you be willing to say that, as regards truth and untruth, the division is in this ratio: As the opinable is to the knowable, so the likeness is to the thing that it is like?

b Certainly.

Consider now how the section of the intelligible is to be divided.

How?

As follows: In one subsection, the soul, using as images the things that were imitated before, is forced to investigate from hypotheses, proceeding not to a first principle but to a conclusion. In the other subsection, however, it makes its way to a first principle that is *not* a hypothesis, proceeding from a hypothesis but without the images used in the previous subsection, using forms themselves and making its investigation through them.

I don't yet fully understand what you mean.

c Let's try again. You'll understand it more easily after this explanation. I think you know that students of geometry, calculation, and the like hypothesize the odd and the even, the various figures, the three kinds of angles, and other things akin to these in each of their investigations, as if they were known. They make these their hypotheses and don't think it necessary to give any account of them, either to themselves or to others, as if they were clear to everyone. And going from these first principles through the remaining steps, they arrive validly at a conclusion about what

d they set out to investigate.

I certainly know that much.

Then you also know that, although they use visible figures and talk about them, their thought isn't directed to these but to those other things that they are like. The claims they make are about the square itself and the diagonal itself, not about the diagonal they draw, and similarly with

e the others. These figures that they make and draw, of which shadows and reflections in water are images, they now in turn use as images, in seeking to see those others themselves that one cannot see except by means of

511 thought.

That's true.

This, then, is the kind of thing that, on the one hand, I said is intelligible, and, on the other, is such that the soul is forced to use hypotheses in the investigation of it, not travelling up to a first principle, since it cannot reach beyond its hypotheses, but using as images those very things of which images were made in the section below, and which, by comparison to their images, were thought to be clear and to be valued as such.

b I understand that you mean what happens in geometry and related sciences.

Then also understand that, by the other subsection of the intelligible, I mean that which reason itself grasps by the power of dialectic. It does not consider these hypotheses as first principles but as stepping stones to take off from, enabling it to reach the unhypothetical first principle of everything. Having grasped this principle, it reverses itself and, keeping hold of what follows from it, comes down to a conclusion without making use of anything visible at all, but only of forms themselves, moving on   *c* from forms to forms, and ending in forms.

I understand, if not yet adequately (for in my opinion you're speaking of an enormous task), that you want to distinguish the intelligible part of that which is, the part studied by the science of dialectic, as clearer than the part studied by the so-called sciences, for which their hypotheses are first principles. And although those who study the objects of these sciences are forced to do so by means of thought rather than sense perception, still, because they do not go back to a genuine first principle, but proceed from   *d* hypotheses, you don't think that they understand them, even though, given such a principle, they are intelligible. And you seem to me to call the state of the geometers thought but not understanding, thought being intermediate between opinion and understanding.

Your exposition is most adequate. Thus there are four such conditions in the soul, corresponding to the four subsections of our line: Understanding for the highest, thought for the second, belief for the third, and imaging for the last. Arrange them in a ratio, and consider that each shares in   *e* clarity to the degree that the subsection it is set over shares in truth.

I understand, agree, and arrange them as you say.

BOOK VII

Book VII begins with another unforgettable image, the allegory of the Cave, which fits together with the Sun and Line (517b) and which illustrates the effects of education on the soul (514a). It leads to a brief but important discussion of education (518b–519b) in which Socrates makes it clear that the aim of education is to turn the soul around by changing its desires.

The next topic is the education of the philosopher-kings. (1) Their initial education is in music and poetry, physical training, and elementary mathematics (535a–537b). (2) This is followed by two or three years of compulsory physical training, rather like the military service that some countries still require (537b–c). (3) Those who are most successful in these studies next receive ten years of education in mathematical science (537c–d, 522c–531d). (4) Those who are again most successful receive five years of training in dialectic (537d–540a, 531e–535a). (5) Those who are still most successful receive fifteen years of practical political training (539e–540a). Finally, (6) those who are also successful in practical politics are "compelled to lift up the radiant light of their souls" to the good itself (540a) and are equipped to be philosopher-kings.

The centrality of mathematics in the philosopher's education is somewhat surprising, as is the restriction of dialectic to mature people who have mastered science. But the fact that the largest component of this education consists of practical political training should reassure those who think that philosopher-kings would not even begin to know how to rule a city. It is an interesting question as to why this training must take place before they can see the good itself. Plato's discussion of users, makers, and imitators in Book X (601d–602b) is surely relevant to this question, for it suggests that only those who use an entire city (see 428c–d) could know what a good city is.

The city that contains philosopher-kings and the educational institutions necessary to produce them is the third and final stage in Plato's construction of the kallipolis (535a–536d, 543c–544a).

Next, I said, compare the effect of education and of the lack of it on our
514 nature to an experience like this: Imagine human beings living in an underground, cavelike dwelling, with an entrance a long way up, which is both open to the light and as wide as the cave itself. They've been there

186

since childhood, fixed in the same place, with their necks and legs fettered, able to see only in front of them, because their bonds prevent them from turning their heads around. Light is provided by a fire burning far above and behind them. Also behind them, but on higher ground, there is a path *b* stretching between them and the fire. Imagine that along this path a low wall has been built, like the screen in front of puppeteers above which they show their puppets.

I'm imagining it.

Then also imagine that there are people along the wall, carrying all kinds of artifacts that project above it—statues of people and other animals, made out of stone, wood, and every material. And, as you'd expect, some *c* of the carriers are talking, and some are silent.   *515*

It's a strange image you're describing, and strange prisoners.

They're like us. Do you suppose, first of all, that these prisoners see anything of themselves and one another besides the shadows that the fire casts on the wall in front of them?

How could they, if they have to keep their heads motionless throughout life?   *b*

What about the things being carried along the wall? Isn't the same true of them?

Of course.

And if they could talk to one another, don't you think they'd suppose that the names they used applied to the things they see passing before them?[1]

They'd have to.

And what if their prison also had an echo from the wall facing them? Don't you think they'd believe that the shadows passing in front of them were talking whenever one of the carriers passing along the wall was doing so?

I certainly do.

Then the prisoners would in every way believe that the truth is nothing *c* other than the shadows of those artifacts.

They must surely believe that.

Consider, then, what being released from their bonds and cured of their ignorance would naturally be like. When one of them was freed and suddenly compelled to stand up, turn his head, walk, and look up toward the light, he'd be pained and dazzled and unable to see the things whose shadows he'd seen before. What do you think he'd say, if we told him that *d* what he'd seen before was inconsequential, but that now—because he is

1. Reading *parionta autous nomizein anomazein*. E.g. they would think that the name "human being" applied to the shadow of a statue of a human being.

a bit closer to the things that are and is turned towards things that are more—he sees more correctly? Or, to put it another way, if we pointed to each of the things passing by, asked him what each of them is, and compelled him to answer, don't you think he'd be at a loss and that he'd believe that the things he saw earlier were truer than the ones he was now being shown?

Much truer.

And if someone compelled him to look at the light itself, wouldn't his
e eyes hurt, and wouldn't he turn around and flee towards the things he's able to see, believing that they're really clearer than the ones he's being shown?

He would.

And if someone dragged him away from there by force, up the rough, steep path, and didn't let him go until he had dragged him into the sunlight, wouldn't he be pained and irritated at being treated that way?
516 And when he came into the light, with the sun filling his eyes, wouldn't he be unable to see a single one of the things now said to be true?

He would be unable to see them, at least at first.

I suppose, then, that he'd need time to get adjusted before he could see things in the world above. At first, he'd see shadows most easily, then images of men and other things in water, then the things themselves. Of these, he'd be able to study the things in the sky and the sky itself more easily at night, looking at the light of the stars and the moon, than during
b the day, looking at the sun and the light of the sun.

Of course.

Finally, I suppose, he'd be able to see the sun, not images of it in water or some alien place, but the sun itself, in its own place, and be able to study it.

Necessarily so.

And at this point he would infer and conclude that the sun provides the seasons and the years, governs everything in the visible world, and is in
c some way the cause of all the things that he used to see.

It's clear that would be his next step.

What about when he reminds himself of his first dwelling place, his fellow prisoners, and what passed for wisdom there? Don't you think that he'd count himself happy for the change and pity the others?

Certainly.

And if there had been any honors, praises, or prizes among them for the one who was sharpest at identifying the shadows as they passed by and who best remembered which usually came earlier, which later, and which
d simultaneously, and who could thus best divine the future, do you think that our man would desire these rewards or envy those among the prisoners

who were honored and held power? Instead, wouldn't he feel, with Homer, that he'd much prefer to "work the earth as a serf to another, one without possessions,"[2] and go through any sufferings, rather than share their opinions and live as they do?

I suppose he would rather suffer anything than live like that.   *e*

Consider this too. If this man went down into the cave again and sat down in his same seat, wouldn't his eyes—coming suddenly out of the sun like that—be filled with darkness?

They certainly would.

And before his eyes had recovered—and the adjustment would not be quick—while his vision was still dim, if he had to compete again with the perpetual prisoners in recognizing the shadows, wouldn't he invite ridi-   *517* cule? Wouldn't it be said of him that he'd returned from his upward journey with his eyesight ruined and that it isn't worthwhile even to try to travel upward? And, as for anyone who tried to free them and lead them upward, if they could somehow get their hands on him, wouldn't they kill him?

They certainly would.

This whole image, Glaucon, must be fitted together with what we said   *b* before. The visible realm should be likened to the prison dwelling, and the light of the fire inside it to the power of the sun. And if you interpret the upward journey and the study of things above as the upward journey of the soul to the intelligible realm, you'll grasp what I hope to convey, since that is what you wanted to hear about. Whether it's true or not, only the god knows. But this is how I see it: In the knowable realm, the form of the good is the last thing to be seen, and it is reached only with difficulty. Once one has seen it, however, one must conclude that it is the cause of all that is correct and beautiful in anything, that it produces both light and   *c* its source in the visible realm, and that in the intelligible realm it controls and provides truth and understanding, so that anyone who is to act sensibly in private or public must see it.

I have the same thought, at least as far as I'm able.

Come, then, share with me this thought also: It isn't surprising that the ones who get to this point are unwilling to occupy themselves with human affairs and that their souls are always pressing upwards, eager to spend their time above, for, after all, this is surely what we'd expect, if indeed things fit the image I described before.   *d*

It is.

What about what happens when someone turns from divine study to

---

2. *Odyssey* 11.489–90. The shade of the dead Achilles speaks these words to Odysseus, who is visiting Hades. Plato is, therefore, likening the cave dwellers to the dead.

the evils of human life? Do you think it's surprising, since his sight is still dim, and he hasn't yet become accustomed to the darkness around him, that he behaves awkwardly and appears completely ridiculous if he's compelled, either in the courts or elsewhere, to contend about the shadows of justice or the statues of which they are the shadows and to dispute about the way these things are understood by people who have never seen
e justice itself?

That's not surprising at all.

518 No, it isn't. But anyone with any understanding would remember that the eyes may be confused in two ways and from two causes, namely, when they've come from the light into the darkness *and* when they've come from the darkness into the light. Realizing that the same applies to the soul, when someone sees a soul disturbed and unable to see something, he won't laugh mindlessly, but he'll take into consideration whether it has come from a brighter life and is dimmed through not having yet become accustomed to the dark or whether it has come from greater ignorance into greater light and is dazzled by the increased brilliance. Then he'll declare the first soul happy in its experience and life, and he'll pity the
b latter—but even if he chose to make fun of it, at least he'd be less ridiculous than if he laughed at a soul that has come from the light above.

What you say is very reasonable.

If that's true, then here's what we must think about these matters: Education isn't what some people declare it to be, namely, putting knowl-
c edge into souls that lack it, like putting sight into blind eyes.

They do say that.

But our present discussion, on the other hand, shows that the power to learn is present in everyone's soul and that the instrument with which each learns is like an eye that cannot be turned around from darkness to light without turning the whole body. This instrument cannot be turned around from that which is coming into being without turning the whole soul until it is able to study that which is and the brightest thing that is,
d namely, the one we call the good. Isn't that right?

Yes.

Then education is the craft concerned with doing this very thing, this turning around, and with how the soul can most easily and effectively be made to do it. It isn't the craft of putting sight into the soul. Education takes for granted that sight is there but that it isn't turned the right way or looking where it ought to look, and it tries to redirect it appropriately.

So it seems.

Now, it looks as though the other so-called virtues of the soul are akin to those of the body, for they really aren't there beforehand but are added
e later by habit and practice. However, the virtue of reason seems to belong

above all to something more divine,³ which never loses its power but is either useful and beneficial or useless and harmful, depending on the way it is turned. Or have you never noticed this about people who are said to *519* be vicious but clever, how keen the vision of their little souls is and how sharply it distinguishes the things it is turned towards? This shows that its sight isn't inferior but rather is forced to serve evil ends, so that the sharper it sees, the more evil it accomplishes.

Absolutely.

However, if a nature of this sort had been hammered at from childhood and freed from the bonds of kinship with becoming, which have been fastened to it by feasting, greed, and other such pleasures and which, like leaden weights, pull its vision downwards—if, being rid of these, it turned *b* to look at true things, then I say that the same soul of the same person would see these most sharply, just as it now does the things it is presently turned towards.

Probably so.

And what about the uneducated who have no experience of truth? Isn't it likely—indeed, doesn't it follow necessarily from what was said before— that they will never adequately govern a city? But neither would those who've been allowed to spend their whole lives being educated. The former would fail because they don't have a single goal at which all their *c* actions, public and private, inevitably aim; the latter would fail because they'd refuse to act, thinking that they had settled while still alive in the faraway Isles of the Blessed.⁴

That's true.

It is our task as founders, then, to compel the best natures to reach the study we said before is the most important, namely, to make the ascent and see the good. But when they've made it and looked sufficiently, we mustn't allow them to do what they're allowed to do today. *d*

What's that?

To stay there and refuse to go down again to the prisoners in the cave and share their labors and honors, whether they are of less worth or of greater.

Then are we to do them an injustice by making them live a worse life when they could live a better one?

You are forgetting again that it isn't the law's concern to make any one *e* class in the city outstandingly happy but to contrive to spread happiness throughout the city by bringing the citizens into harmony with each other

---

3. See 589d, 590d, 611b ff.

4. A place where good people are said to live in eternal happiness, normally after death.

through persuasion or compulsion and by making them share with each other the benefits that each class can confer on the community.[5] The law
520 produces such people in the city, not in order to allow them to turn in whatever direction they want, but to make use of them to bind the city together.

That's true, I had forgotten.

Observe, then, Glaucon, that we won't be doing an injustice to those who've become philosophers in our city and that what we'll say to them, when we compel them to guard and care for the others, will be just. We'll say: "When people like you come to be in other cities, they're justified in
b   not sharing in their city's labors, for they've grown there spontaneously, against the will of the constitution. And what grows of its own accord and owes no debt for its upbringing has justice on its side when it isn't keen to pay anyone for that upbringing. But we've made you kings in our city and leaders of the swarm, as it were, both for yourselves and for the rest of the city. You're better and more completely educated than the others
c   and are better able to share in both types of life.[6] Therefore each of you in turn must go down to live in the common dwelling place of the others and grow accustomed to seeing in the dark. When you are used to it, you'll see vastly better than the people there. And because you've seen the truth about fine, just, and good things, you'll know each image for what it is and also that of which it is the image. Thus, for you and for us, the city will be governed, not like the majority of cities nowadays, by people who fight over shadows and struggle against one another in order to rule—as if that were a great good—but by people who are awake rather than dreaming,[7]
d   for the truth is surely this: A city whose prospective rulers are least eager to rule must of necessity be most free from civil war, whereas a city with the opposite kind of rulers is governed in the opposite way."

Absolutely.

Then do you think that those we've nurtured will disobey us and refuse to share the labors of the city, each in turn, while living the greater part of their time with one another in the pure realm?
e   It isn't possible, for we'll be giving just orders to just people. Each of them will certainly go to rule as to something compulsory, however, which is exactly the opposite of what's done by those who now rule in each city. This is how it is. If you can find a way of life that's better than ruling for the prospective rulers, your well-governed city will become a possibility,

5. See 420b–421c, 462a–466c.

6. I.e. the practical life of ruling the city and the theoretical life of studying the good itself.

7. See 476c–d.

for only in it will the truly rich rule—not those who are rich in gold but *521* those who are rich in the wealth that the happy must have, namely, a good and rational life. But if beggars hungry for private goods go into public life, thinking that the good is there for the seizing, then the well-governed city is impossible, for then ruling is something fought over, and this civil and domestic war destroys these people and the rest of the city as well.

That's very true.

Can you name any life that despises political rule besides that of the *b* true philosopher?

No, by god, I can't.

But surely it is those who are not lovers of ruling who must rule, for if they don't, the lovers of it, who are rivals, will fight over it.

Of course.

Then who will you compel to become guardians of the city, if not those who have the best understanding of what matters for good government and who have other honors than political ones, and a better life as well?

No one.

Do you want us to consider now how such people will come to be in our city and how—just as some are said to have gone up from Hades to *c* the gods—we'll lead them up to the light?

Of course I do.

This isn't, it seems, a matter of spinning a potsherd,[8] but of turning a soul from a day that is a kind of night to the true day—the ascent to what is, which we say is true philosophy.

Indeed.

Then mustn't we try to discover the subjects that have the power to bring this about?   *d*

Of course.

So what subject is it, Glaucon, that draws the soul from the realm of becoming to the realm of what is? And it occurs to me as I'm speaking that we said, didn't we, that it is necessary for the prospective rulers to be athletes in war when they're young?

Yes, we did.

Then the subject we're looking for must also have this characteristic in addition to the former one.

---

8. A proverbial expression, referring to a children's game. The players were divided into two groups. A shell or potsherd, white on one side and black on the other, was thrown into the space between them to the cry of "night or day" (note the reference to night and day which follows). According as the white or black fell uppermost, one group ran away, pursued by the other. The meaning here is much the same as that of our expression "tossing a coin."

Which one?

It mustn't be useless to warlike men.

If it's at all possible, it mustn't.

Now, prior to this, we educated them in music and poetry and physical
e   training.

We did.

And physical training is concerned with what comes into being and dies,
for it oversees the growth and decay of the body.

Apparently.

So it couldn't be the subject we're looking for.
522   No, it couldn't.

Then, could it be the music and poetry we described before?

But that, if you remember, is just the counterpart of physical training.
It educated the guardians through habits. Its harmonies gave them a
certain harmoniousness, not knowledge; its rhythms gave them a certain
rhythmical quality; and its stories, whether fictional or nearer the truth,
cultivated other habits akin to these. But as for the subject you're looking
b   for now, there's nothing like that in music and poetry.

Your reminder is exactly to the point; there's really nothing like that in
music and poetry. But, Glaucon, what is there that does have this? The
crafts all seem to be base or mechanical.

How could they be otherwise? But apart from music and poetry, physical
training, and the crafts, what subject is left?

Well, if we can't find anything apart from these, let's consider one of
the subjects that touches all of them.

What sort of thing?

For example, that common thing that every craft, every type of thought,
c   and every science uses and that is among the first compulsory subjects for
everyone.

What's that?

That inconsequential matter of distinguishing the one, the two, and the
three. In short, I mean number and calculation, for isn't it true that every
craft and science must have a share in that?

They certainly must.

Then so must warfare.

Absolutely.

In the tragedies, at any rate, Palamedes[9] is always showing up Agamemnon as a totally ridiculous general. Haven't you noticed? He says that, by
d   inventing numbers, he established how many troops there were in the

9. Palamades is a proverbially clever warrior best known for his cunning while serving
under Agamemnon.

Trojan army and counted their ships and everything else—implying that they were uncounted before and that Agamemnon (if indeed he didn't know how to count) didn't even know how many feet he had? What kind of general do you think that made him?

A very strange one, if that's true.

Then won't we set down this subject as compulsory for a warrior, so   *e* that he is able to count and calculate?

More compulsory than anything. If, that is, he's to understand anything about setting his troops in order or if he's even to be properly human.

Then do you notice the same thing about this subject that I do?

What's that?

That this turns out to be one of the subjects we were looking for that naturally lead to understanding. But no one uses it correctly, namely, as something that is really fitted in every way to draw one towards being.   *523*

What do you mean?

I'll try to make my view clear as follows: I'll distinguish for myself the things that do or don't lead in the direction we mentioned, and you must study them along with me and either agree or disagree, and that way we may come to know more clearly whether things are indeed as I divine.

Point them out.

I'll point out, then, if you can grasp it, that some sense perceptions *don't* summon the understanding to look into them, because the judgment of sense perception is itself adequate, while others encourage it in every way   *b* to look into them, because sense perception seems to produce no sound result.

You're obviously referring to things appearing in the distance and to *trompe l'oeil* paintings.

You're not quite getting my meaning.

Then what do you mean?

The ones that don't summon the understanding are all those that don't go off into opposite perceptions at the same time. But the ones that do go off in that way I call *summoners*—whenever sense perception doesn't   *c* declare one thing any more than its opposite, no matter whether the object striking the senses is near at hand or far away. You'll understand my meaning better if I put it this way: These, we say, are three fingers—the smallest, the second, and the middle finger.

That's right.

Assume that I'm talking about them as being seen from close by. Now, this is my question about them.

What?

It's apparent that each of them is equally a finger, and it makes no difference in this regard whether the finger is seen to be in the middle or

d at either end, whether it is dark or pale, thick or thin, or anything else of
that sort, for in all these cases, an ordinary soul isn't compelled to ask the
understanding what a finger is, since sight doesn't suggest to it that a
finger is at the same time the opposite of a finger.

No, it doesn't.

Therefore, it isn't likely that anything of that sort would summon or
e awaken the understanding.

No, it isn't.

But what about the bigness and smallness of fingers? Does sight perceive
them adequately? Does it make no difference to it whether the finger is
in the middle or at the end? And is it the same with the sense of touch,
as regards the thick and the thin, the hard and the soft? And do the other
senses reveal such things clearly and adequately? Doesn't each of them
524 rather do the following: The sense set over the hard is, in the first place,
of necessity also set over the soft, and it reports to the soul that the same
thing is perceived by it to be both hard and soft?

That's right.

And isn't it necessary that in such cases the soul is puzzled as to what
this sense means by the hard, if it indicates that the same thing is also
soft, or what it means by the light and the heavy, if it indicates that the
heavy is light, or the light, heavy?

b Yes, indeed, these are strange reports for the soul to receive, and they
do demand to be looked into.

Then it's likely that in such cases the soul, summoning calculation
and understanding, first tries to determine whether each of the things
announced to it is one or two.

Of course.

If it's evidently two, won't each be evidently distinct and one?

Yes.

Then, if each is one, and both two, the soul will understand that the
two are separate, for it wouldn't understand the inseparable to be two, but
c rather one.

That's right.

Sight, however, saw the big and small, not as separate, but as mixed up
together. Isn't that so?

Yes.

And in order to get clear about all this, understanding was compelled
to see the big and the small, not as mixed up together, but as separate—
the opposite way from sight.

True.

And isn't it from these cases that it first occurs to us to ask what the big
is and what the small is?

Absolutely.

And, because of this, we called the one the intelligible and the other the visible.

That's right. *d*

This, then, is what I was trying to express before, when I said that some things summon thought, while others don't. Those that strike the relevant sense at the same time as their opposites I call summoners, those that don't do this do not awaken understanding.

Now I understand, and I think you're right.

Well, then, to which of them do number and the one belong?

I don't know.

Reason it out from what was said before. If the one is adequately seen itself by itself or is so perceived by any of the other senses, then, as we were saying in the case of fingers, it wouldn't draw the soul towards being. But if something opposite to it is always seen at the same time, so that *e* nothing is apparently any more one than the opposite of one, then something would be needed to judge the matter. The soul would then be puzzled, would look for an answer, would stir up its understanding, and would ask what the one itself is. And so this would be among the subjects that lead the soul and turn it around towards the study of that which is. *525*

But surely the sight of the one does possess this characteristic to a remarkable degree, for we see the same thing to be both one and an unlimited number at the same time.

Then, if this is true of the one, won't it also be true of all numbers?

Of course.

Now, calculation and arithmetic are wholly concerned with numbers.

That's right.

Then evidently they lead us towards truth. *b*

Supernaturally so.

Then they belong, it seems, to the subjects we're seeking. They are compulsory for warriors because of their orderly ranks and for philosophers because they have to learn to rise up out of becoming and grasp being, if they are ever to become rational.

That's right.

And our guardian must be both a warrior and a philosopher.

Certainly.

Then it would be appropriate, Glaucon, to legislate this subject for those who are going to share in the highest offices in the city and to persuade them to turn to calculation and take it up, not as laymen do, but staying with it until they reach the study of the natures of the numbers by *c* means of understanding itself, nor like tradesmen and retailers, for the sake of buying and selling, but for the sake of war and for ease in turning the soul around, away from becoming and towards truth and being.

Well put.

Moreover, it strikes me, now that it has been mentioned, how sophisticated the subject of calculation is and in how many ways it is useful for
d our purposes, provided that one practices it for the sake of knowing rather than trading.

How is it useful?

In the very way we were talking about. It leads the soul forcibly upward and compels it to discuss the numbers themselves, never permitting anyone to propose for discussion numbers attached to visible or tangible bodies. You know what those who are clever in these matters are like: If, in the course of the argument, someone tries to divide the one itself, they laugh
e and won't permit it. If you divide it, they multiply it, taking care that one thing never be found to be many parts rather than one.

That's very true.

Then what do you think would happen, Glaucon, if someone were to
526 ask them: "What kind of numbers are you talking about, in which the one is as you assume it to be, each one equal to every other, without the least difference and containing no internal parts?"

I think they'd answer that they are talking about those numbers that can be grasped only in thought and can't be dealt with in any other way.
b Then do you see that it's likely that this subject really is compulsory for us, since it apparently compels the soul to use understanding itself on the truth itself?

Indeed, it most certainly does do that.

And what about those who are naturally good at calculation or reasoning? Have you already noticed that they're naturally sharp, so to speak, in all subjects, and that those who are slow at it, if they're educated and exercised in it, even if they're benefited in no other way, nonetheless improve and become generally sharper than they were?

That's true.

Moreover, I don't think you'll easily find subjects that are harder to
c learn or practice than this.

No, indeed.

Then, for all these reasons, this subject isn't to be neglected, and the best natures must be educated in it.

I agree.

Let that, then, be one of our subjects. Second, let's consider whether the subject that comes next is also appropriate for our purposes.

What subject is that? Do you mean geometry?

That's the very one I had in mind.
d Insofar as it pertains to war, it's obviously appropriate, for when it comes to setting up camp, occupying a region, concentrating troops, deploying them, or with regard to any of the other formations an army adopts in

battle or on the march, it makes all the difference whether someone is a geometer or not.

But, for things like that, even a little geometry—or calculation for that matter—would suffice. What we need to consider is whether the greater and more advanced part of it tends to make it easier to see the form of the good. And we say that anything has that tendency if it compels the   *e* soul to turn itself around towards the region in which lies the happiest of the things that are, the one the soul must see at any cost.

You're right.

Therefore, if geometry compels the soul to study being, it's appropriate, but if it compels it to study becoming, it's inappropriate.

So we've said, at any rate.

Now, no one with even a little experience of geometry will dispute that *527* this science is entirely the opposite of what is said about it in the accounts of its practitioners.

How do you mean?

They give ridiculous accounts of it, though they can't help it, for they speak like practical men, and all their accounts refer to doing things. They talk of "squaring," "applying," "adding," and the like, whereas the entire subject is pursued for the sake of knowledge.   *b*

Absolutely.

And mustn't we also agree on a further point?

What is that?

That it is knowledge of what always is, not of what comes into being and passes away.

That's easy to agree to, for geometry *is* knowledge of what always is.

Then it draws the soul towards truth and produces philosophic thought by directing upwards what we now wrongly direct downwards.

As far as anything possibly can.

Then as far as *we* possibly can, we must require those in your fine city   *c* not to neglect geometry in any way, for even its by-products are not insignificant.

What are they?

The ones concerned with war that you mentioned. But we also surely know that, when it comes to better understanding any subject, there is a world of difference between someone who has grasped geometry and someone who hasn't.

Yes, by god, a world of difference.

Then shall we set this down as a second subject for the young?

Let's do so, he said.

And what about astronomy? Shall we make it the third? Or do you disagree?   *d*

That's fine with me, for a better awareness of the seasons, months, and years is no less appropriate for a general than for a farmer or navigator.

You amuse me: You're like someone who's afraid that the majority will think he is prescribing useless subjects. It's no easy task—indeed it's very difficult—to realize that in every soul there is an instrument that is purified and rekindled by such subjects when it has been blinded and destroyed
e by other ways of life, an instrument that it is more important to preserve than ten thousand eyes, since only with it can the truth be seen. Those who share your belief that this is so will think you're speaking incredibly well, while those who've never been aware of it will probably think you're talking nonsense, since they see no benefit worth mentioning in these subjects. So decide right now which group you're addressing. Or are your
528 arguments for neither of them but mostly for your own sake—though you won't begrudge anyone else whatever benefit he's able to get from them?

The latter: I want to speak, question, and answer mostly for my own sake.

Then let's fall back to our earlier position, for we were wrong just now about the subject that comes after geometry.

What was our error?

After plane surfaces, we went on to revolving solids before dealing with solids by themselves. But the right thing to do is to take up the third
b dimension right after the second. And this, I suppose, consists of cubes and of whatever shares in depth.

You're right, Socrates, but this subject hasn't been developed yet.

There are two reasons for that: First, because no city values it, this difficult subject is little researched. Second, the researchers need a director, for, without one, they won't discover anything. To begin with, such a director is hard to find, and, then, even if he could be found, those who
c currently do research in this field would be too arrogant to follow him. If an entire city helped him to supervise it, however, and took the lead in valuing it, then he would be followed. And, if the subject was consistently and vigorously pursued, it would soon be developed. Even now, when it isn't valued and is held in contempt by the majority and is pursued by researchers who are unable to give an account of its usefulness, nevertheless, in spite of all these handicaps, the force of its charm has caused it to develop somewhat, so that it wouldn't be surprising if it were further developed even as things stand.

d The subject *has* outstanding charm. But explain more clearly what you were saying just now. The subject that deals with plane surfaces you took to be geometry.

Yes.

And at first you put astronomy after it, but later you went back on that.

In my haste to go through them all, I've only progressed more slowly. The subject dealing with the dimension of depth was next. But because it is in a ridiculous state, I passed it by and spoke of astronomy (which deals with the motion of things having depth) after geometry.   *e*

That's right.

Let's then put astronomy as the fourth subject, on the assumption that solid geometry will be available if a city takes it up.

That seems reasonable. And since you reproached me before for praising astronomy in a vulgar manner, I'll now praise it your way, for I think it's clear to everyone that astronomy compels the soul to look upward and *529* leads it from things here to things there.

It may be obvious to everyone except me, but that's not my view about it.

Then what *is* your view?

As it's practiced today by those who teach philosophy, it makes the soul look very much downward.

How do you mean?

In my opinion, your conception of "higher studies" is a good deal too generous, for if someone were to study something by leaning his head back and studying ornaments on a ceiling, it looks as though you'd say he's studying not with his eyes but with his understanding. Perhaps you're   *b* right, and I'm foolish, but I can't conceive of any subject making the soul look upward except one concerned with that which is, and that which is is invisible. If anyone attempts to learn something about sensible things, whether by gaping upward or squinting downward, I'd claim—since there's no knowledge of such things—that he never learns anything and that, even if he studies lying on his back on the ground or floating on it   *c* in the sea, his soul is looking not up but down.

You're right to reproach me, and I've been justly punished, but what did you mean when you said that astronomy must be learned in a different way from the way in which it is learned at present if it is to be a useful subject for our purposes?

It's like this: We should consider the ornaments that brighten the sky to be the most beautiful and most exact of visible things, seeing that they're embroidered on a visible surface. But we should consider their motions to fall far short of the true ones—motions that are really fast or slow as   *d* measured in true numbers, that trace out true geometrical figures, that are all in relation to one another, and that are the true motions of the things carried along in them. And these, of course, must be grasped by reason and thought, not by sight. Or do you think otherwise?

Not at all.

Therefore, we should use the embroidery in the sky as a model in the

study of these other things.[10] If someone experienced in geometry were
to come upon plans very carefully drawn and worked out by Daedalus or
e   some other craftsman or artist, he'd consider them to be very finely
executed, but he'd think it ridiculous to examine them seriously in order
530 to find the truth in them about the equal, the double, or any other ratio.
How could it be anything other than ridiculous?

Then don't you think that a real astronomer will feel the same when he
looks at the motions of the stars? He'll believe that the craftsman of the
heavens arranged them and all that's in them in the finest way possible
for such things. But as for the ratio of night to day, of days to a month,
of a month to a year, or of the motions of the stars to any of them or to
each other, don't you think he'll consider it strange to believe that they're
b   always the same and never deviate anywhere at all or to try in any sort of
way to grasp the truth about them, since they're connected to body and
visible?

That's my opinion anyway, now that I hear it from you.

Then if, by really taking part in astronomy, we're to make the naturally
intelligent part of the soul useful instead of useless, let's study astronomy
by means of problems, as we do geometry, and leave the things in the sky
c   alone.

The task you're prescribing is a lot harder than anything now attempted
in astronomy.

And I suppose that, if we are to be of any benefit as lawgivers, our
prescriptions for the other subjects will be of the same kind. But have you
any other appropriate subject to suggest?

Not offhand.

Well, there isn't just one form of motion but several. Perhaps a wise
d   person could list them all, but there are two that are evident even to us.

What are they?

Besides the one we've discussed, there is also its counterpart.

What's that?

It's likely that, as the eyes fasten on astronomical motions, so the ears
fasten on harmonic ones, and that the sciences of astronomy and harmonics are closely akin. This is what the Pythagoreans[11] say, Glaucon, and we
agree, don't we?

---

10. See 510d–511a.

11. Pythagoras of Samos (sixth century) taught a way of life (see *Republic* 600b) in
which natural science became a religion. He is credited with discovering the mathematical ratios determining the principal intervals of the musical scale. He seems to have
been led by this to believe that all natural phenomena are explicable in terms of
numbers. He may have discovered some version of the theorem about right triangles
that bears his name.

We do.

Therefore, since the subject is so huge, shouldn't we ask them what   *e*
they have to say about harmonic motions and whether there is anything
else besides them, all the while keeping our own goal squarely in view?

What's that?

That those whom we are rearing should never try to learn anything
incomplete, anything that doesn't reach the end that everything should
reach—the end we mentioned just now in the case of astronomy. Or don't
you know that people do something similar in harmonics? Measuring *531*
audible consonances and sounds against one another, they labor in vain,
just like present-day astronomers.

Yes, by the gods, and pretty ridiculous they are too. They talk about
something they call a "dense interval" or quartertone[12]—putting their ears
to their instruments like someone trying to overhear what the neighbors
are saying. And some say that they hear a tone in between and that *it* is
the shortest interval by which they must measure, while others argue
that this tone sounds the same as a quarter tone. Both put ears before   *b*
understanding.

You mean those excellent fellows who torment their strings, torturing
them, and stretching them on pegs. I won't draw out the analogy by
speaking of blows with the plectrum or the accusations or denials and
boastings on the part of the strings; instead I'll cut it short by saying that
these aren't the people I'm talking about. The ones I mean are the ones
we just said we were going to question about harmonics, for they do the
same as the astronomers. They seek out the numbers that are to be found   *c*
in these audible harmonies, but they do not make the ascent to problems.
They don't investigate, for example, which numbers are in harmony and
which aren't or what the explanation is of each.

But that would be a superhuman task.

Yet it's useful in the search for the beautiful and the good. But pursued
for any other purpose, it's useless.

Probably so.

Moreover, I take it that, if inquiry into all the subjects we've mentioned
brings out their association and relationship with one another and draws
conclusions about their kinship, it does contribute something to our goal   *d*
and isn't labor in vain, but that otherwise it is in vain.

I, too, divine that this is true. But you're still talking about a very big
task, Socrates.

Do you mean the prelude, or what? Or don't you know that all these
subjects are merely preludes to the song itself that must also be learned?

---

12. A dense interval is evidently the smallest difference in pitch recognized in ancient
music.

Surely you don't think that people who are clever in these matters are
e   dialecticians.

No, by god, I don't. Although I have met a few exceptions.

But did it ever seem to you that those who can neither give nor follow
an account know anything at all of the things we say they must know?

My answer to that is also no.

532   Then isn't this at last, Glaucon, the song that dialectic sings? It is
intelligible, but it is imitated by the power of sight. We said that sight tries
at last to look at the animals themselves, the stars themselves, and, in the
end, at the sun itself.[13] In the same way, whenever someone tries through
argument and apart from all sense perceptions to find the being itself
of each thing and doesn't give up until he grasps the good itself with
b   understanding itself, he reaches the end of the intelligible, just as the
other reached the end of the visible.

Absolutely.

And what about this journey? Don't you call it dialectic?

I do.

Then the release from bonds and the turning around from shadows to
statues and the light of the fire and, then, the way up out of the cave to
the sunlight and, there, the continuing inability to look at the animals, the
plants, and the light of the sun, but the newly acquired ability to look at
c   divine images in water and shadows of the things that are, rather than, as
before, merely at shadows of statues thrown by another source of light
that is itself a shadow in relation to the sun—all this business of the crafts
we've mentioned has the power to awaken the best part of the soul and
lead it upward to the study of the best among the things that are, just as,
before, the clearest thing in the body was led to the brightest thing in the
d   bodily and visible realm.

I accept that this is so, even though it seems very hard to accept in one
way and hard not to accept in another. All the same, since we'll have to
return to these things often in the future, rather than having to hear them
just once now, let's assume that what you've said is so and turn to the song
itself, discussing it in the same way as we did the prelude. So tell us the
way in which the power of dialectic works, what forms it is divided into,
e   and what paths it follows, for these lead at last, it seems, towards that
place which is a rest from the road, so to speak, and an end of journeying
for the one who reaches it.

533   You won't be able to follow me any longer, Glaucon, even though there
is no lack of eagerness on my part to lead you, for you would no longer
be seeing an image of what we're describing, but the truth itself. At any
rate, that's how it seems to me. That it is really so is not worth insisting

13. See 516a–b.

on any further. But that there is some such thing to be seen, *that* is something we must insist on. Isn't that so?

Of course.

And mustn't we also insist that the power of dialectic could reveal it only to someone experienced in the subjects we've described and that it cannot reveal it in any other way?

That too is worth insisting on.

At any rate, no one will dispute it when we say that there is no other   *b*
inquiry that systematically attempts to grasp with respect to each thing itself what the being of it is, for all the other crafts are concerned with human opinions and desires, with growing or construction, or with the care of growing or constructed things. And as for the rest, I mean geometry and the subjects that follow it, we described them as to some extent grasping what is, for we saw that, while they do dream about what is, they are unable to command a waking view of it as long as they make use of hypotheses that they leave untouched and that they cannot give any account   *c*
of. What mechanism could possibly turn any agreement into knowledge when it begins with something unknown and puts together the conclusion and the steps in between from what is unknown?

None.

Therefore, dialectic is the only inquiry that travels this road, doing away with hypotheses and proceeding to the first principle itself, so as to be   *d*
secure. And when the eye of the soul is really buried in a sort of barbaric bog,[14] dialectic gently pulls it out and leads it upwards, using the crafts we described to help it and cooperate with it in turning the soul around. From force of habit, we've often called these crafts sciences or kinds of knowledge, but they need another name, clearer than opinion, darker than knowledge. We called them thought somewhere before.[15] But I presume that we won't dispute about a name when we have so many more important matters to investigate.   *e*

Of course not.

It will therefore be enough to call the first section knowledge, the second thought, the third belief, and the fourth imaging, just as we did before. The last two together we call opinion, the other two, intellect.[16] Opinion is *534*

14. See 519a–b.

15. See 511d–e.

16. The reference is to 511d–e, but there the first section is called understanding (*noēsis*) rather than knowledge (*epistēmē*). However, since we've just been told that thought (*dianoia*) is not a kind of knowledge, understanding and knowing have in effect become identified. It is harder to explain why knowledge and thought are now referred to jointly as *noēsis*. But presumably it is because that whole section of the line is earlier referred to as the intelligible (*noēton*). See 509d–e. To prevent misunderstanding, therefore, I have translated *noēsis* as 'intellect' here.

concerned with becoming, intellect with being. And as being is to becoming, so intellect is to opinion, and as intellect is to opinion, so knowledge is to belief and thought to imaging. But as for the ratios between the things these are set over and the division of either the opinable or the intelligible section into two, let's pass them by, Glaucon, lest they involve us in arguments many times longer than the ones we've already gone through.

b I agree with you about the others in any case, insofar as I'm able to follow.

Then, do you call someone who is able to give an account of the being of each thing dialectical? But insofar as he's unable to give an account of something, either to himself or to another, do you deny that he has any understanding of it?

How could I do anything else?

Then the same applies to the good. Unless someone can distinguish in an account the form of the good from everything else, can survive all *c* refutation, as if in a battle, striving to judge things not in accordance with opinion but in accordance with being, and can come through all this with his account still intact, you'll say that he doesn't know the good itself or any other good. And if he gets hold of some image of it, you'll say that it's through opinion, not knowledge, for he is dreaming and asleep throughout his present life, and, before he wakes up here, he will arrive in Hades and *d* go to sleep forever.

Yes, by god, I'll certainly say all of that.

Then, as for those children of yours whom you're rearing and educating in theory, if you ever reared them in fact, I don't think that you'd allow them to rule in your city or be responsible for the most important things while they are as irrational as incommensurable lines.

Certainly not.

Then you'll legislate that they are to give most attention to the education that will enable them to ask and answer questions most knowledgeably? *e* I'll legislate it along with you.

Then do you think that we've placed dialectic at the top of the other subjects like a coping stone and that no other subject can rightly be placed above it, but that our account of the subjects that a future ruler must learn 535 has come to an end?

Probably so.

Then it remains for you to deal with the distribution of these subjects, with the question of to whom we'll assign them and in what way.

That's clearly next.

Do you remember what sort of people we chose in our earlier selection of rulers?[17]

17. See 412b ff.

Of course I do.

In the other respects, the same natures have to be chosen: we have to select the most stable, the most courageous, and as far as possible the most graceful. In addition, we must look not only for people who have a noble and tough character but for those who have the natural qualities   *b* conducive to this education of ours.

Which ones exactly?

They must be keen on the subjects and learn them easily, for people's souls give up much more easily in hard study than in physical training, since the pain—being peculiar to them and not shared with their body— is more their own.

That's true.

We must also look for someone who has got a good memory, is persis-   *c* tent, and is in every way a lover of hard work. How else do you think he'd be willing to carry out both the requisite bodily labors and also complete so much study and practice?

Nobody would, unless his nature was in every way a good one.

In any case, the present error, which as we said before explains why philosophy isn't valued, is that she's taken up by people who are unworthy of her, for illegitimate students shouldn't be allowed to take her up, but only legitimate ones.

How so?

In the first place, no student should be lame in his love of hard work,   *d* really loving one half of it, and hating the other half. This happens when someone is a lover of physical training, hunting, or any kind of bodily labor and isn't a lover of learning, listening, or inquiry, but hates the work involved in them. And someone whose love of hard work tends in the opposite direction is also lame.

That's very true.

Similarly with regard to truth, won't we say that a soul is maimed if it hates a voluntary falsehood, cannot endure to have one in itself, and is greatly angered when it exists in others, but is nonetheless content to accept   *e* an involuntary falsehood, isn't angry when it is caught being ignorant, and bears its lack of learning easily, wallowing in it like a pig?[18]

Absolutely.   536

And with regard to moderation, courage, high-mindedness, and all the other parts of virtue, it is also important to distinguish the illegitimate from the legitimate, for when either a city or an individual doesn't know how to do this, it unwittingly employs the lame and illegitimate as friends or rulers for whatever services it wants done.

That's just how it is.

18. See 382a ff.

So we must be careful in all these matters, for if we bring people who are sound of limb and mind to so great a subject and training, and educate
b them in it, even justice itself won't blame us, and we'll save the city and its constitution. But if we bring people of a different sort, we'll do the opposite, and let loose an even greater flood of ridicule upon philosophy.

And it would be shameful to do that.

It certainly would. But I seem to have done something a bit ridiculous myself just now.

What's that?

I forgot that we were only playing, and so I spoke too vehemently.
c But I looked upon philosophy as I spoke, and seeing her undeservedly besmirched, I seem to have lost my temper and said what I had to say too earnestly, as if I were angry with those responsible for it.

That certainly wasn't my impression as I listened to you.

But it was mine as I was speaking. In any case, let's not forget that in our earlier selection we chose older people but that that isn't permitted in this one, for we mustn't believe Solon[19] when he says that as someone
d grows older he's able to learn a lot. He can do that even less well than he can run races, for all great and numerous labors belong to the young.

Necessarily.

Therefore, calculation, geometry, and all the preliminary education required for dialectic must be offered to the future rulers in childhood, and not in the shape of compulsory learning either.

Why's that?
e Because no free person should learn anything like a slave. Forced bodily labor does no harm to the body, but nothing taught by force stays in the soul.

That's true.

Then don't use force to train the children in these subjects; use play instead. That way you'll also see better what each of them is naturally
537 fitted for.

That seems reasonable.

Do you remember that we stated that the children were to be led into war on horseback as observers and that, wherever it is safe to do so, they should be brought close and taste blood, like puppies?

I remember.

In all these things—in labors, studies, and fears—the ones who always show the greatest aptitude are to be inscribed on a list.
b At what age?

When they're released from compulsory physical training, for during

19. Athenian statesman, lawgiver, and poet (c. 640–560).

that period, whether it's two or three years, young people are incapable of doing anything else, since weariness and sleep are enemies of learning. At the same time, how they fare in this physical training is itself an important test.

Of course it is.

And after that, that is to say, from the age of twenty, those who are chosen will also receive more honors than the others. Moreover, the subjects they learned in no particular order as children they must now bring together to form a unified vision of their kinship both with one *c* another and with the nature of that which is.

At any rate, only learning of that sort holds firm in those who receive it.

It is also the greatest test of who is naturally dialectical and who isn't, for anyone who can achieve a unified vision is dialectical, and anyone who can't isn't.

I agree.

Well, then, you'll have to look out for the ones who most of all have this ability in them and who also remain steadfast in their studies, in war, and in the other activities laid down by law. And after they have reached their *d* thirtieth year, you'll select them in turn from among those chosen earlier and assign them yet greater honors. Then you'll have to test them by means of the power of dialectic, to discover which of them can relinquish his eyes and other senses, going on with the help of truth to that which by itself is. And this is a task that requires great care.

What's the main reason for that?

Don't you realize what a great evil comes from dialectic as it is currently practiced? *e*

What evil is that?

Those who practice it are filled with lawlessness.

They certainly are.

Do you think it's surprising that this happens to them? Aren't you sympathetic?

Why isn't it surprising? And why should I be sympathetic?

Because it's like the case of a child brought up surrounded by much wealth and many flatterers in a great and numerous family, who finds out, when he has become a man, that he isn't the child of his professed parents *538* and that he can't discover his real ones. Can you divine what the attitude of someone like that would be to the flatterers, on the one hand, and to his supposed parents, on the other, before he knew about his parentage, and what it would be when he found out? Or would you rather hear what I divine about it?

I'd rather hear your views.

Well, then, I divine that during the time that he didn't know the truth, he'd honor his father, mother, and the rest of his supposed family more

b than he would the flatterers, that he'd pay greater attention to their needs, be less likely to treat them lawlessly in word or deed, and be more likely to obey them than the flatterers in any matters of importance.

Probably so.

When he became aware of the truth, however, his honor and enthusiasm would lessen for his family and increase for the flatterers, he'd obey the latter far more than before, begin to live in the way that they did, and keep

c company with them openly, and, unless he was very decent by nature, he'd eventually care nothing for that father of his or any of the rest of his supposed family.

All this would probably happen as you say, but in what way is it an image of those who take up arguments?

As follows. We hold from childhood certain convictions about just and fine things; we're brought up with them as with our parents, we obey and honor them.

Indeed, we do.

d There are other ways of living, however, opposite to these and full of pleasures, that flatter the soul and attract it to themselves but which don't persuade sensible people, who continue to honor and obey the convictions of their fathers.

That's right.

And then a questioner comes along and asks someone of this sort, "What is the fine?" And, when he answers what he has heard from the traditional lawgiver, the argument refutes him, and by refuting him often and in many places shakes him from his convictions, and makes him believe that the fine is no more fine than shameful, and the same with the

e just, the good, and the things he honored most. What do you think his attitude will be then to honoring and obeying his earlier convictions?

Of necessity he won't honor or obey them in the same way.

Then, when he no longer honors and obeys those convictions and can't discover the true ones, will he be likely to adopt any other way of life than

539 that which flatters him?

No, he won't.

And so, I suppose, from being law-abiding he becomes lawless.

Inevitably.

Then, as I asked before, isn't it only to be expected that this is what happens to those who take up arguments in this way, and don't they therefore deserve a lot of sympathy?

Yes, and they deserve pity too.

Then, if you don't want your thirty-year-olds to be objects of such pity, you'll have to be extremely careful about how you introduce them to arguments.

That's right.

And isn't it one lasting precaution not to let them taste arguments while they're young? I don't suppose that it has escaped your notice that, when young people get their first taste of arguments, they misuse it by treating *b* it as a kind of game of contradiction. They imitate those who've refuted them by refuting others themselves, and, like puppies, they enjoy dragging and tearing those around them with their arguments.

They're excessively fond of it.

Then, when they've refuted many and been refuted by them in turn, they forcefully and quickly fall into disbelieving what they believed before. And, as a result, they themselves and the whole of philosophy are discred- *c* ited in the eyes of others.

That's very true.

But an older person won't want to take part in such madness. He'll imitate someone who is willing to engage in discussion in order to look for the truth, rather than someone who plays at contradiction for sport. He'll be more sensible himself and will bring honor rather than discredit to the philosophical way of life. *d*

That's right.

And when we said before that those allowed to take part in arguments should be orderly and steady by nature, not as nowadays, when even the unfit are allowed to engage in them—wasn't all that also said as a precaution?

Of course.

Then if someone continuously, strenuously, and exclusively devotes himself to participation in arguments, exercising himself in them just as he did in the bodily physical training, which is their counterpart, would that be enough?

Do you mean six years or four? *e*

It doesn't matter. Make it five. And after that, you must make them go down into the cave again, and compel them to take command in matters of war and occupy the other offices suitable for young people, so that they won't be inferior to the others in experience. But in these, too, they must be tested to see whether they'll remain steadfast when they're pulled this way and that or shift their ground. *540*

How much time do you allow for that?

Fifteen years. Then, at the age of fifty, those who've survived the tests and been successful both in practical matters and in the sciences must be led to the goal and compelled to lift up the radiant light of their souls to what itself provides light for everything. And once they've seen the good

b

c

itself, they must each in turn put the city, its citizens, and themselves in order, using it as their model. Each of them will spend most of his time with philosophy, but, when his turn comes, he must labor in politics and rule for the city's sake, not as if he were doing something fine, but rather something that has to be done. Then, having educated others like himself to take his place as guardians of the city, he will depart for the Isles of the Blessed and dwell there. And, if the Pythia agrees, the city will publicly establish memorials and sacrifices to him as a daimon, but if not, then as a happy and divine human being.

Like a sculptor,[20] Socrates, you've produced ruling men that are completely fine.

And ruling women, too, Glaucon, for you mustn't think that what I've said applies any more to men than it does to women who are born with the appropriate natures.

That's right, if indeed they are to share everything equally with the men, as we said they should.

d

e

Then, do you agree that the things we've said about the city and its constitution aren't altogether wishful thinking, that it's hard for them to come about, but not impossible? And do you also agree that they can come about only in the way we indicated, namely, when one or more true philosophers come to power in a city, who despise present honors, thinking them slavish and worthless, and who prize what is right and the honors that come from it above everything, and regard justice as the most important and most essential thing, serving it and increasing it as they set their city in order?

How will they do that?

They'll send everyone in the city who is over ten years old into the *541* country. Then they'll take possession of the children, who are now free from the ethos of their parents, and bring them up in their own customs and laws, which are the ones we've described. This is the quickest and easiest way for the city and constitution we've discussed to be established, become happy, and bring most benefit to the people among whom it's established.

That's by far the quickest and easiest way. And in my opinion, Socrates, *b* you've described well how it would come into being, if it ever did.

Then, isn't that enough about this city and the man who is like it? Surely it is clear what sort of man we'll say he has to be.

It is clear, he said. And as for your question, I think that we have reached the end of this topic.

20. See 361d.

Book VIII

The description of the kallipolis and of the man whose character resembles it— the philosopher-king—is now complete, and Socrates returns to the argument interrupted at the beginning of Book V. He describes four individual character types and the four types of constitutions that result when people who possess them rule in a city (544d–545d). He presents these as four stages in the increasing corruption or decline of the kallipolis, and he explains, by appeal to the mathematical myth of the geometrical number (546a–b), why the kallipolis will decline. However, embedded in the myth is the serious philosophical suggestion that the kallipolis will decline because the philosopher-kings have to rely on sense perception in putting their eugenics policy into practice (546b–c).

The first of the bad cities Socrates describes is a timocracy. It is ruled by people whose souls are themselves ruled by the spirited part of their soul, in which the desire for honor, victories, and good reputation are located (550b). It is the second-best city to the kallipolis. The third-best city is an oligarchy. It is ruled by people whose souls are ruled by their necessary appetites (554a). The fourth-best city is a democracy. It is ruled by people whose souls are ruled by unnecessary appetites (561a–b). The worst city of all is a tyranny. It is ruled by someone whose soul is ruled by its lawless and unnecessary appetites (571a).

Well, then, Glaucon, we've agreed to the following: If a city is to achieve the height of good government, wives must be in common, children and 543 all their education must be in common, their way of life, whether in peace or war, must be in common, and their kings must be those among them who have proved to be best, both in philosophy and in warfare.

We have agreed to that, he said.

Moreover, we also agreed that, as soon as the rulers are established, they will lead the soldiers and settle them in the kind of dwellings we *b* described, which are in no way private but common to all. And we also agreed, if you remember, what kind of possessions they will have.

I remember that we thought that none of them should acquire any of the things that the other rulers now do but that, as athletes of war and guardians, they should receive their yearly upkeep from the other citizens

c   as a wage for their guardianship and look after themselves and the rest of
the city.[1]
      That's right. But since we have completed this discussion, let's recall
the point at which we began the digression that brought us here, so that
we can continue on the same path from where we left off.
      That isn't difficult, for, much the same as now, you were talking as if
you had completed the description of the city.[2] You said that you would
class both the city you described and the man who is like it as good, even
d   though, as it seems, you had a still finer city and man to tell us about. But,
544 in any case, you said that, if this city was the right one, the others were
faulty. You said, if I remember, that there were four types of constitution
remaining that are worth discussing, each with faults that we should
observe, and we should do the same for the people who are like them.
Our aim was to observe them all, agree which man is best and which
worst, and then determine whether the best is happiest and the worst
most wretched or whether it's otherwise. I was asking you which four
constitutions you had in mind when Polemarchus and Adeimantus inter-
b   rupted.[3] And that's when you took up the discussion that led here.
      That's absolutely right.
      Well, then, like a wrestler, give me the same hold again, and when I ask
the same question, try to give the answer you were about to give before.
      If I can.
      I'd at least like to hear what four constitutions you meant.
c   That won't be difficult since they're the ones for which we have names.
First, there's the constitution praised by most people, namely, the Cretan
or Laconian.[4] The second, which is also second in the praise it receives,
is called oligarchy and is filled with a host of evils. The next in order, and
antagonistic to it, is democracy. And finally there is genuine tyranny,
surpassing all of them, the fourth and last of the diseased cities. Or can
you think of another type of constitution—I mean another whose form is
distinct from these? Dynasties and purchased kingships and other consti-
d   tutions of that sort, which one finds no less among the barbarians than
among the Greeks, are somewhere intermediate between these four.
      At any event, many strange ones are indeed talked about.
      And do you realize that of necessity there are as many forms of human
character as there are of constitutions? Or do you think that constitutions

---

1. See 414d–20b.
2. See 445c–e.
3. See 449b ff.
4. I.e. the Spartan constitution.

are born "from oak or rock"[5] and not from the characters of the people who live in the cities governed by them, which tip the scales, so to speak, and drag the rest along with them?   *e*

No, I don't believe they come from anywhere else.

Then, if there are five forms of city, there must also be five forms of the individual soul.

Of course.

Now, we've already described the one that's like aristocracy, which is rightly said to be good and just.

We have.   *545*

Then mustn't we next go through the inferior ones, namely, the victory-loving and honor-loving (which corresponds to the Laconian form of constitution), followed by the oligarchic, the democratic, and the tyrannical, so that, having discovered the most unjust of all, we can oppose him to the most just? In this way, we can complete our investigation into how pure justice and pure injustice stand, with regard to the happiness or wretchedness of those who possess them, and either be persuaded by Thrasymachus to practice injustice or by the argument that is now coming to light to practice justice.   *b*

That's absolutely what we have to do.

Then, just as we began by looking for the virtues of character in a constitution, before looking for them in the individual, thinking that they'd be clearer in the former,[6] shouldn't we first examine the honor-loving constitution? I don't know what other name there is for it, but it should be called either timocracy or timarchy. Then shouldn't we examine an individual who is related to that constitution, and, after that, oligarchy and an oligarchic person, and democracy and a democratic person? And finally, having come to a city under a tyrant and having examined it, shouldn't we   *c* look into a tyrannical soul, trying in this way to become adequate judges of the topic we proposed to ourselves?

That would be a reasonable way for us to go about observing and judging, at any rate.

Well, then, let's try to explain how timocracy emerges from aristocracy. Or is it a simple principle that the cause of change in any constitution is civil war breaking out within the ruling group itself, but that if this group— however small it is—remains of one mind, the constitution cannot be   *d* changed?

Yes, that's right.

How, then, Glaucon, will our city be changed? How will civil war arise,

5. See e.g. *Odyssey* 19.163.
6. See 368c ff.

either between the auxiliaries and the rulers or within either group? Or
do you want us to be like Homer and pray to the Muses to tell us "how
e   civil war first broke out?"[7] And shall we say that they speak to us in tragic
tones, as if they were in earnest, playing and jesting with us as if we were
children?

What will they say?

546   Something like this. "It is hard for a city composed in this way to change,
but everything that comes into being must decay. Not even a constitution
such as this will last for ever. It, too, must face dissolution. And this is
how it will be dissolved. All plants that grow in the earth, and also all
animals that grow upon it, have periods of fruitfulness and barrenness of
both soul and body as often as the revolutions complete the circumferences
of their circles. These circumferences are short for the short-lived, and
the opposite for their opposites.[8] Now, the people you have educated to
be leaders in your city, even though they are wise, still won't, through
b   calculation together with sense perception, hit upon the fertility and barrenness of the human species, but it will escape them, and so they will at
some time beget children when they ought not to do so. For the birth of
a divine creature, there is a cycle comprehended by a perfect number.[9]
For a human being, it is the first number in which are found root and
square increases, comprehending three lengths and four terms, of elements that make things like and unlike, that cause them to increase and
decrease, and that render all things mutually agreeable and rational in
c   their relations to one another. Of these elements, four and three, married
with five, give two harmonies when thrice increased. One of them is a
square, so many times a hundred. The other is of equal length one way
but oblong. One of its sides is one hundred squares of the rational diameter
of five diminished by one each or one hundred squares of the irrational
diameter diminished by two each. The other side is a hundred cubes of
three. This whole geometrical number controls better and worse births.[10]

---

7. This seems to be an adaptation of *Iliad* 16.112. Cf. 1.575.

8. I.e. plants and animals have fixed gestation periods, represented by circles whose
circumferences revolve. If a seed is sown in the fertile part of the cycle, it grows to
proper maturity, but if a seed is sown during the barren part of the cycle, it will either
not germinate or produce an inferior crop. The reason that the length of these periods—
the size of the corresponding circle—is proportional to the length of the life of the
thing whose period or circle they are is that longer-lived things were thought to have
longer gestation periods.

9. The divine creature seems to be the world or universe. See *Timaeus* 30b–d, 32d,
34a–b. Plato does not specify what its number is.

10. The human geometrical number is the product of 3, 4, and 5 "thrice increased,"
multiplied by itself three times, i.e. $(3 \cdot 4 \cdot 5)^4$ or 12,960,000. This can be represented
geometrically as a square whose sides are 3600 or as an oblong or rectangle whose
sides are 4800 and 2700. The first is "so many times a hundred," viz. 36 times. The

And when your rulers, through ignorance of these births, join brides and
grooms at the wrong time, the children will be neither good natured nor   *d*
fortunate. The older generation will choose the best of these children but
they are unworthy nevertheless, and when they acquire their fathers'
powers, they will begin, as guardians, to neglect us Muses. First, they will
have less consideration for music and poetry than they ought, then they
will neglect physical training, so that your young people will become less
well educated in music and poetry. Hence, rulers chosen from among
them won't be able to guard well the testing of the golden, silver, bronze,   *e*
and iron races, which are Hesiod's and your own.[11] The intermixing of
iron with silver and bronze with gold that results will engender lack of *547*
likeness and unharmonious inequality, and these always breed war and
hostility wherever they arise. Civil war, we declare, is always and everywhere 'of this lineage'."[12]

And we'll declare that what the Muses say is right.

It must be, since they're Muses.

What do the Muses say after that?   *b*

Once civil war breaks out, both the iron and bronze types[13] pull the
constitution towards money-making and the acquisition of land, houses,
gold, and silver, while both the gold and silver types[14]—not being poor,
but by nature rich or rich in their souls—lead the constitution towards
virtue and the old order. And thus striving and struggling with one another,
they compromise on a middle way: They distribute the land and houses
as private property, enslave and hold as serfs and servants those whom
they previously guarded as free friends and providers of upkeep,[15] and
occupy themselves with war and with guarding against those whom they've   *c*
enslaved.

I think that is the way this transformation begins.

Then, isn't this constitution a sort of midpoint between aristocracy and
oligarchy?

Absolutely.

Then, if that's its place in the transformation, how will it be managed

latter is obtained as follows. The "rational diameter" of 5 is the nearest rational number
to the real diagonal of a square whose sides are 5, i.e. to $\sqrt{50}$. This number is 7. Since
the square of 7 is 49, we get the longer side of the rectangle by diminishing 49 by 1
and multiplying the result by 100. This gives 4800. The "irrational diameter" of 5 is
$\sqrt{50}$. When squared, diminished by 2, and multiplied by 100 this, too, is 4800. The
short side, "a hundred cubes of three," is 2700.

11. See *Works and Days* 109–202.

12. See e.g. *Iliad* 6.211.

13. I.e. the rulers into whose souls iron or bronze have been mixed.

14. I.e. the rulers whose souls are either silver or gold.

15. See 463b.

after the change? Isn't it obvious that it will imitate the aristocratic constitu-
d   tion in some respects and oligarchy in others, since it's between them, and
that it will also have some features of its own?

That's right.

The rulers will be respected; the fighting class will be prevented from
taking part in farming, manual labor, or other ways of making money; it
will eat communally and devote itself to physical training and training for
war; and in all such ways, won't the constitution be like the aristocratic
one?

Yes.

On the other hand, it will be afraid to appoint wise people as rulers, on
e   the grounds that they are no longer simple and earnest but mixed, and
will incline towards spirited and simpler people, who are more naturally
suited for war than peace; it will value the tricks and stratagems of war
548 and spend all its time making war. Aren't most of these qualities peculiar
to it?

Yes.

Such people will desire money just as those in oligarchies do, passion-
ately adoring gold and silver in secret. They will possess private treasuries
and storehouses, where they can keep it hidden, and have houses to
enclose them, like private nests, where they can spend lavishly either on
b   women or on anyone else they wish.

That's absolutely true.

They'll be mean with their own money, since they value it and are not
allowed to acquire it openly, but they'll love to spend other people's
because of their appetites. They'll enjoy their pleasures in secret, running
away from the law like boys from their father, for since they've neglected
the true Muse—that of discussion and philosophy—and have valued
physical training more than music and poetry, they haven't been educated
c   by persuasion but by force.

The constitution you're discussing is certainly a mixture of good and
bad.

Yes, it is mixed, but because of the predominance of the spirited
element, one thing alone is most manifest in it, namely, the love of victory
and the love of honor.

Very much so.

This, then, is the way this constitution would come into being and what
it would be like, for, after all, we're only sketching the shape of the
constitution in theory, not giving an exact account of it, since even from
d   a sketch we'll be able to discern the most just and the most unjust
person. And, besides, it would be an intolerably long task to describe every
constitution and every character without omitting any detail.

That's right.

Then who is the man that corresponds to this constitution? How does he come to be, and what sort of man is he?

I think, said Adeimantus, that he'd be very like Glaucon here, as far as the love of victory is concerned.

In that respect, I said, he might be, but, in the following ones, I don't think his nature would be similar.

Which ones?   e

He'd be more obstinate and less well trained in music and poetry, though he's a lover of it, and he'd love to listen to speeches and arguments, though he's by no means a rhetorician. He'd be harsh to his slaves rather than merely looking down on them as an adequately educated person does. He'd be gentle to free people and very obedient to rulers, being 549 himself a lover of ruling and a lover of honor. However, he doesn't base his claim to rule on his ability as a speaker or anything like that, but, as he's a lover of physical training and a lover of hunting, on his abilities and exploits in warfare and warlike activities.

Yes, that's the character that corresponds to this constitution.

Wouldn't such a person despise money when he's young but love it more and more as he grows older, because he shares in the money-loving nature and isn't pure in his attitude to virtue? And isn't that because he   b lacks the best of guardians?

What guardian is that? Adeimantus said.

Reason, I said, mixed with music and poetry, for it alone dwells within the person who possesses it as the lifelong preserver of his virtue.

Well put.

That, then, is a timocratic youth; he resembles the corresponding city.

Absolutely.   c

And he comes into being in some such way as this. He's the son of a good father who lives in a city that isn't well governed, who avoids honors, office, lawsuits, and all such meddling in other people's affairs, and who is even willing to be put at a disadvantage in order to avoid trouble.

Then how does he come to be timocratic?

When he listens, first, to his mother complaining that her husband isn't one of the rulers and that she's at a disadvantage among the other women as a result. Then she sees that he's not very concerned about money and that he doesn't fight back when he's insulted, whether in private or in   d public in the courts, but is indifferent to everything of that sort. She also sees him concentrating his mind on his own thoughts, neither honoring nor dishonoring her overmuch. Angered by all this, she tells her son that his father is unmanly, too easy-going, and all the other things that women repeat over and over again in such cases.   e

Yes, Adeimantus said, it's like them to have many such complaints.

You know, too, I said, that the servants of men like that—the ones who are thought to be well disposed to the family—also say similar things to the son in private. When they see the father failing to prosecute someone who owes him money or has wronged him in some other way, they urge the son to take revenge on all such people when he grows up and to be 550 more of a man than his father. The boy hears and sees the same kind of things when he goes out: Those in the city who do their own work are called fools and held to be of little account, while those who meddle in other people's affairs are honored and praised. The young man hears and sees all this, but he also listens to what his father says, observes what he does from close at hand, and compares his ways of living with those of the b others. So he's pulled by both. His father nourishes the rational part of his soul and makes it grow; the others nourish the spirited and appetitive parts. Because he isn't a bad man by nature but keeps bad company, when he's pulled in these two ways, he settles in the middle and surrenders the rule over himself to the middle part—the victory-loving and spirited part— and becomes a proud and honor-loving man.

I certainly think that you've given a full account of how this sort of man comes to be.

c   Then we now have the second constitution and the second man.

We have.

Then shall we next talk, as Aeschylus says, of "another man ordered like another city,"[16] or shall we follow our plan and talk about the city first?

We must follow our plan.

And I suppose that the one that comes after the present constitution is oligarchy.

And what kind of constitution would you call oligarchy?

The constitution based on a property assessment, in which the rich d rule, and the poor man has no share in ruling.

I understand.

So mustn't we first explain how timarchy is transformed into oligarchy?

Yes.

And surely the manner of this transformation is clear even to the blind.

What is it like?

The treasure house filled with gold, which each possesses, destroys the constitution. First, they find ways of spending money for themselves, then they stretch the laws relating to this, then they and their wives disobey the laws altogether.

---

16. The line does not occur in the extant plays, but it may be an adaptation of *Seven against Thebes* 451.

They would do that.

And as one person sees another doing this and emulates him, they make the majority of the others like themselves.   *e*

They do.

From there they proceed further into money-making, and the more they value it, the less they value virtue. Or aren't virtue and wealth so opposed that if they were set on a scales, they'd always incline in opposite directions?

That's right.

So, when wealth and the wealthy are valued or honored in a city, virtue and good people are valued less.   *551*

Clearly.

And what is valued is always practiced, and what isn't valued is neglected.

That's right.

Then, in the end, victory-loving and honor-loving men become lovers of making money, or money-lovers. And they praise and admire wealthy people and appoint them as rulers, while they dishonor poor ones.

Certainly.

Then, don't they pass a law that is characteristic of an oligarchic constitution, one that establishes a wealth qualification—higher where the constitution is more oligarchic, less where it's less so—and proclaims that those whose property doesn't reach the stated amount aren't qualified to   *b* rule? And they either put this through by force of arms, or else, before it comes to that, they terrorize the people and establish their constitution that way. Isn't that so?

Of course it is.

Generally speaking, then, that's the way this kind of constitution is established.

Yes, but what is its character? And what are the faults that we said it contained?   *c*

First of all, the very thing that defines it is one, for what would happen if someone were to choose the captains of ships by their wealth, refusing to entrust the ship to a poor person even if he was a better captain?

They would make a poor voyage of it.

And isn't the same true of the rule of anything else whatsoever?

I suppose so.

Except a city? Or does it also apply to a city?

To it most of all, since it's the most difficult and most important kind of rule.

That, then, is one major fault in oligarchy.   *d*

Apparently.

And what about this second fault? Is it any smaller than the other?
What fault?

That of necessity it isn't one city but two—one of the poor and one of
the rich—living in the same place and always plotting against one another.

By god, that's just as big a fault as the first.

And the following is hardly a fine quality either, namely, that oligarchs
probably aren't able to fight a war, for they'd be compelled either to arm
and use the majority, and so have more to fear from them than the enemy,

e   or not to use them and show up as true oligarchs—few in number—on
the battlefield. At the same time, they'd be unwilling to pay mercenaries,
because of their love of money.

That certainly isn't a fine quality either.

And what about the meddling in other people's affairs that we condemned before? Under this constitution, won't the same people be farmers, money-makers, and soldiers simultaneously? And do you think it's

552 right for things to be that way?

Not at all.

Now, let's see whether this constitution is the first to admit the greatest
of all evils.

Which one is that?

Allowing someone to sell all his possessions and someone else to buy
them and then allowing the one who has sold them to go on living in the
city, while belonging to none of its parts, for he's neither a money-maker,
a craftsman, a member of the cavalry, or a hoplite, but a poor person
without means.

b   It is the first to allow that.

At any rate, this sort of thing is not forbidden in oligarchies. If it were,
some of their citizens wouldn't be excessively rich, while others are totally
impoverished.

That's right.

Now, think about this. When the person who sells all his possessions
was rich and spending his money, was he of any greater use to the city in
the ways we've just mentioned than when he'd spent it all? Or did he
merely seem to be one of the rulers of the city, while in truth he was
neither ruler nor subject there, but only a squanderer of his property?

That's right. He seemed to be part of the city, but he was nothing but

c   a squanderer.

Should we say, then, that, as a drone exists in a cell and is an affliction
to the hive, so this person is a drone in the house and an affliction to the
city?

That's certainly right, Socrates.

Hasn't the god made all the winged drones stingless, Adeimantus, as

well as some wingless ones, while other wingless ones have dangerous
stings? And don't the stingless ones continue as beggars into old age, while
those with stings become what we call evildoers?   *d*
    That's absolutely true.
    Clearly, then, in any city where you see beggars, there are thieves,
pickpockets, temple-robbers, and all such evildoers hidden.
    That is clear.
    What about oligarchic cities? Don't you see beggars in them?
    Almost everyone except the rulers is a beggar there.
    Then mustn't we suppose that they also include many evildoers with   *e*
stings, whom the rulers carefully keep in check by force?
    We certainly must.
    And shall we say that the presence of such people is the result of lack
of education, bad rearing, and a bad constitutional arrangement?
    We shall.
    This, then, or something like it, is the oligarchic city. It contains all
these evils and probably others in addition.
    That's pretty well what it's like.
    Then, let's take it that we've disposed of the constitution called oligar-
chy—I mean the one that gets its rulers on the basis of a property assess- *553*
ment—and let's examine the man who is like it, both how he comes to be
and what sort of man he is.
    All right.
    Doesn't the transformation from the timocrat we described to an oli-
garch occur mostly in this way?
    Which way?
    The timocrat's son at first emulates his father and follows in his foot-
steps. Then he suddenly sees him crashing against the city like a ship
against a reef, spilling out all his possessions, even his life. He had held   *b*
a generalship or some other high office, was brought to court by false
witnesses, and was either put to death or exiled or was disenfranchised
and had all his property confiscated.
    That's quite likely.
    The son sees all this, suffers from it, loses his property, and, fearing for
his life, immediately drives from the throne in his own soul the honor-
loving and spirited part that ruled there. Humbled by poverty, he turns
greedily to making money, and, little by little, saving and working, he   *c*
amasses property. Don't you think that this person would establish his
appetitive and money-making part on the throne, setting it up as a great
king within himself, adorning it with golden tiaras and collars and girding
it with Persian swords?
    I do.

He makes the rational and spirited parts sit on the ground beneath
d   appetite, one on either side, reducing them to slaves. He won't allow the
first to reason about or examine anything except how a little money can
be made into great wealth. And he won't allow the second to value or
admire anything but wealth and wealthy people or to have any ambition
other than the acquisition of wealth or whatever might contribute to getting
it.

There is no other transformation of a young man who is an honor-lover
into one who is a money-lover that's as swift and sure as this.

e   Then isn't this an oligarchic man?

Surely, he developed out of a man who resembled the constitution from
which oligarchy came.

Then let's consider whether he resembles the oligarchic constitution?
554   All right.

Doesn't he resemble it, in the first place, by attaching the greatest
importance to money?

Of course.

And, further, by being a thrifty worker, who satisfies only his necessary
appetites, makes no other expenditures, and enslaves his other desires as
vain.

That's right.

A somewhat squalid fellow, who makes a profit from everything and
hoards it—the sort the majority admires. Isn't this the man who resembles
b   such a constitution?

That's my opinion, anyway. At any rate, money is valued above everything by both the city and the man.

I don't suppose that such a man pays any attention to education.

Not in my view, for, if he did, he wouldn't have chosen a blind leader
for his chorus and honored him most.[17]

Good. But consider this: Won't we say that, because of his lack of
education, the dronish appetites—some beggarly and others evil—exist in
c   him, but that they're forcibly held in check by his carefulness?

Certainly.

Do you know where you should look to see the evildoings of such
people?

Where?

To the guardianship of orphans or something like that, where they have
ample opportunity to do injustice with impunity.

True.

---

17. The blind leader is Plutus, the god of wealth, who is represented as being blind,
e.g. in Aristophanes' *Plutus*.

And doesn't this make it clear that, in those other contractual obligations, where he has a good reputation and is thought to be just, he's forcibly holding his other evil appetites in check by means of some decent part of himself? He holds them in check, not by persuading them that it's *d* better not to act on them or taming them with arguments, but by compulsion and fear, trembling for his other possessions.

That's right.

And, by god, you'll find that most of them have appetites akin to those of the drone, once they have other people's money to spend.

You certainly will.

Then someone like that wouldn't be entirely free from internal civil war and wouldn't be one but in some way two,[18] though generally his better desires are in control of his worse.   *e*

That's right.

For this reason, he'd be more respectable than many, but the true virtue of a single-minded and harmonious soul far escapes him.

I suppose so.

Further, this thrifty man is a poor individual contestant for victory in a city or for any other fine and much-honored thing, for he's not willing to spend money for the sake of a fine reputation or on contests for such *555* things. He's afraid to arouse his appetites for spending or to call on them as allies to obtain victory, so he fights like an oligarch, with only a few of his resources. Hence he's mostly defeated but remains rich.

That's right.

Then have we any further doubt that a thrifty money-maker is like an oligarchic city?   *b*

None at all.

It seems, then, that we must next consider democracy, how it comes into being, and what character it has when it does, so that, knowing in turn the character of a man who resembles it, we can present him for judgment.

That would be quite consistent with what we've been doing.

Well, isn't the city changed from an oligarchy to a democracy in some such way as this, because of its insatiable desire to attain what it has set before itself as the good, namely, the need to become as rich as possible?

In what way?

Since those who rule in the city do so because they own a lot, I suppose *c* they're unwilling to enact laws to prevent young people who've had no discipline from spending and wasting their wealth, so that by making loans

18. See 443c–444.

to them, secured by the young people's property, and then calling those
loans in, they themselves become even richer and more honored.

That's their favorite thing to do.

So isn't it clear by now that it is impossible for a city to honor wealth
and at the same time for its citizens to acquire moderation, but one or the
d other is inevitably neglected?

That's pretty clear.

Because of this neglect and because they encourage bad discipline,
oligarchies not infrequently reduce people of no common stamp to poverty.

That's right.

And these people sit idle in the city, I suppose, with their stings and
weapons—some in debt, some disenfranchised, some both—hating those
who've acquired their property, plotting against them and others, and
e longing for a revolution.

They do.

The money-makers, on the other hand, with their eyes on the ground,
pretend not to see these people,[19] and by lending money they disable any
of the remainder who resist, exact as interest many times the principal
sum, and so create a considerable number of drones and beggars in the
556 city.

A considerable number indeed.

In any case, they are unwilling to quench this kind of evil as it flares up
in the city, either in the way we mentioned, by preventing people from
doing whatever they like with their own property or by another law which
would also solve the problem.

What law?

The second-best one, which compels the citizens to care about virtue
by prescribing that the majority of voluntary contracts be entered into at
b the lender's own risk, for lenders would be less shameless then in their
pursuit of money in the city and fewer of those evils we were mentioning
just now would develop.

Far fewer.

But as it is, for all these reasons, the rulers in the city treat their subjects
in the way we described. But as for themselves and their children, don't
they make their young fond of luxury, incapable of effort either mental or
c physical, too soft to stand up to pleasures or pains, and idle besides?

Of course.

And don't they themselves neglect everything except making money,
caring no more for virtue than the poor do?

19. Their eyes are on the ground because their appetite for money forces their souls
to look downward. See 518c–519b.

Yes.

But when rulers and subjects in this condition meet on a journey or some other common undertaking—it might be a festival, an embassy, or a campaign, or they might be shipmates or fellow soldiers—and see one another in danger, in these circumstances are the poor in any way despised by the rich? Or rather isn't it often the case that a poor man, lean and   *d* suntanned, stands in battle next to a rich man, reared in the shade and carrying a lot of excess flesh, and sees him panting and at a loss? And don't you think that he'd consider that it's through the cowardice of the poor that such people are rich and that one poor man would say to another when they met in private: "These people are at our mercy; they're good for nothing"?   *e*

I know very well that's what they would do.

Then, as a sick body needs only a slight shock from outside to become ill and is sometimes at civil war with itself even without this, so a city in the same condition needs only a small pretext—such as one side bringing in allies from an oligarchy or the other from a democracy—to fall ill and to fight with itself and is sometimes in a state of civil war even without any external influence.

Absolutely.   *557*

And I suppose that democracy comes about when the poor are victorious, killing some of their opponents and expelling others, and giving the rest an equal share in ruling under the constitution, and for the most part assigning people to positions of rule by lot.

Yes, that's how democracy is established, whether by force of arms or because those on the opposing side are frightened into exile.

Then how do these people live? What sort of constitution do they have? It's clear that a man who is like it will be democratic.   *b*

That is clear.

First of all, then, aren't they free? And isn't the city full of freedom and freedom of speech? And doesn't everyone in it have the license to do what he wants?

That's what they say, at any rate.

And where people have this license, it's clear that each of them will arrange his own life in whatever manner pleases him.

It is.

Then I suppose that it's most of all under this constitution that one finds people of all varieties.   *c*

Of course.

Then it looks as though this is the finest or most beautiful of the constitutions, for, like a coat embroidered with every kind of ornament, this city, embroidered with every kind of character type, would seem to be the most beautiful. And many people would probably judge it to be so, as women and children do when they see something multicolored.

They certainly would.

d It's also a convenient place to look for a constitution.

Why's that?

Because it contains all kinds of constitutions on account of the license it gives its citizens. So it looks as though anyone who wants to put a city in order, as we were doing, should probably go to a democracy, as to a supermarket of constitutions, pick out whatever pleases him, and establish that.

e He probably wouldn't be at a loss for models, at any rate.

In this city, there is no requirement to rule, even if you're capable of it, or again to be ruled if you don't want to be, or to be at war when the others are, or at peace unless you happen to want it. And there is no requirement in the least that you not serve in public office as a juror, if you happen to want to serve, even if there is a law forbidding you to do *558* so. Isn't that a divine and pleasant life, while it lasts?

It probably is—while it lasts.

And what about the calm of some of their condemned criminals? Isn't that a sign of sophistication? Or have you never seen people who've been condemned to death or exile under such a constitution stay on at the center of things, strolling around like the ghosts of dead heroes, without anyone staring at them or giving them a thought?

Yes, I've seen it a lot.

b And what about the city's tolerance? Isn't it so completely lacking in small-mindedness that it utterly despises the things we took so seriously when we were founding our city, namely, that unless someone had transcendent natural gifts, he'd never become good unless he played the right games and followed a fine way of life from early childhood? Isn't it magnificent the way it tramples all this underfoot, by giving no thought to what someone was doing before he entered public life and by honoring *c* him if only he tells them that he wishes the majority well?

Yes, it's altogether splendid!

Then these and others like them are the characteristics of democracy. And it would seem to be a pleasant constitution, which lacks rulers but not variety and which distributes a sort of equality to both equals and unequals alike.

We certainly know what you mean.

Consider, then, what private individual resembles it. Or should we first inquire, as we did with the city, how he comes to be?

Yes, we should.

Well, doesn't it happen like this? Wouldn't the son of that thrifty oligarch *d* be brought up in his father's ways?

Of course.

Then he too rules his spendthrift pleasures by force—the ones that aren't money-making and are called unnecessary.

Clearly.

But, so as not to discuss this in the dark, do you want us first to define which desires are necessary and which aren't?

I do.

Aren't those we can't desist from and those whose satisfaction benefits us rightly called necessary, for we are by nature compelled to satisfy them both? Isn't that so?   *e*

Of course.

So we'd be right to apply the term "necessary" to them?   *559*

We would.

What about those that someone could get rid of if he practiced from youth on, those whose presence leads to no good or even to the opposite? If we said that all of them were unnecessary, would we be right?

We would.

Let's pick an example of each, so that we can grasp the patterns they exhibit.

We should do that.

Aren't the following desires necessary: the desire to eat to the point of health and well-being and the desire for bread and delicacies?   *b*

I suppose so.

The desire for bread is necessary on both counts; it's beneficial, and unless it's satisfied, we die.[20]

Yes.

The desire for delicacies is also necessary to the extent that it's beneficial to well-being.

Absolutely.

What about the desire that goes beyond these and seeks other sorts of foods, that most people can get rid of, if it's restrained and educated while they're young, and that's harmful both to the body and to the reason and moderation of the soul? Would it be rightly called unnecessary?   *c*

It would indeed.

Then wouldn't we also say that such desires are spendthrift, while the earlier ones are money-making, because they profit our various projects?

Certainly.

And won't we say the same about the desire for sex and about other desires?

Yes.

And didn't we say that the person we just now called a drone is full of

20. Bread is here the "stuff of life." That's why one dies for want of it.

d
such pleasures and desires, since he is ruled by the unnecessary ones,
while a thrifty oligarch is ruled by his necessary desires?

We certainly did.

Let's go back, then, and explain how the democratic man develops out
of the oligarchic one. It seems to me as though it mostly happens as
follows.

How?

When a young man, who is reared in the miserly and uneducated
manner we described, tastes the honey of the drones and associates with
wild and dangerous creatures who can provide every variety of multicolored pleasure in every sort of way, this, as you might suppose, is the
beginning of his transformation from having an oligarchic constitution
within him to having a democratic one.

e

It's inevitable that this is how it starts.

And just as the city changed when one party received help from like-
minded people outside, doesn't the young man change when one party of
his desires receives help from external desires that are akin to them and
of the same form?

Absolutely.

And I suppose that, if any contrary help comes to the oligarchic party
within him, whether from his father or from the rest of his household,
who exhort and reproach him, then there's civil war and counterrevolution
within him, and he battles against himself.

560

That's right.

Sometimes the democratic party yields to the oligarchic, so that some
of the young man's appetites are overcome, others are expelled, a kind of
shame rises in his soul, and order is restored.

That does sometimes happen.

But I suppose that, as desires are expelled, others akin to them are
being nurtured unawares, and because of his father's ignorance about how
to bring him up, they grow numerous and strong.

b

That's what tends to happen.

These desires draw him back into the same bad company and in secret
intercourse breed a multitude of others.

Certainly.

And, seeing the citadel of the young man's soul empty of knowledge,
fine ways of living, and words of truth (which are the best watchmen and
guardians of the thoughts of those men whom the gods love), they finally
occupy that citadel themselves.

c

They certainly do.

And in the absence of these guardians, false and boastful words and
beliefs rush up and occupy this part of him.

Indeed, they do.

Won't he then return to these lotus-eaters and live with them openly? And if some help comes to the thrifty part of his soul from his household, won't these boastful words close the gates of the royal wall within him to prevent these allies from entering and refuse even to receive the words of older private individuals as ambassadors? Doing battle and controlling things themselves, won't they call reverence foolishness and moderation   *d* cowardice, abusing them and casting them out beyond the frontiers like disenfranchised exiles? And won't they persuade the young man that measured and orderly expenditure is boorish and mean, and, joining with many useless desires, won't they expel it across the border?

They certainly will.

Having thus emptied and purged these from the soul of the one they've possessed and initiated in splendid rites, they proceed to return insolence, anarchy, extravagance, and shamelessness from exile in a blaze of torch-   *e* light, wreathing them in garlands and accompanying them with a vast chorus of followers. They praise the returning exiles and give them fine names, calling insolence good breeding, anarchy freedom, extravagance magnificence, and shamelessness courage. Isn't it in some such way as this that someone who is young changes, after being brought up with necessary desires, to the liberation and release of useless and unnecessary *561* pleasures?

Yes, that's clearly the way it happens.

And I suppose that after that he spends as much money, effort, and time on unnecessary pleasures as on necessary ones. If he's lucky, and his frenzy doesn't go too far, when he grows older, and the great tumult within him has spent itself, he welcomes back some of the exiles, ceases to surrender himself completely to the newcomers, and puts his pleasures   *b* on an equal footing. And so he lives, always surrendering rule over himself to whichever desire comes along, as if it were chosen by lot.[21] And when that is satisfied, he surrenders the rule to another, not disdaining any but satisfying them all equally.

That's right.

And he doesn't admit any word of truth into the guardhouse, for if someone tells him that some pleasures belong to fine and good desires and others to evil ones and that he must pursue and value the former and   *c* restrain and enslave the latter, he denies all this and declares that all pleasures are equal and must be valued equally.

---

21. Many public officials were elected by lot in Athens. Socrates seems to have been opposed to this practice. See Aristotle, *Rhetoric* 1393b5–9 and Xenophon, *Memorabilia* I.ii.9–10.

That's just what someone in that condition would do.

And so he lives on, yielding day by day to the desire at hand. Sometimes he drinks heavily while listening to the flute; at other times, he drinks only water and is on a diet; sometimes he goes in for physical training; at other
d times, he's idle and neglects everything; and sometimes he even occupies himself with what he takes to be philosophy. He often engages in politics, leaping up from his seat and saying and doing whatever comes into his mind. If he happens to admire soldiers, he's carried in that direction, if money-makers, in that one. There's neither order nor necessity in his life, but he calls it pleasant, free, and blessedly happy, and he follows it for as long as he lives.

e You've perfectly described the life of a man who believes in legal equality.

I also suppose that he's a complex man, full of all sorts of characters, fine and multicolored, just like the democratic city, and that many men and women might envy his life, since it contains the most models of constitutions and ways of living.

That's right.

Then shall we set this man beside democracy as one who is rightly
562 called democratic?

Let's do so.

The finest constitution and the finest man remain for us to discuss, namely, tyranny and a tyrannical man.

They certainly do.

Come, then, how does tyranny come into being? It's fairly clear that it evolves from democracy.

It is.

And doesn't it evolve from democracy in much the same way that
b democracy does from oligarchy?

What way is that?

The good that oligarchy puts before itself and because of which it is established is wealth, isn't it?

Yes.

And its insatiable desire for wealth and its neglect of other things for the sake of money-making is what destroyed it, isn't it?

That's true.

And isn't democracy's insatiable desire for what it defines as the good also what destroys it?

What do you think it defines as the good?

Freedom: Surely you'd hear a democratic city say that this is the finest
c thing it has, so that as a result it is the only city worth living in for someone who is by nature free.

Yes, you often hear that.

Then, as I was about to say, doesn't the insatiable desire for freedom and the neglect of other things change this constitution and put it in need of a dictatorship?

In what way?

I suppose that, when a democratic city, athirst for freedom, happens to get bad cupbearers for its leaders, so that it gets drunk by drinking more than it should of the unmixed wine of freedom,[22] then, unless the rulers   *d* are very pliable and provide plenty of that freedom, they are punished by the city and accused of being accursed oligarchs.

Yes, that is what it does.

It insults those who obey the rulers as willing slaves and good-for-nothings and praises and honors, both in public and in private, rulers who behave like subjects and subjects who behave like rulers. And isn't it inevitable that freedom should go to all lengths in such a city?   *e*

Of course.

It makes its way into private households and in the end breeds anarchy even among the animals.

What do you mean?

I mean that a father accustoms himself to behave like a child and fear his sons, while the son behaves like a father, feeling neither shame nor fear in front of his parents, in order to be free. A resident alien or a foreign visitor is made equal to a citizen, and he is their equal.   *563*

Yes, that is what happens.

It does. And so do other little things of the same sort. A teacher in such a community is afraid of his students and flatters them, while the students despise their teachers or tutors. And, in general, the young imitate their elders and compete with them in word and deed, while the old stoop to the level of the young and are full of play and pleasantry, imitating the young for fear of appearing disagreeable and authoritarian.   *b*

Absolutely.

The utmost freedom for the majority is reached in such a city when bought slaves, both male and female, are no less free than those who bought them. And I almost forgot to mention the extent of the legal equality of men and women and of the freedom in the relations between them.

What about the animals? Are we, with Aeschylus, going to "say whatever it was that came to our lips just now" about them?[23]   *c*

Certainly. I put it this way: No one who hasn't experienced it would

22. The Greeks drank their wine mixed with water.
23. We no longer possess the play from which this fragment comes.

believe how much freer domestic animals are in a democratic city than anywhere else. As the proverb says, dogs become like their mistresses; horses and donkeys are accustomed to roam freely and proudly along the streets, bumping into anyone who doesn't get out of their way; and all the
d rest are equally full of freedom.

You're telling me what I already know. I've often experienced that sort of thing while travelling in the country.

To sum up: Do you notice how all these things together make the citizens' souls so sensitive that, if anyone even puts upon *himself* the least degree of slavery, they become angry and cannot endure it. And in the end, as you know, they take no notice of the laws, whether written or
e unwritten, in order to avoid having any master at all.

I certainly do.

This, then, is the fine and impetuous origin from which tyranny seems to me to evolve.

It is certainly impetuous. But what comes next?

The same disease that developed in oligarchy and destroyed it also develops here, but it is more widespread and virulent because of the general permissiveness, and it eventually enslaves democracy. In fact, excessive action in one direction usually sets up a reaction in the opposite direction. This happens in seasons, in plants, in bodies, and, last but not
564 least, in constitutions.

That's to be expected.

Extreme freedom can't be expected to lead to anything but a change to extreme slavery, whether for a private individual or for a city.

No, it can't.

Then I don't suppose that tyranny evolves from any constitution other than democracy—the most severe and cruel slavery from the utmost freedom.

Yes, that's reasonable.

But I don't think that was your question. You asked what was the disease
b that developed in oligarchy and also in democracy, enslaving it.

That's true.

And what I had in mind as an answer was that class of idle and extravagant men, whose bravest members are leaders and the more cowardly ones followers. We compared them to stinged and stingless drones, respectively.

That's right.

Now, these two groups cause problems in any constitution, just as phlegm and bile do in the body. And it's against them that the good doctor
c and lawgiver of a city must take advance precautions, first, to prevent their presence and, second, to cut them out of the hive as quickly as possible, cells and all, if they should happen to be present.

Yes, by god, he must cut them out altogether.

Then let's take up the question in the following way, so that we can see what we want more clearly.

In what way?

Let's divide a democratic city into three parts in theory, this being the way that it is in fact divided. One part is this class of idlers, that grows here no less than in an oligarchy, because of the general permissiveness.   *d*

So it does.

But it is far fiercer in democracy than in the other.

How so?

In an oligarchy it is fierce because it's disdained, but since it is prevented from having a share in ruling, it doesn't get any exercise and doesn't become vigorous. In a democracy, however, with a few exceptions, this class is the dominant one. Its fiercest members do all the talking and acting, while the rest settle near the speaker's platform and buzz and refuse to tolerate the opposition of another speaker, so that, under a democratic constitution, with the few exceptions I referred to before, this class manages everything.   *e*

That's right.

Then there's a second class that always distinguishes itself from the majority of people.

Which is that?

When everybody is trying to make money, those who are naturally most organized generally become the wealthiest.

Probably so.

Then they would provide the most honey for the drones and the honey that is most easily extractable by them.

Yes, for how could anyone extract it from those who have very little?

Then I suppose that these rich people are called drone-fodder.

Something like that.

The people—those who work with their own hands—are the third class.   *565*
They take no part in politics and have few possessions, but, when they are assembled, they are the largest and most powerful class in a democracy.

They are. But they aren't willing to assemble often unless they get a share of the honey.

And they always do get a share, though the leaders, in taking the wealth of the rich and distributing it to the people, keep the greater part for themselves.

Yes, that is the way the people get their share.   *b*

And I suppose that those whose wealth is taken away are compelled to defend themselves by speaking before the people and doing whatever else they can.

Of course.

And they're accused by the drones of plotting against the people and of being oligarchs, even if they have no desire for revolution at all.

That's right.

So in the end, when they see the people trying to harm them, they truly
c do become oligarchs and embrace oligarchy's evils, whether they want to or not. But neither group does these things willingly. Rather the people act as they do because they are ignorant and are deceived by the drones, and the rich act as they do because they are driven to it by the stinging of those same drones.

Absolutely.

And then there are impeachments, judgments, and trials on both sides.

That's right.

Now, aren't the people always in the habit of setting up one man as their special champion, nurturing him and making him great?

They are.

d And it's clear that, when a tyrant arises, this special leadership is the sole root from which he sprouts.

It is.

What is the beginning of the transformation from leader of the people to tyrant? Isn't it clear that it happens when the leader begins to behave like the man in the story told about the temple of the Lycaean Zeus[24] in Arcadia?

What story is that?

That anyone who tastes the one piece of human innards that's chopped up with those of other sacrificial victims must inevitably become a wolf.
e Haven't you heard that story?

I have.

Then doesn't the same happen with a leader of the people who dominates a docile mob and doesn't restrain himself from spilling kindred blood? He brings someone to trial on false charges and murders him (as tyrants so often do), and, by thus blotting out a human life, his impious tongue and lips taste kindred citizen blood. He banishes some, kills others, and drops hints to the people about the cancellation of debts and the
566 redistribution of land. And because of these things, isn't a man like that inevitably fated either to be killed by his enemies or to be transformed from a man into a wolf by becoming a tyrant?

It's completely inevitable.

He's the one who stirs up civil wars against the rich.

He is.

---

24. Zeus the wolf-god.

And if he's exiled but manages, despite his enemies, to return, doesn't he come back as a full-fledged tyrant?[25]

Clearly.

And if these enemies are unable to expel him or to put him to death by accusing him before the city, they plot secretly to kill him.

That's usually what happens at least.

And all who've reached this stage soon discover the famous request of the tyrant, namely, that the people give him a bodyguard to keep their defender safe for them.

That's right.

And the people give it to him, I suppose, because they *are* afraid for his safety but aren't worried at all about their own.

That's right.

And when a wealthy man sees this and is charged with being an enemy of the people because of his wealth, then, as the oracle to Croesus put it, he

> *Flees to the banks of the many-pebbled Hermus,*
> *Neither staying put nor being ashamed of his cowardice.*[26]

He wouldn't get a second chance of being ashamed.

That's true, for if he was caught, he'd be executed.

He most certainly would.

But, as for the leader, he doesn't lie on the ground "mighty in his might,"[27] but, having brought down many others, he stands in the city's chariot, a complete tyrant rather than a leader.

What else?

Then let's describe the happiness of this man and of the city in which a mortal like him comes to be.

Certainly, let's do so.

During the first days of his reign and for some time after, won't he smile in welcome at anyone he meets, saying that he's no tyrant, making all sorts of promises both in public and in private, freeing the people from debt, redistributing the land to them and to his followers, and pretending to be gracious and gentle to all?

He'd have to.

---

25. Plato seems to be alluding to the tyrant Peisistratus. In 560 B.C. he made himself tyrant with the help of a bodyguard granted to him by the Athenian people. After five years, he was expelled. Eventually he returned to Athens and used mercenaries to establish himself firmly as tyrant. He died in 527. See Herodotus 1.59–64.

26. The story of the Delphic oracle to Croesus is found in Herodotus 1.55.

27. See *Iliad* 16.776.

But I suppose that, when he has dealt with his exiled enemies by making peace with some and destroying others, so that all is quiet on that front, the first thing he does is to stir up a war, so that the people will continue to feel the need of a leader.

Probably so.

But also so that they'll become poor through having to pay war taxes, 567 for that way they'll have to concern themselves with their daily needs and be less likely to plot against him.

Clearly.

Besides, if he suspects some people of having thoughts of freedom and of not favoring his rule, can't he find a pretext for putting them at the mercy of the enemy in order to destroy them? And for all these reasons, isn't it necessary for a tyrant to be always stirring up war?

It is.

b   And because of this, isn't he all the more readily hated by the citizens?

Of course.

Moreover, don't the bravest of those who helped to establish his tyranny and who hold positions of power within it speak freely to each other and to him, criticizing what's happening?

They probably do.

Then the tyrant will have to do away with all of them if he intends to rule, until he's left with neither friend nor enemy of any worth.

Clearly.

He must, therefore, keep a sharp lookout for anyone who is brave, large-minded, knowledgeable, or rich. And so happy is he that he must c   be the enemy of them all, whether he wants to be or not, and plot against them until he has purged them from the city.

That's a fine sort of purge!

Yes, for it's the opposite of the one that doctors perform on the body. They draw off the worst and leave the best, but he does just the opposite.

Yet I expect he'll have to do this, if he's really going to rule.

d   It's a blessedly happy necessity he's bound by, since it requires him either to live with the inferior majority, even though they hate him, or not to live at all.

Yet that's exactly his condition.

And won't he need a larger and more loyal bodyguard, the more his actions make the citizens hate him?

Of course.

And who will these trustworthy people be? And where will he get them from?

They'll come swarming of their own accord, if he pays them.

Drones, by the dog! All manner of foreign drones! That's what I think e   you're talking about.

You're right.

But what about in the city itself? Wouldn't he be willing . . .

Willing to what?

To deprive citizens of their slaves by freeing them and enlisting them in his bodyguard?

He certainly would, since they'd be likely to prove most loyal to him.

What a blessedly happy sort of fellow you make the tyrant out to be, if these are the sort of people he employs as friends and loyal followers after he's done away with the earlier ones.   *568*

Nonetheless, they're the sort he employs.

And these companions and new citizens admire and associate with him, while the decent people hate and avoid him.

Of course.

It isn't for nothing, then, that tragedy in general has the reputation of being wise and that Euripides is thought to be outstandingly so.

Why's that?

Because among other shrewd things he said that "tyrants are wise who associate with the wise." And by "the wise" he clearly means the sort of people that we've seen to be the tyrant's associates.[28]   *b*

Yes. And he and the other poets eulogize tyranny as godlike and say lots of other such things about it.

Then, surely, since the tragic poets are wise, they'll forgive us and those whose constitutions resemble ours, if we don't admit them into our city, since they praise tyranny.

I suppose that the more sophisticated among them will.   *c*

And so I suppose that they go around to other cities, draw crowds, hire people with fine, big, persuasive voices, and lead their constitutions to tyranny and democracy.

They do indeed.

And besides this, they receive wages and honors, especially—as one might expect—from the tyrants and, in second place, from the democracies, but the higher they go on the ascending scale of constitutions, the more their honor falls off, as if unable to keep up with them for lack of   *d* breath.

Absolutely.

But we digress. So let's return to that fine, numerous, diverse, and ever-changing bodyguard of the tyrant and explain how he'll pay for it.

Clearly, if there are sacred treasuries in the city, he'll use them for as

---

28. The fragment is from an unknown play. Euripides meant that tyrants gain wisdom from the wise people who, as Simonides said, "knock at the doors of the rich" (see 489b). But Plato twists his words to mean that the drones and slaves, who are the tyrant's last resort, must be deemed wise, since they associate with him.

long as they last, as well as the property of the people he has destroyed, thus requiring smaller taxes from the people.

e   What about when these give out?

Clearly, both he and his fellow revellers—his companions, male or female—will have to feed off his father's estate.

I understand. You mean that the people, who fathered the tyrant, will have to feed him and his companions.

They'll be forced to do so.

And what would you have to say about this? What if the people get angry and say, first, that it isn't just for a grown-up son to be fed by his father but, on the contrary, for the father to be fed by his son; second, that they didn't father him and establish him in power so that, when he'd become

569 strong, they'd be enslaved to their own slave and have to feed both him and his slaves, along with other assorted rabble, but because they hoped that, with him as their leader, they'd be free from the rich and the so-called fine and good people in the city; third, that they therefore order him and his companions to leave the city, just as a father might drive a son and his troublesome fellow revellers from his house?

Then, by god, the people will come to know what kind of creature they have fathered, welcomed, and made strong and that they are the weaker

b   trying to drive out the stronger.

What do you mean? Will the tyrant dare to use violence against his father or to hit him if he doesn't obey?

Yes—once he's taken away his father's weapons.

You mean that the tyrant is a parricide and a harsh nurse of old age, that his rule has become an acknowledged tyranny at last, and that—as the saying goes—by trying to avoid the frying pan of enslavement to free men, the people have fallen into the fire of having slaves as their masters,

c   and that in the place of the great but inappropriate freedom they enjoyed under democracy, they have put upon themselves the harshest and most bitter slavery to slaves.

That's exactly what I mean.

Well, then, aren't we justified in saying that we have adequately described how tyranny evolves from democracy and what it's like when it has come into being?

We certainly are, he said.

BOOK IX

Book VIII ended with the description of tyranny. Book IX begins with a long and brilliant description of the tyrannical person himself, notable for its psychological realism and insight. When it is complete, Socrates is ready to respond to the challenge Glaucon raised in Book II.

His response consists of three complex arguments. The first appeals to the foregoing description of the five cities and the five character types. It concludes that a philosopher-king is the happiest and most just of people, a timocrat is second in virtue and happiness, an oligarch third, a democrat fourth, and a tyrant fifth, the most unjust and most wretched of all (580a–c).

The second argument (580d–583b) appeals to the tripartition of the soul. In it Socrates argues that a philosopher's assessment of the relative pleasantness of his life and those of money-lovers and honor-lovers is more reliable than their assessments of the relative pleasantness of his life and theirs.

The third argument (583b–588a), described by Socrates as "the greatest and most decisive of the overthrows," is also the most complex. It uses the metaphysical theory developed in Books V–VII, together with the psychological theory of Book IV, to develop a complex theory of pleasure. It concludes that a philosopher's pleasures are truer and purer than those of a money-lover or honor-lover.

The book ends with a powerful image of what the soul of an unjust person is like.

It remains, I said, to consider the tyrannical man himself, how he evolves from a democrat, what he is like when he has come into being, and whether *571* he is wretched or blessedly happy.

Yes, he said, he is the one who is still missing.

And do you know what else I think is still missing?

What?

I don't think we have adequately distinguished the kinds and numbers of our desires, and, if that subject isn't adequately dealt with, our entire investigation will be less clear. *b*

Well, isn't now as fine a time as any to discuss the matter?

It certainly is. Consider, then, what I want to know about our desires. It's this: Some of our unnecessary pleasures and desires seem to me to be lawless. They are probably present in everyone, but they are held in check by the laws and by the better desires in alliance with reason. In a few people, they have been eliminated entirely or only a few weak ones remain,

c while in others they are stronger and more numerous.

What desires do you mean?

Those that are awakened in sleep, when the rest of the soul—the rational, gentle, and ruling part—slumbers. Then the beastly and savage part, full of food and drink, casts off sleep and seeks to find a way to gratify itself. You know that there is nothing it won't dare to do at such a time, free of all control by shame or reason. It doesn't shrink from trying to

d have sex with a mother, as it supposes, or with anyone else at all, whether man, god, or beast. It will commit any foul murder, and there is no food it refuses to eat. In a word, it omits no act of folly or shamelessness.

That's completely true.

On the other hand, I suppose that someone who is healthy and moderate with himself goes to sleep only after having done the following: First, he rouses his rational part and feasts it on fine arguments and speculations;

e second, he neither starves nor feasts his appetites, so that they will slumber and not disturb his best part with either their pleasure or their pain, but

572 they'll leave it alone, pure and by itself, to look for something—it knows not what—and to try to perceive it,[1] whether it is past, present, or future; third, he soothes his spirited part in the same way, for example, by not falling asleep with his spirit still aroused after an outburst of anger. And when he has quieted these two parts and aroused the third, in which reason resides, and so takes his rest, you know that it is then that he best grasps the truth and that the visions that appear in his dreams are least

b lawless.

Entirely so.

However, we've been carried away from what we wanted to establish, which is this: Our dreams make it clear that there is a dangerous, wild, and lawless form of desire in everyone, even in those of us who seem to be entirely moderate or measured. See whether you think I'm talking sense and whether or not you agree with me.

I do agree.

Recall, then, what we said a democratic man is like. He was produced by being brought up from youth by a thrifty father who valued only those

c desires that make money and who despised the unnecessary ones that aim at frivolity and display. Isn't that right?

Yes.

And by associating with more sophisticated men, who are full of the latter desires, he starts to indulge in every kind of insolence and to adopt

---

1. Reading *skopein kai oregesthai tou kai aisthanesthai ho mē oiden.*

their form of behavior, because of his hatred of his father's thrift. But, because he has a better nature than his corrupters, he is pulled in both directions and settles down in the middle between his father's way of life and theirs. And enjoying each in moderation, as he supposes, he leads a life that is neither slavish nor lawless and from having been oligarchic he *d* becomes democratic.

That was and is our opinion about this type of man.

Suppose now that this man has in turn become older and that *he* has a son who is brought up in *his* father's ethos.

All right.

And further suppose that the same things that happened to his father now happen to him. First, he is led to all the kinds of lawlessness that those who are leading him call freedom. Then his father and the rest of *e* the household come to the aid of the middle desires, while the others help the other ones. Then, when those clever enchanters and tyrant-makers have no hope of keeping hold of the young man in any other way, they contrive to plant in him a powerful erotic love, like a great winged drone, to be the leader of those idle desires that spend whatever is at hand. Or do you think that erotic love is anything other than an enormous drone in *573* such people?

I don't think that it could be anything else.

And when the other desires—filled with incense, myrrh, wreaths, wine, and the other pleasures found in their company—buzz around the drone, nurturing it and making it grow as large as possible, they plant the sting of longing in it. Then this leader of the soul adopts madness as its bodyguard and becomes frenzied. If it finds any beliefs or desires in the *b* man that are thought to be good or that still have some shame, it destroys them and throws them out, until it's purged him of moderation and filled him with imported madness.

You've perfectly described the evolution of a tyrannical man.

Is this the reason that erotic love has long been called a tyrant?

It looks that way.

Then doesn't a drunken man have something of a tyrannical mind? *c*

Yes, he has.

And a man who is mad and deranged attempts to rule not just human beings, but gods as well, and expects that he will be able to succeed.

He certainly does.

Then a man becomes tyrannical in the precise sense of the term when either his nature or his way of life or both of them together make him drunk, filled with erotic desire, and mad.

Absolutely.

This, then, it seems, is how a tyrannical man comes to be. But what way does he live?

d   No doubt *you're* going to tell *me*, just as posers of riddles usually do.

I am. I think that someone in whom the tyrant of erotic love dwells and in whom it directs everything next goes in for feasts, revelries, luxuries, girlfriends, and all that sort of thing.

Necessarily.

And don't many terrible desires grow up day and night beside the tyrannical one, needing many things to satisfy them?

Indeed they do.

Hence any income someone like that has is soon spent.

Of course.

e   Then borrowing follows, and expenditure of capital.

What else?

And when everything is gone, won't the violent crowd of desires that has nested within him inevitably shout in protest? And driven by the stings of the other desires and especially by erotic love itself (which leads all of them as its bodyguard), won't he become frenzied and look to see who
574 possesses anything that he could take, by either deceit or force?

He certainly will.

Consequently, he must acquire wealth from every source or live in great pain and suffering.

He must.

And just as the pleasures that are latecomers outdo the older ones and steal away their satisfactions, won't the man himself think that he deserves to outdo[2] his father and mother, even though he is younger than they are—to take and spend his father's wealth when he's spent his own share?

Of course.

And if they won't give it to him, won't he first try to steal it from them
b   by deceitful means?

Certainly.

And if that doesn't work, wouldn't he seize it by force?

I suppose so.

And if the old man and woman put up a fight, would he be careful to refrain from acting like a tyrant?

I'm not very optimistic about their fate, if they do.

But, good god, Adeimantus, do you think he'd sacrifice his long-loved and irreplaceable mother for a recently acquired girlfriend whom he can do without? Or that for the sake of a newfound and replaceable boyfriend
c   in the bloom of youth, he'd strike his aged and irreplaceable father, his oldest friend? Or that he'd make his parents the slaves of these others, if he brought them under the same roof?

Yes, indeed he would.

---

2. *pleon echein.* See 343e n. 18.

It seems to be a very great blessing to produce a tyrannical son!

It certainly does!

What about when the possessions of his father and mother give out?
With that great swarm of pleasures inside him, won't he first try to break *d*
into someone's house or snatch someone's coat late at night? Then won't
he try to loot a temple? And in all this, the old traditional opinions that he
had held from childhood about what is fine or shameful—opinions that
are accounted just—are overcome by the opinions, newly released from
slavery, that are now the bodyguard of erotic love and hold sway along
with it.[3] When he himself was subject to the laws and his father and had *e*
a democratic constitution within him, these opinions used only to be
freed in sleep. Now, however, under the tyranny of erotic love, he has
permanently become while awake what he used to become occasionally
while asleep, and he won't hold back from any terrible murder or from
any kind of food or act. But, rather, erotic love lives like a tyrant within
him, in complete anarchy and lawlessness as his sole ruler, and drives *575*
him, as if he were a city, to dare anything that will provide sustenance for
itself and the unruly mob around it (some of whose members have come
in from the outside as a result of his keeping bad company, while others
have come from within, freed and let loose by his own bad habits). Isn't
this the life that a tyrannical man leads?

It is indeed.

Now, if there are only a few such men in a city, and the rest of the
people are moderate, this mob will leave the city in order to act as a
bodyguard to some other tyrant or to serve as mercenaries if there happens *b*
to be a war going on somewhere. But if they chance to live in a time of
peace and quiet, they'll remain in the city and bring about lots of little
evils.

What sort of evils do you mean?

They steal, break into houses, snatch purses, steal clothes, rob temples,
and sell people into slavery. Sometimes, if they are good speakers, they
become sycophants and bear false witness and accept bribes.[4]

These evils *are* small, provided that there happen to be only a few such
people.   *c*

Yes, for small things are small by comparison to big ones. And when it
comes to producing wickedness and misery in a city, all these evils together

---

3. See 538c ff.

4. Athens had nothing corresponding to our public prosecutors. By and large, private
citizens prosecuted each other. By the middle of the fifth century, some people began
to make a profession of prosecuting others for financial, political, or personal reasons.
These people were called sycophants. A vivid sense of their power and importance is
conveyed in L. B. Carter, *The Quiet Athenian* (Oxford: Clarendon Press, 1986).

don't, as the saying goes, come within a mile of the rule of a tyrant. But
when such people become numerous and conscious of their numbers, it
is they—aided by the foolishness of the people—who create a tyrant. And
he, more than any of them, has in his soul the greatest and strongest tyrant
d   of all.

Naturally, for he'd be the most tyrannical.

That's if the city happens to yield willingly, but if it resists him, then,
just as he once chastised his mother and father, he'll now chastise his
fatherland, if he can, by bringing in new friends and making his fatherland
and his dear old motherland (as the Cretans call it) their slaves and keeping
them that way, for this is surely the end at which such a man's desires are
directed.

e   It most certainly is.

Now, in private life, before a tyrannical man attains power, isn't he this
sort of person—one who associates primarily with flatterers who are ready
to obey him in everything? Or if he himself happens to need anything from
other people, isn't he willing to fawn on them and make every gesture of
friendship, as if he were dealing with his own family? But once he gets
576 what he wants, don't they become strangers again?

Yes, they certainly do.

So someone with a tyrannical nature lives his whole life without being
friends with anyone, always a master to one man or a slave to another and
never getting a taste of either freedom or true friendship.

That's right.

Wouldn't we be right to call someone like that untrustworthy?

Of course.

And isn't he as unjust as anyone can be? If indeed what we earlier
b   agreed about justice was right.

And it certainly was right.

Then, let's sum up the worst type of man: His waking life is like the
nightmare we described earlier.[5]

That's right.

And he evolves from someone by nature most tyrannical who achieves
sole rule. And the longer he remains tyrant, the more like the nightmare
he becomes.

That's inevitable, said Glaucon, taking over the argument.

Well, then, I said, isn't the man who is clearly most vicious also clearly
most wretched? And isn't the one who for the longest time is most of all
c   a tyrant, most wretched for the longest time? If, that is to say, truth rather
than majority opinion is to settle these questions.

5. See 571c–d.

That much is certain, at any rate.

And isn't a tyrannical man like a city ruled by a tyrant, a democratic man like a city ruled by a democracy, and similarly with the others?

Of course.

And won't the relations between the cities with respect to virtue and happiness be the same as those between the men?

Certainly.   *d*

Then how does the city ruled by a tyrant compare to the city ruled by kings that we described first?

They are total opposites: one is the best, and the other the worst.

I won't ask you which is which, since it's obvious. But is your judgment the same with regard to their happiness and wretchedness? And let's not be dazzled by looking at one man—a tyrant—or at the few who surround him, but since it is essential to go into the city and study the whole of it, let's not give our opinion, till we've gone down and looked into every corner.   *e*

That's right, for it's clear to everyone that there is no city more wretched than one ruled by a tyrant and none more happy than one ruled by kings.

Would I be right, then, to make the same challenge about the individuals, assuming, first, that the person who is fit to judge them is someone who in *577* thought can go down into a person's character and examine it thoroughly, someone who doesn't judge from outside, the way a child does, who is dazzled by the façade that tyrants adopt for the outside world to see, but is able to see right through that sort of thing? And, second, that he's someone—since we'd all listen to him if he were—who is competent to judge, because he has lived in the same house with a tyrant and witnessed his behavior at home and his treatment of each member of his household when he is stripped of his theatrical façade, and has also seen how he behaves when in danger from the people? Shouldn't we ask the person   *b* who has seen all that to tell us how the tyrant compares to the others in happiness and wretchedness?

That's also right.

Then do you want us to pretend that we are among those who can give such a judgment and that we have already met tyrannical people, so that we'll have someone to answer our questions?

I certainly do.

Come, then, and look at it this way for me: Bearing in mind the   *c* resemblance between the city and the man, look at each in turn and describe its condition.

What kinds of things do you want me to describe?

First, speaking of the city, would you say that a tyrannical city is free or enslaved?

It is as enslaved as it is possible to be.

Yet you see in it people who are masters and free.

I do see a few like that, but the whole city, so to speak, and the most decent part of it are wretched, dishonored slaves.

d   Then, if man and city are alike, mustn't the same structure be in him too? And mustn't his soul be full of slavery and unfreedom, with the most decent parts enslaved and with a small part, the maddest and most vicious, as their master?

It must.

What will you say about such a soul then? Is it free or slave?

Slave, of course.

And isn't the enslaved and tyrannical city least likely to do what it wants?

Certainly.

Then a tyrannical soul—I'm talking about the whole soul—will also be least likely to do what it wants and, forcibly driven by the stings of a *e*   dronish gadfly, will be full of disorder and regret.

How could it be anything else?

Is a tyrannically ruled city rich or poor?

Poor.

578   Then a tyrannical soul, too, must always be poor and unsatisfiable.

That's right.

What about fear? Aren't a tyrannical city and man full of it?

Absolutely.

And do you think that you'll find more wailing, groaning, lamenting, and grieving in any other city?

Certainly not.

Then, are such things more common in anyone besides a tyrannical man, who is maddened by his desires and erotic loves?

How could they be?

b   It is in view of all these things, I suppose, and others like them, that you judged this to be the most wretched of cities.

And wasn't I right?

Of course you were. But what do you say about a tyrannical man, when you look at these same things?

He's by far the most wretched of all of them.

There you're no longer right.

How is that?

I don't think that this man has yet reached the extreme of wretchedness.

Then who has?

Perhaps you'll agree that this next case is even more wretched.

Which one?

c   The one who is tyrannical but doesn't live a private life, because some misfortune provides him with the opportunity to become an actual tyrant.

On the basis of what was said before, I assume that what you say is true.

Yes, but in matters of this sort, it isn't enough just to assume these things; one needs to investigate carefully the two men in question by means of argument, for the investigation concerns the most important thing, namely, the good life and the bad one.

That's absolutely right.

Then consider whether I'm talking sense or not, for I think our investigation will be helped by the following examples.   *d*

What are they?

We should look at all the wealthy private citizens in our cities who have many slaves, for, like a tyrant, they rule over many, although not over so many as he does.

That's right.

And you know that they're secure and do not fear their slaves.

What have they got to be afraid of?

Nothing. And do you know why?

Yes. It's because the whole city is ready to defend each of its individual citizens.

You're right. But what if some god were to lift one of these men, his   *e*
fifty or more slaves, and his wife and children out of the city and deposit him with his slaves and other property in a deserted place, where no free person could come to his assistance? How frightened would he be that he himself and his wife and children would be killed by the slaves?

Very frightened indeed.

And wouldn't he be compelled to fawn on some of his own slaves, promise them lots of things, and free them, even though he didn't want *579* to? And wouldn't he himself have become a panderer to slaves?

He'd have to or else be killed.

What if the god were to settle many other neighbors around him, who wouldn't tolerate anyone to claim that he was the master of another and who would inflict the worst punishments on anyone they caught doing it?

I suppose that he'd have even worse troubles, since he'd be surrounded   *b*
by nothing but vigilant enemies.

And isn't this the kind of prison in which the tyrant is held—the one whose nature is such as we have described it, filled with fears and erotic loves of all kinds? Even though his soul is really greedy for it, he's the only one in the whole city who can't travel abroad or see the sights that other free people want to see. Instead, he lives like a woman, mostly confined to his own house, and envying any other citizen who happens to travel abroad and see something worthwhile.   *c*

That's entirely so.

Then, isn't this harvest of evils a measure of the difference between a tyrannical man who is badly governed on the inside—whom you judged

to be most wretched just now—and one who doesn't live a private life but is compelled by some chance to be a tyrant, who tries to rule others when he can't even control himself. He's just like an exhausted body without any self-control, which, instead of living privately, is compelled to compete
d   and fight with other bodies all its life.

That's exactly what he's like, Socrates, and what you say is absolutely true.

And so, Glaucon, isn't this a completely wretched condition to be in, and doesn't the reigning tyrant have an even harder life than the one you judged to be hardest?

He certainly does.

In truth, then, and whatever some people may think, a real tyrant is really a slave, compelled to engage in the worst kind of fawning, slavery, and pandering to the worst kind of people. He's so far from satisfying his
e   desires in any way that it is clear—if one happens to know that one must study his whole soul—that he's in the greatest need of most things and truly poor. And, if indeed his state is like that of the city he rules, then he's full of fear, convulsions, and pains throughout his life. And it is like it, isn't it?

Of course it is.

580   And we'll also attribute to the man what we mentioned before, namely, that he is inevitably envious, untrustworthy, unjust, friendless, impious, host and nurse to every kind of vice, and that his ruling makes him even more so. And because of all these, he is extremely unfortunate and goes on to make those near him like himself.

No one with any understanding could possibly contradict you.

Come, then, and like the judge who makes the final decision,[6] tell me who among the five—the king, the timocrat, the oligarch, the democrat,
b   and the tyrant—is first in happiness, who second, and so on in order.

That's easy. I rank them in virtue and vice, in happiness and its opposite, in the order of their appearance, as I might judge choruses.

Shall we, then, hire a herald, or shall I myself announce that the son of Ariston has given as his verdict that the best, the most just, and the most
c   happy is the most kingly, who rules like a king over himself, and that the worst, the most unjust, and the most wretched is the most tyrannical, who most tyrannizes himself and the city he rules.

Let it be so announced.

And shall I add to the announcement that it holds, whether these things remain hidden from every god and human being or not?

Add it.

---

6. This probably refers to the way in which plays were judged at festivals.

Good. Then that is one of our proofs. And there'd be a second, if you happen to think that there is anything in this.   *d*

In what?

In the fact that the soul of each individual is divided into three parts, in just the way that a city is, for that's the reason I think that there is another proof.

What is it?

This: it seems to me that there are three pleasures corresponding to the three parts of the soul, one peculiar to each part, and similarly with desires and kinds of rule.

What do you mean?

The first, we say, is the part with which a person learns, and the second the part with which he gets angry. As for the third, we had no one special name for it, since it's multiform, so we named it after the biggest and strongest thing in it. Hence we called it the appetitive part, because of the   *e* intensity of its appetites for food, drink, sex, and all the things associated with them, but we also called it the money-loving part, because such appetites are most easily satisfied by means of money.   *581*

And rightly so.

Then, if we said that its pleasure and love are for profit, wouldn't that best determine its central feature for the purposes of our argument and insure that we are clear about what we mean when we speak of this part of the soul, and wouldn't we be right to call it money-loving and profit-loving?

That's how it seems to me, at least.

What about the spirited part? Don't we say that it is wholly dedicated to the pursuit of control, victory, and high repute?

Certainly.   *b*

Then wouldn't it be appropriate for us to call it victory-loving and honor-loving?

It would be most appropriate.

Now, it is clear to everyone that the part with which we learn is always wholly straining to know where the truth lies and that, of the three parts, it cares least for money and reputation.

By far the least.

Then wouldn't it be appropriate for us to call it learning-loving and philosophical?

Of course.

And doesn't this part rule in some people's souls, while one of the other parts—whichever it happens to be—rules in other people's?   *c*

That's right.

And isn't that the reason we say that there are three primary kinds of people: philosophic, victory-loving, and profit-loving?

That's it precisely.

And also three forms of pleasure, one assigned to each of them?

Certainly.

And do you realize that, if you chose to ask three such people in turn to tell you which of their lives is most pleasant, each would give the highest praise to his own? Won't a money-maker say that the pleasure of being *d* honored and that of learning are worthless compared to that of making a profit, if he gets no money from them?

He will.

What about an honor-lover? Doesn't he think that the pleasure of making money is vulgar and that the pleasure of learning—except insofar as it brings him honor—is smoke and nonsense?

He does.

And as for a philosopher, what do you suppose he thinks the other pleasures are worth compared to that of knowing where the truth lies and *e* always being in some such pleasant condition while learning? Won't he think that they are far behind? And won't he call them really necessary, since he'd have no need for them if they weren't necessary for life?

He will: we can be sure of that.

Then, since there's a dispute between the different forms of pleasure and between the lives themselves, not about which way of living is finer or more shameful or better or worse, but about which is more pleasant *582* and less painful, how are we to know which of them is speaking most truly?

Don't ask me.

Look at it this way: How are we to judge things if we want to judge them well? Isn't it by experience, reason, and argument? Or could anyone have better criteria than these?

How could he?

Consider, then: Which of the three men has most experience of the pleasures we mentioned? Does a profit-lover learn what the truth itself is like or acquire more experience of the pleasure of knowing it than a *b* philosopher does of making a profit?

There's a big difference between them. A philosopher has of necessity tasted the other pleasures since childhood, but it isn't necessary for a profit-lover to taste or experience the pleasure of learning the nature of the things that are and how sweet it is. Indeed, even if he were eager to taste it, he couldn't easily do so.

Then a philosopher is far superior to a profit-lover in his experience of both their pleasures.

c   He certainly is.

What about an honor-lover? Has he more experience of the pleasure of knowing than a philosopher has of the pleasure of being honored?

No, for honor comes to each of them, provided that he accomplishes his aim. A rich man is honored by many people, so is a courageous one and a wise one, but the pleasure of studying the things that are cannot be tasted by anyone except a philosopher.

Then, as far as experience goes, he is the finest judge of the three.   *d*

By far.

And he alone has gained his experience in the company of reason.

Of course.

Moreover, the instrument one must use to judge isn't the instrument of a profit-lover or an honor-lover but a philosopher.

What instrument is that?

Arguments, for didn't we say that we must judge by means of them?

Yes.

And argument is a philosopher's instrument most of all.

Of course.

Now, if wealth and profit were the best means of judging things, the praise and blame of a profit-lover would necessarily be truest.   *e*

That's right.

And if honor, victory, and courage were the best means, wouldn't it be the praise and blame of an honor-lover?

Clearly.

But since the best means are experience, reason, and argument . . .

The praise of a wisdom-lover and argument-lover is necessarily truest.

Then, of the three pleasures, the most pleasant is that of the part of the soul with which we learn, and the one in whom that part rules has the *583* most pleasant life.

How could it be otherwise? A person with knowledge at least speaks with authority when he praises his own life.

To what life and to what pleasure does the judge give second place?

Clearly, he gives it to those of a warrior and honor-lover, since they're closer to his own than those of a money-maker.

Then the life and pleasure of a profit-lover come last, it seems.

Of course they do.

These, then, are two proofs in a row, and the just person has defeated   *b* the unjust one in both. The third is dedicated in Olympic fashion to Olympian Zeus the Savior.[7] Observe then that, apart from those of a knowledgeable person, the other pleasures are neither entirely true nor pure but are like a shadow-painting, as I think I've heard some wise person say. And yet, if this were true, it would be the greatest and most decisive of the overthrows.

---

7. The first toast at a banquet was to the Olympian Zeus, the third to Zeus the Savior. By combining the two aspects of Zeus in a single form of address, Plato seems to be emphasizing the importance of this final proof.

It certainly would. But what exactly do you mean?

c   I'll find out, if I ask the questions, and you answer.

Ask, then.

Tell me, don't we say that pain is the opposite of pleasure?

Certainly.

And is there such a thing as feeling neither pleasure nor pain?

There is.

Isn't it intermediate between these two, a sort of calm of the soul by comparison to them? Or don't you think of it that way?

I do.

And do you recall what sick people say when they're ill?

Which saying of theirs do you have in mind?

That nothing gives more pleasure than being healthy, but that they

d   hadn't realized that it was most pleasant until they fell ill.

I do recall that.

And haven't you also heard those who are in great pain say that nothing is more pleasant than the cessation of their suffering?

I have.

And there are many similar circumstances, I suppose, in which you find people in pain praising, not enjoyment, but the absence of pain and relief from it as most pleasant.

That may be because at such times a state of calm becomes pleasant enough to content them.

e   And when someone ceases to feel pleasure, this calm will be painful to him.

Probably so.

Then the calm we described as being intermediate between pleasure and pain will sometimes be both.

So it seems.

Now, is it possible for that which is neither to become both?

Not in my view.

Moreover, the coming to be of either the pleasant or the painful in the soul is a sort of motion, isn't it?

Yes.

And didn't what is neither painful nor pleasant come to light just now

584 as a calm state, intermediate between them?

Yes, it did.

Then, how can it be right to think that the absence of pain is pleasure or that the absence of pleasure is pain?

There's no way it can be.

Then it isn't right. But when the calm is next to the painful it appears pleasant, and when it is next to the pleasant it appears painful. However, there is nothing sound in these appearances as far as the truth about pleasure is concerned, only some kind of magic.

That's what the argument suggests, at any rate.

Take a look at the pleasures that don't come out of pains, so that you   *b*
won't suppose in their case also that it is the nature of pleasure to be the cessation of pain or of pain to be the cessation of pleasure.

Where am I to look? What pleasures do you mean?

The pleasures of smell are especially good examples to take note of, for they suddenly become very intense without being preceded by pain, and when they cease they leave no pain behind. But there are plenty of other examples as well.

That's absolutely true.

Then let no one persuade us that pure pleasure is relief from pain or that pure pain is relief from pleasure.   *c*

No, let's not.

However, most of the so-called pleasures that reach the soul through the body, as well as the most intense ones are of this form—they are some kind of relief from pain.

Yes, they are.

And aren't the pleasures and pains of anticipation, which arise from the expectation of future pleasures or pains, also of this form?

They are.

Do you know what kind of thing they are and what they most resemble?   *d*

No, what is it?

Do you believe that there is an up, a down, and a middle in nature?

I do.

And do you think that someone who was brought from down below to the middle would have any other belief than that he was moving upward? And if he stood in the middle and saw where he had come from, would he believe that he was anywhere other than the upper region, since he hasn't seen the one that is truly upper?

By god, I don't see how he could think anything else.

And if he was brought back, wouldn't he suppose that he was being brought down? And wouldn't he be right?   *e*

Of course.

Then wouldn't all this happen to him because he is inexperienced in what is really and truly up, down, and in the middle?

Clearly.

Is it any surprise, then, if those who are inexperienced in the truth have unsound opinions about lots of other things as well, or that they are so disposed to pleasure, pain, and the intermediate state that, when they descend to the painful, they believe truly and are really in pain, but that,

585 when they ascend from the painful to the intermediate state, they firmly believe that they have reached fulfillment and pleasure? They are inexperienced in pleasure and so are deceived when they compare pain to painlessness, just as they would be if they compared black to grey without having experienced white.

No, by god, I wouldn't be surprised. In fact, I'd be very surprised if it were any other way.

b   Think of it this way: Aren't hunger, thirst, and the like some sort of empty states of the body?

They are.

And aren't ignorance and lack of sense empty states of the soul?

Of course.

And wouldn't someone who partakes of nourishment or strengthens his understanding be filled?

Certainly.

Does the truer filling up fill you with that which is less or that which is more?

Clearly, it's with that which is more.

And which kinds partake more of pure being? Kinds of filling up such as filling up with bread or drink or delicacies or food in general? Or the kind of filling up that is with true belief, knowledge, understanding, and, in sum, with all of virtue? Judge it this way: That which is related to what

c   is always the same, immortal, and true, is itself of that kind, and comes to be in something of that kind—this is more, don't you think, than that which is related to what is never the same and mortal, is itself of that kind, and comes to be in something of that kind?

That which is related to what is always the same is far more.

And does the being of what is always the same participate more in being than in knowledge?

Not at all.

Or more than in truth?

Not that either.

And if less in truth, then less in being also?

Necessarily.

And isn't it generally true that the kinds of filling up that are concerned

d   with the care of the body share less in truth and being than those concerned with the care of the soul?

Yes, much less.

And don't you think that the same holds of the body in comparison to the soul?

Certainly.

And isn't that which is more, and is filled with things that are more, really more filled than that which is less, and is filled with things that are less?

Of course.

Therefore, if being filled with what is appropriate to our nature is pleasure, that which is more filled with things that are more enjoys more really and truly a more true pleasure, while that which partakes of things *e* that are less is less truly and surely filled and partakes of a less trustworthy and less true pleasure.

That's absolutely inevitable.

Therefore, those who have no experience of reason or virtue, but are always occupied with feasts and the like, are brought down and then back *586* up to the middle, as it seems, and wander in this way throughout their lives, never reaching beyond this to what is truly higher up, never looking up at it or being brought up to it, and so they aren't filled with that which really is and never taste any stable or pure pleasure. Instead, they always look down at the ground like cattle, and, with their heads bent over the dinner table, they feed, fatten, and fornicate. To outdo[8] others in these things, they kick and butt them with iron horns and hooves, killing each *b* other, because their desires are insatiable. For the part that they're trying to fill is like a vessel full of holes, and neither it nor the things they are trying to fill it with are among the things that are.

Socrates, you've exactly described the life of the majority of people, just like an oracle.

Then isn't it necessary for these people to live with pleasures that are mixed with pains, mere images and shadow-paintings of true pleasures? And doesn't the juxtaposition of these pleasures and pains make them appear intense, so that they give rise to mad erotic passions in the foolish, *c* and are fought over in just the way that Stesichorus tells us the phantom of Helen was fought over at Troy by men ignorant of the truth?[9]

Something like that must be what happens.

And what about the spirited part? Mustn't similar things happen to someone who satisfies it? Doesn't his love of honor make him envious and his love of victory make him violent, so that he pursues the satisfaction of his anger and of his desires for honors and victories without calculation *d* or understanding?

Such things must happen to him as well.

Then can't we confidently assert that those desires of even the money-loving and honor-loving parts that follow knowledge and argument and pursue with their help those pleasures that reason approves will attain the truest

8. *Pleonexias.* See 343e n. 18.

9. According to the story, Stesichorus wrote a poem defaming Helen and was punished by being struck with blindness. His sight was restored when he added a verse to the poem in which he claimed that it was a phantom of Helen and not Helen herself who was at Troy. See *Phaedrus* 243a.

pleasures possible for them, because they follow truth, and the ones that are
e   most their own, if indeed what is best for each thing is most its own?

And indeed it is best.

Therefore, when the entire soul follows the philosophic part, and there
is no civil war in it, each part of it does its own work exclusively and is
just, and in particular it enjoys its own pleasures, the best and truest
587 pleasures possible for it.

Absolutely.

But when one of the other parts gains control, it won't be able to secure
its own pleasure and will compel the other parts to pursue an alien and
untrue pleasure.

That's right.

And aren't the parts that are most distant from philosophy and reason
the ones most likely to do this sort of compelling?

They're much more likely.

And isn't whatever is most distant from reason also most distant from
law and order?

Clearly.

And didn't the erotic and tyrannical desires emerge as most distant
b   from these things?

By far.

And weren't the kingly and orderly ones least distant?

Yes.

Then I suppose that a tyrant will be most distant from a pleasure that
is both true and his own and that a king will be least distant.

Necessarily.

So a tyrant will live most unpleasantly, and a king most pleasantly.

Necessarily.

Do you know how much more unpleasant a tyrant's life is than a king's?

I will if you tell me.

There are, it seems, three pleasures, one genuine and two illegitimate,
and a tyrant is at the extreme end of the illegitimate ones, since he flees
c   both law and reason and lives with a bodyguard of certain slavish pleasures.
But it isn't easy, all the same, to say just how inferior he is to a king, except
perhaps as follows. A tyrant is somehow third from an oligarch, for a
democrat was between them.

Yes.

Then, if what we said before is true, doesn't he live with an image of
pleasure that is third from an oligarch's with respect to truth?[10]

---

10. Third because the Greeks always counted the first as well as the last member of
a series, e.g. the day after tomorrow was the third day.

He does.

Now, an oligarch, in turn, is third from a king,[11] if we identify a king
and an aristocrat.   *d*

Yes, he's third.

So a tyrant is three times three times removed from true pleasure.

Apparently so.

It seems then, on the basis of the magnitude of its number, that the
image of tyrannical pleasure is a plane figure.

Exactly.

But then it's clear that, by squaring and cubing it, we'll discover how
far a tyrant's pleasure is from that of a king.

It is clear to a mathematician, at any rate.

Then, turning it the other way around, if someone wants to say how far
a king's pleasure is from a tyrant's, he'll find, if he completes the calculation, that a king lives seven hundred and twenty-nine times more pleasantly   *e*
than a tyrant and that a tyrant is the same number of times more wretched.[12]

That's an amazing calculation of the difference between the pleasure
and pain of the two men, the just and the unjust.   *588*

Yet it's a true one, and one appropriate to human lives, if indeed days,
nights, months, and years are appropriate to them.

And of course they are appropriate.

Then, if a good and just person's life is that much more pleasant than
the life of a bad and unjust person, won't its grace, fineness, and virtue
be incalculably greater?

By god, it certainly will.

All right, then. Since we've reached this point in the argument, let's   *b*

---

11. Because the timocrat is between them.

12. Socrates' mathematics is difficult to follow. He seems to have something like this
in mind. The tyrant's image of pleasure is two-dimensional, whereas the true pleasure
of the philosopher is three-dimensional. Hence, if a one-unit square represents the
degree of closeness to true pleasure of an image nine times removed from it, true
pleasure should be represented by a nine-unit cube. It follows that the king lives 729
times more pleasantly than the tyrant. However, in order to reach the number 729,
which seems to have been significant to Pythagoras and his followers (there were,
allegedly, 729 days and nights in the year, and 729 months in the "great year" recognized
by the Pythagorean philosopher Philolaus), Socrates has made two fast moves. First,
he has illegitimately capitalized on the Greek manner of counting series in order to
count the oligarch twice, once as the last term in his first series (tyrant, democrat,
oligarch) and again as the first term in his second series (oligarch, timocrat, king).
Second, he has *multiplied* the number of times the tyrant is removed from the oligarch
by the number of times the oligarch is removed from the king, when he should have
added them. The tyrant is therefore only five times removed from the king and lives
only 125 times less pleasantly!

return to the first things we said, since they are what led us here. I think someone said at some point that injustice profits a completely unjust person who is believed to be just. Isn't that so?

It certainly is.

Now, let's discuss this with him, since we've agreed on the respective powers that injustice and justice have.

How?

By fashioning an image of the soul in words, so that the person who says this sort of thing will know what he is saying.

c   What sort of image?

One like those creatures that legends tell us used to come into being in ancient times, such as the Chimera, Scylla, Cerberus,[13] or any of the multitude of others in which many different kinds of things are said to have grown together naturally into one.

Yes, the legends do tell us of such things.

Well, then, fashion a single kind of multicolored beast with a ring of many heads that it can grow and change at will—some from gentle, some from savage animals.

d   That's work for a clever artist. However, since words are more malleable than wax and the like, consider it done.

Then fashion one other kind, that of a lion, and another of a human being. But make the first much the largest and the other second to it in size.

That's easier—the sculpting is done.

Now join the three of them into one, so that that they somehow grow together naturally.

They're joined.

Then, fashion around them the image of one of them, that of a human being so that anyone who sees only the outer covering and not what's e   inside will think it is a single creature, a human being.

It's done.

Then, if someone maintains that injustice profits this human being and that doing just things brings no advantage, let's tell him that he is simply saying that it is beneficial for him, first, to feed the multiform beast well and make it strong, and also the lion and all that pertains to him; second, 589   to starve and weaken the human being within, so that he is dragged along wherever either of the other two leads; and, third, to leave the parts to

---

13. The Chimera was "lion in the front, serpent in the back, and she-goat in the middle" (*Iliad* 6.181). Scylla had six heads, each with three rows of teeth, and twelve feet (see *Odyssey* 12.85 ff., 245 ff.). Cerberus was a huge dog guarding the entrance to Hades; he had three heads and a serpent's tail.

bite and kill one another rather than accustoming them to each other and making them friendly.

Yes, that's absolutely what someone who praises injustice is saying.

But, on the other hand, wouldn't someone who maintains that just things are profitable be saying, first, that all our words and deeds should insure that the human being within this human being has the most control; second, that he should take care of the many-headed beast as a farmer does   *b* his animals, feeding and domesticating the gentle heads and preventing the savage ones from growing; and, third, that he should make the lion's nature his ally, care for the community of all his parts, and bring them up in such a way that they will be friends with each other and with himself?

Yes, that's exactly what someone who praises justice is saying.

From every point of view, then, anyone who praises justice speaks truly, and anyone who praises injustice speaks falsely. Whether we look at the matter from the point of view of pleasure, good reputation, or advantage, a praiser of justice tells the truth, while one who condemns it has nothing   *c* sound to say and condemns without knowing what he is condemning.

In my opinion, at least, he knows nothing about it.

Then let's persuade him gently—for he isn't wrong of his own will— by asking him these questions. Should we say that this is the original basis for the conventions about what is fine and what is shameful? Fine things are those that subordinate the beastlike parts of our nature to the human— or better, perhaps, to the divine; shameful ones are those that enslave the   *d* gentle to the savage? Will he agree or what?

He will, if he takes my advice.

In light of this argument, can it profit anyone to acquire gold unjustly if, by doing so, he enslaves the best part of himself to the most vicious? If he got the gold by enslaving his son or daughter to savage and evil men, it wouldn't profit him, no matter how much gold he got. How, then, could   *e* he fail to be wretched if he pitilessly enslaves the most divine part of himself to the most godless and polluted one and accepts golden gifts in return for a more terrible destruction than Eriphyle's when she took the   *590* necklace in return for her husband's soul?[14]

A much more terrible one, Glaucon said. I'll answer for him.

And don't you think that licentiousness has long been condemned for just these reasons, namely, that because of it, that terrible, large, and multiform beast is let loose more than it should be?

Clearly.

---

14. Eriphyle was bribed by Polynices to persuade her husband, Amphiaraus, to take part in an attack on Thebes. He was killed, and she was murdered by her son in revenge. See *Odyssey* 11.326–7; Pindar, *Nemean* 9.37 ff.

And aren't stubbornness and irritability condemned because they inhar-
b   moniously increase and stretch the lionlike and snakelike[15] part?

Certainly.

And aren't luxury and softness condemned because the slackening and
loosening of this same part produce cowardice in it?

Of course.

And aren't flattery and slavishness condemned because they subject the
spirited part to the moblike beast, accustoming it from youth on to being
insulted for the sake of the money needed to satisfy the beast's insatiable
appetites, so that it becomes an ape instead of a lion?

c   They certainly are.

Why do you think that the condition of a manual worker is despised?
Or is it for any other reason than that, when the best part is naturally weak
in someone, it can't rule the beasts within him but can only serve them
and learn to flatter them?

Probably so.

Therefore, to insure that someone like that is ruled by something similar
to what rules the best person, we say that he ought to be the slave of that
best person who has a divine ruler within himself. It isn't to harm the slave
d   that we say he must be ruled, which is what Thrasymachus thought to be
true of all subjects, but because it is better for everyone to be ruled by
divine reason, preferably within himself and his own, otherwise imposed
from without, so that as far as possible all will be alike and friends,
governed by the same thing.

Yes, that's right.

This is clearly the aim of the law, which is the ally of everyone. But it's
also our aim in ruling our children, we don't allow them to be free until
we establish a constitution in them, just as in a city, and—by fostering
their best part with our own—equip them with a guardian and ruler similar
591   to our own to take our place. Then, and only then, we set them free.

Clearly so.

Then how can we maintain or argue, Glaucon, that injustice, licentiousness, and doing shameful things are profitable to anyone, since, even
though he may acquire more money or other sort of power from them,
they make him more vicious?

There's no way we can.

Or that to do injustice without being discovered and having to pay the
penalty is profitable? Doesn't the one who remains undiscovered become

15. The snakelike part hasn't been previously mentioned, although it may be included
in "all that pertains to" the lion (588e). It symbolizes some of the meaner components
of the spirited part, such as irritability, which it would be unnatural to attribute to the
noble lion.

even more vicious, while the bestial part of the one who is discovered is   *b*
calmed and tamed and his gentle part freed, so that his entire soul settles
into its best nature, acquires moderation, justice, and reason, and attains
a more valuable state than that of having a fine, strong, healthy body, since
the soul itself is more valuable than the body?

That's absolutely certain.

Then won't a person of understanding direct all his efforts to attaining
that state of his soul? First, he'll value the studies that produce it and   *c*
despise the others.

Clearly so.

Second, he won't entrust the condition and nurture of his body to the
irrational pleasure of the beast within or turn his life in that direction, but
neither will he make health his aim or assign first place to being strong,
healthy, and beautiful, unless he happens to acquire moderation as a
result. Rather, it's clear that he will always cultivate the harmony of his
body for the sake of the consonance in his soul.   *d*

He certainly will, if indeed he's to be truly trained in music and poetry.

Will he also keep order and consonance in his acquisition of money,
with that same end in view? Or, even though he isn't dazzled by the size
of the majority into accepting their idea of blessed happiness, will he
increase his wealth without limit and so have unlimited evils?

Not in my view.

Rather, he'll look to the constitution within him and guard against   *e*
disturbing anything in it, either by too much money or too little. And, in
this way, he'll direct both the increase and expenditure of his wealth, as
far as he can.

That's exactly what he'll do.

And he'll look to the same thing where honors are concerned. He'll
willingly share in and taste those that he believes will make him better, *592*
but he'll avoid any public or private honor that might overthrow the
established condition of his soul.

If that's his chief concern, he won't be willing to take part in politics.

Yes, by the dog, he certainly will, at least in his own kind of city. But
he may not be willing to do so in his fatherland, unless some divine good
luck chances to be his.

I understand. You mean that he'll be willing to take part in the politics
of the city we were founding and describing, the one that exists in theory,
for I don't think it exists anywhere on earth.   *b*

But perhaps, I said, there is a model of it in heaven, for anyone who
wants to look at it and to make himself its citizen on the strength of what
he sees. It makes no difference whether it is or ever will be somewhere,
for he would take part in the practical affairs of that city and no other.

Probably so, he said.

BOOK X

The main argument of the Republic *is now complete. Hence Socrates is in a position to discuss the kind of poetry about human beings that is permitted in the kallipolis, a discussion that had to be postponed in Book III (392a–c). Given the importance Socrates attributes to music and poetry and physical training (424b–425a) and the importance of Homer and Hesiod in Greek education, the return to this topic is hardly an anticlimax. It is rather the moment at which the new philosophy-based education confronts the traditional education based on poetry.*

Central to this discussion is a new account of mimēsis, *or imitation, based on the metaphysical theories introduced in Books V–VII. Earlier in Book III, imitation was something a person did by impersonating a character in a poem (394d ff.); now imitation is something a poem or a painting does.*

Socrates' critique of poetry is extremely subtle. The question on which it focuses is whether what one needs to know in order to be a good poet qualifies one as a teacher of virtue. Socrates argues that it does not. An imitator, in Plato's new technical sense, is someone whose products are third from the truth (597e), because they imitate the sorts of things the craftsman makes, which are themselves only imitations of what the philosopher-king would make (596e–597e). Hence, if poetry is third from the truth, it too will be imitative, and the poet will be an imitator. But Socrates argues that the poet is an imitator in this sense (598d–607a), and consequently he does not even have true belief about virtue. Makers have true belief through associating with users, who alone have knowledge. But imitators don't even have the kind of insight that makers do; they have only opinion—sometimes true, sometimes false—nothing more. Hence they are not reliable teachers of virtue and, because of their disturbing influence even on good people, should not be admitted into the kallipolis. Socrates' ban on imitative poetry is not final, however. He allows for the possibility that someone might be able to construct a defense of poetry that would change his mind (607b–608b).

Having completed his account of poetry, Socrates turns to the topic of the immortality of the soul and to the previously excluded consequences of justice and injustice (609b–612e). He argues, in part by appeal to the Myth of Er, that the good consequences of justice both in this life and in the next far outweigh those of injustice. This completes his argument that justice belongs in the best of the three classes of goods that Glaucon distinguished at the beginning of Book II, since it is choiceworthy both for its own sake and for its consequences.

Indeed, I said, our city has many features that assure me that we were *595*
entirely right in founding it as we did, and, when I say this, I'm especially
thinking of poetry.

What about it in particular? Glaucon said.

That we didn't admit any that is imitative. Now that we have distinguished the separate parts of the soul, it is even clearer, I think, that such
poetry should be altogether excluded.   *b*

What do you mean?

Between ourselves—for *you* won't denounce me to the tragic poets or
any of the other imitative ones—all such poetry is likely to distort the
thought of anyone who hears it, unless he has the knowledge of what it is
really like, as a drug to counteract it.

What exactly do you have in mind in saying this?

I'll tell you, even though the love and respect I've had for Homer since
I was a child make me hesitate to speak, for he seems to have been the
first teacher and leader of all these fine tragedians. All the same, no one
is to be honored or valued more than the truth. So, as I say, it must be   *c*
told.

That's right.

Listen then, or, rather, answer.

Ask and I will.

Could you tell me what imitation in general is? I don't entirely understand what sort of thing imitations are trying to be.

Is it likely, then, that *I'll* understand?

That wouldn't be so strange, for people with bad eyesight often see
things before those whose eyesight is keener.   *596*

That's so, but even if something occurred to me, I wouldn't be eager
to talk about it in front of you. So I'd rather that you did the looking.

Do you want us to begin our examination, then, by adopting our usual
procedure? As you know, we customarily hypothesize a single form in
connection with each of the many things to which we apply the same
name.[1] Or don't you understand?

I do.

Then let's now take any of the manys you like. For example, there are
many beds and tables.   *b*

Of course.

But there are only two forms of such furniture, one of the bed and one
of the table.

Yes.

And don't we also customarily say that their makers look towards the

---

1. See 475e ff., 507a–b, and 476c n. 29.

appropriate form in making the beds or tables we use, and similarly in the
other cases? Surely no craftsman makes the form itself. How could he?

There's no way he could.

Well, then, see what you'd call *this* craftsman?

c   Which one?

The one who makes all the things that all the other kinds of craftsmen
severally make.

That's a clever and wonderful fellow you're talking about.

Wait a minute, and you'll have even more reason to say that, for this
same craftsman is able to make, not only all kinds of furniture, but all
plants that grow from the earth, all animals (including himself), the earth
itself, the heavens, the gods, all the things in the heavens and in Hades
beneath the earth.

d   *He'd* be amazingly clever!

You don't believe me? Tell me, do you think that there's no way any
craftsman could make all these things, or that in one way he could and in
another he couldn't? Don't you see that there is a way in which you yourself
could make all of them?

What way is that?

It isn't hard: You could do it quickly and in lots of places, especially if
you were willing to carry a mirror with you, for that's the quickest way of
all. With it you can quickly make the sun, the things in the heavens,
e   the earth, yourself, the other animals, manufactured items, plants, and
everything else mentioned just now.

Yes, I could make them appear, but I couldn't make the things themselves as they truly are.

Well put! You've extracted the point that's crucial to the argument. I
suppose that the painter too belongs to this class of makers,[2] doesn't he?

Of course.

But I suppose you'll say that he doesn't truly make the things he makes.
Yet, in a certain way, the painter does make a bed, doesn't he?

Yes, he makes the appearance of one.

What about the carpenter? Didn't you just say that he doesn't make the
597 form—which is our term for the being[3] of a bed—but only *a* bed?

Yes, I did say that.

Now, if he doesn't make the being of a bed, he isn't making that which

---

2. Throughout the following passage, Plato takes advantage of the fact that the Greek
word *poiein* means both "to make" generally and also "to compose poetry." Indeed, the
word *poiētēs* means both "poet" and "maker," so that to class the poet (and the painter)
as "makers" is much more natural in Greek than it is in English.

3. See 507b n. 21.

is, but something which is like that which is, but is not it. So, if someone were to say that the work of a carpenter or any other craftsman is completely that which is, wouldn't he risk saying what isn't true?[4]

That, at least, would be the opinion of those who busy themselves with arguments of this sort.

Then let's not be surprised if the carpenter's bed, too, turns out to be a somewhat dark affair in comparison to the true one.

All right.   *b*

Then, do you want us to try to discover what an imitator is by reference to these same examples?

I do, if you do.

We get, then, these three kinds of beds. The first is in nature a bed, and I suppose we'd say that a god makes it, or does someone else make it?

No one else, I suppose.

The second is the work of a carpenter.

Yes.

And the third is the one the painter makes. Isn't that so?

It is.

Then the painter, carpenter, and god correspond to three kinds of bed?

Yes, three.

Now, the god, either because he didn't want to or because it was necessary for him not to do so, didn't make more than one bed in nature, *c*
but only one, the very one that is the being of a bed. Two or more of these have not been made by the god and never will be.

Why is that?

Because, if he made only two, then again one would come to light whose form they in turn would both possess, and *that* would be the one that is the being of a bed and not the other two.[5]

That's right.

The god knew this, I think, and wishing to be the real maker of the truly real bed and not just *a* maker of *a* bed, he made it to be one in nature. *d*

Probably so.

Do you want us to call him its natural maker or something like that?

It would be right to do so, at any rate, since he is by nature the maker of this and everything else.

---

4. This sentence is best understood as follows: "If the carpenter doesn't make the being of e.g. a bed, he isn't making that which a bed is, but something which, though it is like what a bed is, isn't the same as what a bed is. So if someone were to say that the work of a carpenter or other craftsman is completely that which it is (e.g. a bed), wouldn't he risk saying what isn't true?"

5. Here Socrates uses the principle given at 596a.

What about a carpenter? Isn't he the maker of a bed?

Yes.

And is a painter also a craftsman and maker of such things?

Not at all.

Then what do you think he does do to a bed?

He imitates it. He is an imitator of what the others make. That, in my
e   view, is the most reasonable thing to call him.

All right. Then wouldn't you call someone whose product is third from
the natural one an imitator?[6]

I most certainly would.

Then this will also be true of a tragedian, if indeed he is an imitator.
He is by nature third from the king and the truth, as are all other imitators.

It looks that way.

We're agreed about imitators, then. Now, tell me this about a painter.
Do you think he tries in each case to imitate the thing itself in nature or
598 the works of craftsmen?

The works of craftsmen.

As they are or as they appear? You must be clear about that.

How do you mean?

Like this. If you look at a bed from the side or the front or from
anywhere else is it a different bed each time? Or does it only appear
different, without being at all different? And is that also the case with
other things?

That's the way it is—it appears different without being so.

Then consider this very point: What does painting do in each case?
b   Does it imitate that which is as it is, or does it imitate that which appears
as it appears? Is it an imitation of appearances or of truth?

Of appearances.

Then imitation is far removed from the truth, for it touches only a small
part of each thing and a part that is itself only an image. And that, it seems,
is why it can produce everything. For example, we say that a painter can
paint a cobbler, a carpenter, or any other craftsman, even though he knows
c   nothing about these crafts. Nevertheless, if he is a good painter and
displays his painting of a carpenter at a distance, he can deceive children
and foolish people into thinking that it is truly a carpenter.

Of course.

Then this, I suppose, is what we must bear in mind in all these cases.
Hence, whenever someone tells us that he has met a person who knows
all the crafts as well as all the other things that anyone else knows and that
his knowledge of any subject is more exact than any of theirs is, we must

6. See 587c n. 10.

assume that we're talking to a simple-minded fellow who has apparently   *d*
encountered some sort of magician or imitator and been deceived into
thinking him omniscient and that the reason he has been deceived is that
he himself can't distinguish between knowledge, ignorance, and imitation.

That's absolutely true.

Then, we must consider tragedy and its leader, Homer. The reason is
this: We hear some people say that poets know all crafts, all human affairs
concerned with virtue and vice, and all about the gods as well. They say   *e*
that if a good poet produces fine poetry, he must have knowledge of the
things he writes about, or else he wouldn't be able to produce it at all.
Hence, we have to look to see whether those who tell us this have encountered these imitators and have been so deceived by them that they don't
realize that their works are at the third remove from that which is and are
easily produced without knowledge of the truth (since they are only images, *599*
not things that are), or whether there is something in what these people
say, and good poets really do have knowledge of the things most people
think they write so well about.

We certainly must look into it.

Do you think that someone who could make both the thing imitated
and its image would allow himself to be serious about making images and
put this at the forefront of his life as the best thing to do?   *b*

No, I don't.

I suppose that, if he truly had knowledge of the things he imitates, he'd
be much more serious about actions than about imitations of them, would
try to leave behind many fine deeds as memorials to himself, and would
be more eager to be the subject of a eulogy than the author of one.

I suppose so, for these things certainly aren't equally valuable or equally
beneficial either.

Then let's not demand an account of any of these professions from
Homer or the other poets. Let's not ask whether any of them is a doctor
rather than an imitator of what doctors say, or whether any poet of the old   *c*
or new school has made anyone healthy as Asclepius did, or whether he
has left any students of medicine behind as Asclepius did his sons. And
let's not ask them about the other crafts either. Let's pass over all that.
But about the most important and most beautiful things of which Homer
undertakes to speak—warfare, generalship, city government, and people's
education—about these it *is* fair to question him, asking him this: "Homer,
if you're not third from the truth about virtue, the sort of craftsman of   *d*
images that we defined an imitator to be, but if you're even second and
capable of knowing what ways of life make people better in private or in
public, then tell us which cities are better governed because of you, as
Sparta is because of Lycurgus, and as many others—big and small—are

because of many other men? What city gives you credit for being a good
e lawgiver who benefited it, as Italy and Sicily do to Charondas,[7] and as we
do to Solon? Who gives such credit to you?" Will he be able to name one?
I suppose not, for not even the Homeridae[8] make that claim for him.

Well, then, is any war in Homer's time remembered that was won
600 because of his generalship and advice?

None.

Or, as befits a wise man, are many inventions and useful devices in the
crafts or sciences attributed to Homer, as they are to Thales of Miletus
and Anacharsis the Scythian?[9]

There's nothing of that kind at all.

Then, if there's nothing of a public nature, are we told that, when
Homer was alive, he was a leader in the education of certain people who
took pleasure in associating with him in private and that he passed on a
b Homeric way of life to those who came after him, just as Pythagoras did?
Pythagoras is particularly loved for this, and even today his followers are
conspicuous for what they call the Pythagorean way of life.

Again, we're told nothing of this kind about Homer. If the stories about
him are true, Socrates, his companion, Creophylus,[10] seems to have been
an even more ridiculous example of education than his name suggests, for
they tell us that while Homer was alive, Creophylus completely neglected
c him.

They do tell us that. But, Glaucon, if Homer had really been able to
educate people and make them better, if he'd known about these things
and not merely about how to imitate them, wouldn't he have had many
companions and been loved and honored by them? Protagoras of Abdera,
Prodicus of Ceos,[11] and a great many others are able to convince anyone
who associates with them in private that he wouldn't be able to manage

7. Charondas probably lived in the sixth century B.C. and gave laws to Catane and
other cities in Italy and Sicily.

8. The Homeridae were the rhapsodes and poets who recited and expounded Homer
throughout the Greek world.

9. Thales of Miletus, on the Ionian coast of Asia Minor, is the first philosopher we
know of in ancient Greece. He seems to have regarded water as the fundamental
principle of all things and is said to have predicted the solar eclipse of 585 B.C.
Ancharsis, who lived around 600 B.C. and is often included among the Seven Sages,
is credited with beginning Greek geometry and with being able to calculate the distance
of ships at sea.

10. Creophylus is said to have been an epic poet from Chios. His name comes from
two words, kreas, meaning "meat," and phylon, meaning "race" or "kind." A modern
equivalent, with parallel comic overtones, would be "meathead."

11. Protagoras and Prodicus were two of the most famous fifth-century sophists.

his household or city unless they themselves supervise his education, and
they are so intensely loved because of this wisdom of theirs that their   *d*
disciples do everything but carry them around on their shoulders. So do
you suppose that, if Homer had been able to benefit people and make
them more virtuous, his companions would have allowed either him or
Hesiod to wander around as rhapsodes? Instead, wouldn't they have clung
tighter to them than to gold and compelled them to live with them in their
homes, or, if they failed to persuade them to do so, wouldn't they have
followed them wherever they went until they had received sufficient edu-   *e*
cation?

It seems to me, Socrates, that what you say is entirely true.

Then shall we conclude that all poetic imitators, beginning with Homer,
imitate images of virtue and all the other things they write about and have
no grasp of the truth? As we were saying just now, a painter, though he
knows nothing about cobblery, can make what seems to be a cobbler to
those who know as little about it as he does and who judge things by their   *601*
colors and shapes.

That's right.

And in the same way, I suppose we'll say that a poetic imitator uses
words and phrases to paint colored pictures of each of the crafts. He
himself knows nothing about them, but he imitates them in such a way
that others, as ignorant as he, who judge by words, will think he speaks
extremely well about cobblery or generalship or anything else whatever,
provided—so great is the natural charm of these things—that he speaks
with meter, rhythm, and harmony, for if you strip a poet's works of their
musical colorings and take them by themselves, I think you know what   *b*
they look like. You've surely seen them.

I certainly have.

Don't they resemble the faces of young boys who are neither fine nor
beautiful after the bloom of youth has left them?

Absolutely.

Now, consider this. We say that a maker of an image—an imitator—
knows nothing about that which is but only about its appearance. Isn't that
so?   *c*

Yes.

Then let's not leave the discussion of this point halfway, but examine
it fully.

Go ahead.

Don't we say that a painter paints reins and a mouth-bit?

Yes.

And that a cobbler and a metal-worker makes them?

Of course.

Then, does a painter know how the reins and mouth-bit have to be? Or is it the case that even a cobbler and metal-worker who make them don't know this, but only someone who knows how to use them, namely, a horseman?

That's absolutely true.

And won't we say that the same holds for everything?

What?

d   That for each thing there are these three crafts, one that uses it, one that makes it, and one that imitates it?

Yes.

Then aren't the virtue or excellence, the beauty and correctness of each manufactured item, living creature, and action related to nothing but the use for which each is made or naturally adapted?

They are.

It's wholly necessary, therefore, that a user of each thing has most experience of it and that he tell a maker which of his products performs well or badly in actual use. A flute-player, for example, tells a flute-maker about the flutes that respond well in actual playing and prescribes what *e*   kind of flutes he is to make, while the maker follows his instructions.

Of course.

Then doesn't the one who knows give instructions about good and bad flutes, and doesn't the other rely on him in making them?

Yes.

Therefore, a maker—through associating with and having to listen to the one who knows—has right opinion about whether something he makes *602* is fine or bad, but the one who knows is the user.

That's right.

Does an imitator have knowledge of whether the things he makes are fine or right through having made use of them, or does he have right opinion about them through having to consort with the one who knows and being told how he is to paint them?

Neither.

Therefore an imitator has neither knowledge nor right opinion about whether the things he makes are fine or bad.

Apparently not.

Then a poetic imitator is an accomplished fellow when it comes to wisdom about the subjects of his poetry!

Hardly.

Nonetheless, he'll go on imitating, even though he doesn't know the good or bad qualities of anything, but what he'll imitate, it seems, is what *b*   appears fine or beautiful to the majority of people who know nothing.

Of course.

It seems, then, that we're fairly well agreed that an imitator has no worthwhile knowledge of the things he imitates, that imitation is a kind of game and not something to be taken seriously, and that all the tragic poets, whether they write in iambics or hexameters, are as imitative as they could possibly be.

That's right.

Then is this kind of imitation concerned with something that is third   c from the truth, or what?

Yes, it is.

And on which of a person's parts does it exert its power?

What do you mean?

This: Something looked at from close at hand doesn't seem to be the same size as it does when it is looked at from a distance.

No, it doesn't.

And something looks crooked when seen in water and straight when seen out of it, while something else looks both concave and convex because our eyes are deceived by its colors, and every other similar sort of confusion is clearly present in our soul. And it is because they exploit this weakness in our nature that *trompe l'oeil* painting, conjuring, and other forms of   d trickery have powers that are little short of magical.

That's true.

And don't measuring, counting, and weighing give us most welcome assistance in these cases, so that we aren't ruled by something's looking bigger, smaller, more numerous, or heavier, but by calculation, measurement, or weighing?

Of course.

And calculating, measuring, and weighing are the work of the rational part of the soul.   e

They are.

But when this part has measured and has indicated that some things are larger or smaller or the same size as others, the opposite appears to it at the same time.

Yes.

And didn't we say that it is impossible for the same thing to believe opposites about the same thing at the same time?[12]

We did, and we were right to say it.

Then the part of the soul that forms a belief contrary to the measurements couldn't be the same as the part that believes in accord with them. *603*

No, it couldn't.

12. See 436b–c.

Now, the part that puts its trust in measurement and calculation is the best part of the soul.

Of course.

Therefore, the part that opposes it is one of the inferior parts in us.

Necessarily.

This, then, is what I wanted to get agreement about when I said that painting and imitation as a whole produce work that is far from the truth, namely, that imitation really consorts with a part of us that is far from reason, and the result of their being friends and companions is neither
b sound nor true.

That's absolutely right.

Then imitation is an inferior thing that consorts with another inferior thing to produce an inferior offspring.

So it seems.

Does this apply only to the imitations we see, or does it also apply to the ones we hear—the ones we call poetry?

It probably applies to poetry as well.

However, we mustn't rely solely on a mere probability based on the analogy with painting; instead, we must go directly to the part of our thought with which poetic imitations consort and see whether it is inferior
c or something to be taken seriously.

Yes, we must.

Then let's set about it as follows. We say that imitative poetry imitates human beings acting voluntarily or under compulsion, who believe that, as a result of these actions, they are doing either well or badly and who experience either pleasure or pain in all this. Does it imitate anything apart from this?

Nothing.

Then is a person of one mind in all these circumstances? Or, just as he was at war with himself in matters of sight and held opposite beliefs about
d the same thing at the same time, does he also fight with himself and engage in civil war with himself in matters of action? But there is really no need for us to reach agreement on this question now, for I remember that we already came to an adequate conclusion about all these things in our earlier arguments, when we said that our soul is full of a myriad of such oppositions at the same time.[13]

And rightly so.

It *was* right, but I think we omitted some things then that we must now
e discuss.

What are they?

13. See 439c ff.

We also mentioned somewhere before[14] that, if a decent man happens to lose his son or some other prized possession, he'll bear it more easily than the other sorts of people.

Certainly.

But now let's consider this. Will he not grieve at all, or, if that's impossible, will he be somehow measured in his response to pain?

The latter is closer to the truth.

Now, tell me this about him: Will he fight his pain and put up more resistance to it when his equals can see him or when he's alone by himself *604* in solitude?

He'll fight it far more when he's being seen.

But when he's alone I suppose he'll venture to say and do lots of things that he'd be ashamed to be heard saying or seen doing.

That's right.

And isn't it reason and law that tells him to resist his pain, while his experience of it tells him to give in?   *b*

True.

And when there are two opposite inclinations in a person in relation to the same thing at the same time, we say that he must also have two parts.

Of course.

Isn't one part ready to obey the law wherever it leads him?

How so?

The law says, doesn't it, that it is best to keep as quiet as possible in misfortunes and not get excited about them? First, it isn't clear whether such things will turn out to be good or bad in the end; second, it doesn't make the future any better to take them hard; third, human affairs aren't worth taking very seriously; and, finally, grief prevents the very thing we *c* most need in such circumstances from coming into play as quickly as possible.

What are you referring to?

Deliberation. We must accept what has happened as we would the fall of the dice, and then arrange our affairs in whatever way reason determines to be best. We mustn't hug the hurt part and spend our time weeping and wailing like children when they trip. Instead, we should always accustom our souls to turn as quickly as possible to healing the disease and putting the disaster right, replacing lamentation with cure.   *d*

That would be the best way to deal with misfortune, at any rate.

Accordingly, we say that it is the best part of us that is willing to follow this rational calculation.

Clearly.

14. See 387d–e.

Then won't we also say that the part that leads us to dwell on our misfortunes and to lamentation, and that can never get enough of these things, is irrational, idle, and a friend of cowardice?

We certainly will.

Now, this excitable character admits of many multicolored imitations.

e But a rational and quiet character, which always remains pretty well the same, is neither easy to imitate nor easy to understand when imitated, especially not by a crowd consisting of all sorts of people gathered together at a theater festival, for the experience being imitated is alien to them.

605 Absolutely.

Clearly, then, an imitative poet isn't by nature related to the part of the soul that rules in such a character,[15] and, if he's to attain a good reputation with the majority of people, his cleverness isn't directed to pleasing it. Instead, he's related to the excitable and multicolored character, since it is easy to imitate.

Clearly.

Therefore, we'd be right to take him and put him beside a painter as his counterpart. Like a painter, he produces work that is inferior with respect to truth and that appeals to a part of the soul that is similarly *b* inferior rather than to the best part. So we were right not to admit him into a city that is to be well-governed, for he arouses, nourishes, and strengthens this part of the soul and so destroys the rational one, in just the way that someone destroys the better sort of citizens when he strengthens the vicious ones and surrenders the city to them. Similarly, we'll say that an imitative poet puts a bad constitution in the soul of each individual by making images that are far removed from the truth and by *c* gratifying the irrational part, which cannot distinguish the large and the small but believes that the same things are large at one time and small at another.

That's right.

However, we haven't yet brought the most serious charge against imitation, namely, that with a few rare exceptions it is able to corrupt even decent people, for that's surely an altogether terrible thing.

It certainly is, if indeed it can do that.

Listen, then, and consider whether it can or not. When even the best of us hear Homer or some other tragedian imitating one of the heroes sorrowing and making a long lamenting speech or singing and beating his *d* breast, you know that we enjoy it, give ourselves up to following it, sympathize with the hero, take his sufferings seriously, and praise as a good poet the one who affects us most in this way.

15. See 437d ff.

Of course we do.

But when one of us suffers a private loss, you realize that the opposite happens. We pride ourselves if we are able to keep quiet and master our grief, for we think that this is the manly thing to do and that the behavior we praised before is womanish.   *e*

I do realize that.

Then are we right to praise it? Is it right to look at someone behaving in a way that we would consider unworthy and shameful and to enjoy and praise it rather than being disgusted by it?

No, by god, that doesn't seem reasonable.

No, at least not if you look at it in the following way.   *606*

How?

If you reflect, first, that the part of the soul that is forcibly controlled in our private misfortunes and that hungers for the satisfaction of weeping and wailing, because it desires these things by nature, is the very part that receives satisfaction and enjoyment from poets, and, second, that the part of ourselves that is best by nature, since it hasn't been adequately educated either by reason or habit, relaxes its guard over the lamenting part when it is watching the sufferings of somebody else. The reason it does so is this: It thinks that there is no shame involved for it in praising and pitying   *b* another man who, in spite of his claim to goodness, grieves excessively. Indeed, it thinks that there is a definite gain involved in doing so, namely, pleasure. And it wouldn't want to be deprived of that by despising the whole poem. I suppose that only a few are able to figure out that enjoyment of other people's sufferings is necessarily transferred to our own and that the pitying part, if it is nourished and strengthened on the sufferings of others, won't be easily held in check when we ourselves suffer.

That's very true.   *c*

And doesn't the same argument apply to what provokes laughter? If there are any jokes that you yourself would be ashamed to tell but that you very much enjoy hearing and don't detest as something evil in comic plays or in private, aren't you doing the same thing as in the case of what provokes pity? The part of you that wanted to tell the jokes and that was held back by your reason, for fear of being thought a buffoon, you then release, not realizing that, by making it strong in this way, you will be led into becoming a figure of fun where your own affairs are concerned.

Yes, indeed.

And in the case of sex, anger, and all the desires, pleasures, and pains   *d* that we say accompany all our actions, poetic imitation has the very same effect on us. It nurtures and waters them and establishes them as rulers in us when they ought to wither and be ruled, for that way we'll become better and happier rather than worse and more wretched.

I can't disagree with you.

e   And so, Glaucon, when you happen to meet those who praise Homer and say that he's the poet who educated Greece, that it's worth taking up his works in order to learn how to manage and educate people, and that one should arrange one's whole life in accordance with his teachings, you should welcome these people and treat them as friends, since they're as
607 good as they're capable of being, and you should agree that Homer is the most poetic of the tragedians and the first among them. But you should also know that hymns to the gods and eulogies to good people are the only poetry we can admit into our city. If you admit the pleasure-giving Muse, whether in lyric or epic poetry, pleasure and pain will be kings in your city instead of law or the thing that everyone has always believed to be best, namely, reason.

That's absolutely true.

Then let this be our defense—now that we've returned to the topic of
b   poetry—that, in view of its nature, we had reason to banish it from the city earlier, for our argument compelled us to do so. But in case we are charged with a certain harshness and lack of sophistication, let's also tell poetry that there is an ancient quarrel between it and philosophy, which is evidenced by such expressions as "the dog yelping and shrieking at its master," "great in the empty eloquence of fools," "the mob of wise men
c   that has mastered Zeus,"[16] and "the subtle thinkers, beggars all."[17] Nonetheless, if the poetry that aims at pleasure and imitation has any argument to bring forward that proves it ought to have a place in a well-governed city, we at least would be glad to admit it, for we are well aware of the charm it exercises. But, be that as it may, to betray what one believes to be the truth is impious. What about you, Glaucon, don't you feel the charm of the pleasure-giving Muse, especially when you study her through
d   the eyes of Homer?

Very much so.

Therefore, isn't it just that such poetry should return from exile when it has successfully defended itself, whether in lyric or any other meter?

Certainly.

Then we'll allow its defenders, who aren't poets themselves but lovers of poetry, to speak in prose on its behalf and to show that it not only gives

---

16. Reading *tôn Dia sophôn ochlôs kratôn*. The phrase would apply to such philosophers as Thales, who might seem to have replaced Zeus with natural forces.

17. Philosophers, such as Xenophanes and Heraclitus, attacked Homer and Hesiod for their immoral tales about the gods. Poets, such as Aristophanes in his *Clouds*, attacked philosophers for subverting traditional ethical and religious values. But the sources of these particular quotations are unknown.

pleasure but is beneficial both to constitutions and to human life. Indeed, we'll listen to them graciously, for we'd certainly profit if poetry were shown to be not only pleasant but also beneficial.   *e*

How could we fail to profit?

However, if such a defense isn't made, we'll behave like people who have fallen in love with someone but who force themselves to stay away from him, because they realize that their passion isn't beneficial. In the same way, because the love of this sort of poetry has been implanted in us by the upbringing we have received under our fine constitutions, we are well disposed to any proof that it is the best and truest thing. But if it isn't able to produce such a defense, then, whenever we listen to it, we'll   *608* repeat the argument we have just now put forward like an incantation so as to preserve ourselves from slipping back into that childish passion for poetry which the majority of people have. And we'll go on chanting that such poetry is not to be taken seriously or treated as a serious undertaking with some kind of hold on the truth, but that anyone who is anxious about the constitution within him must be careful when he hears it and must continue to believe what we have said about it.   *b*

I completely agree.

Yes, for the struggle to be good rather than bad is important, Glaucon, much more important than people think. Therefore, we mustn't be tempted by honor, money, rule, or even poetry into neglecting justice and the rest of virtue.

After what we've said, I agree with you, and so, I think, would anyone else.

And yet we haven't discussed the greatest rewards and prizes that have   *c* been proposed for virtue.

They must be inconceivably great, if they're greater than those you've already mentioned.

Could anything really great come to pass in a short time? And isn't the time from childhood to old age short when compared to the whole of time?

It's a mere nothing.

Well, do you think that an immortal thing should be seriously concerned with that short period rather than with the whole of time?   *d*

I suppose not, but what exactly do you mean by this?

Haven't you realized that our soul is immortal and never destroyed?

He looked at me with wonder and said: No, by god, I haven't. Are you really in a position to assert that?

I'd be wrong not to, I said, and so would you, for it isn't difficult.

It is for me, so I'd be glad to hear from you what's not difficult about it.

Listen, then.

Just speak, and I will.

Do you talk about good and bad?

I do.

e   And do you think about them the same way I do?

What way is that?

The bad is what destroys and corrupts, and the good is what preserves and benefits.

I do.

And do you say that there is a good and a bad for everything? For example, ophthalmia for the eyes, sickness for the whole body, blight for
609 grain, rot for wood, rust for iron or bronze. In other words, is there, as I say, a natural badness and sickness for pretty well everything?

There is.

And when one of these attaches itself to something, doesn't it make the thing in question bad, and in the end, doesn't it disintegrate it and destroy it wholly?

Of course.

Therefore, the evil that is natural to each thing and the bad that is peculiar to it destroy it. However, if they don't destroy it, nothing else will, for the good would never destroy anything, nor would anything neither
b   good nor bad.

How could they?

Then, if we discover something that has an evil that makes it bad but isn't able to disintegrate and destroy it, can't we infer that it is naturally incapable of being destroyed?

Probably so.

Well, what about the soul? Isn't there something that makes it bad?

Certainly, all the things we were mentioning: Injustice, licentiousness,
c   cowardice, and lack of learning.

Does any of these disintegrate and destroy the soul? Keep your wits about you, and let's not be deceived into thinking that, when an unjust and foolish person is caught, he has been destroyed by injustice, which is evil in a soul. Let's think about it this way instead: Just as the body is worn out, destroyed, and brought to the point where it is a body no longer by disease, which is evil in a body, so all the things we mentioned just now reach the point at which they cease to be what they are through their own peculiar
d   evil, which attaches itself to them and is present in them. Isn't that so?

Yes.

Then look at the soul in the same way. Do injustice and the other vices that exist in a soul—by their very presence in it and by attaching themselves to it—corrupt it and make it waste away until, having brought it to the point of death, they separate it from the body?

That's not at all what they do.

But surely it's unreasonable to suppose that a thing is destroyed by the badness proper to something else when it is not destroyed by its own?

That is unreasonable.

Keep in mind, Glaucon, that we don't think that a body is destroyed by   *e* the badness of food, whether it is staleness, rottenness, or anything else. But if the badness of the food happens to implant in the body an evil proper to a body, we'll say that the body was destroyed by its own evil, namely, disease. But, since the body is one thing and food another, we'll never judge that the body is destroyed by the badness of food, unless it   *610* implants in it the body's own natural and peculiar evil.

That's absolutely right.

By the same argument, if the body's evil doesn't cause an evil in the soul that is proper to the soul, we'll never judge that the soul, in the absence of its own peculiar evil, is destroyed by the evil of something else. We'd never accept that *anything* is destroyed by an evil proper to something else.

That's also reasonable.

Then let's either refute our argument and show that we were wrong, or, as long as it remains unrefuted, let's never say that the soul is destroyed by a fever or any other disease or by killing either, for that matter, not even if the body is cut up into tiny pieces. We mustn't say that the soul is   *b* even close to being destroyed by these things until someone shows us that these conditions of the body make the soul more unjust and more impious. When something has the evil proper to something else in it, but its own peculiar evil is absent, we won't allow anyone to say that it is destroyed, no matter whether it is a soul or anything else whatever.   *c*

And you may be sure that no one will ever prove that the souls of the dying are made more unjust by death.

But if anyone dares to come to grips with our argument, in order to avoid having to agree that our souls are immortal, and says that a dying man does become more vicious and unjust, we'll reply that, if what he says is true, then injustice must be as deadly to unjust people as a disease, and those who catch it must die of it because of its own deadly nature, with   *d* the worst cases dying quickly and the less serious dying more slowly. As things now stand, however, it isn't like that at all. Unjust people do indeed die of injustice, but at the hands of others who inflict the death penalty on them.

By god, if injustice were actually fatal to those who contracted it, it wouldn't seem so terrible, for it would be an escape from their troubles. But I rather think that it's clearly the opposite, something that kills other people if it can, while, on top of making the unjust themselves lively, it   *e* even brings them out at night. Hence it's very far from being deadly to its possessors.

You're right, for if the soul's own evil and badness isn't enough to kill and destroy it, an evil appointed for the destruction of something else will hardly kill it. Indeed, it won't kill anything at all except the very thing it is appointed to destroy.

"Hardly" is right, or so it seems.

Now, if the soul isn't destroyed by a single evil, whether its own or something else's, then clearly it must always be. And if it always is, it is 611 immortal.

Necessarily so.

So be it. And if it is so, then you realize that there would always be the same souls, for they couldn't be made fewer if none is destroyed, and they couldn't be made more numerous either. If anything immortal is increased, you know that the increase would have to come from the mortal, and then everything would end up being immortal.

That's true.

Then we mustn't think such a thing, for the argument doesn't allow it, nor must we think that the soul in its truest nature is full of multicolored b variety and unlikeness or that it differs with itself.

What do you mean?

It isn't easy for anything composed of many parts to be immortal if it isn't put together in the finest way, yet this is how the soul now appeared to us.

It probably isn't easy.

Yet our recent argument and others as well compel us to believe that the soul *is* immortal. But to see the soul as it is in truth, we must not study it as it is while it is maimed by its association with the body and other c evils—which is what we were doing earlier—but as it is in its pure state, that's how we should study the soul, thoroughly and by means of logical reasoning. We'll then find that it is a much finer thing than we thought and that we can see justice and injustice as well as all the other things we've discussed far more clearly. What we've said about the soul is true of it as it appears at present. But the condition in which we've studied it is like that of the sea god Glaucus, whose primary nature can't easily be d made out by those who catch glimpses of him. Some of the original parts have been broken off, others have been crushed, and his whole body has been maimed by the waves and by the shells, seaweeds, and stones that have attached themselves to him, so that he looks more like a wild animal than his natural self. The soul, too, is in a similar condition when we study it, beset by many evils. That, Glaucon, is why we have to look somewhere else in order to discover its true nature.

To where?

To its philosophy, or love of wisdom. We must realize what it grasps   *e*
and longs to have intercourse with, because it is akin to the divine and
immortal and what always is, and we must realize what it would become
if it followed this longing with its whole being, and if the resulting effort
lifted it out of the sea in which it now dwells, and if the many stones and   *612*
shells (those which have grown all over it in a wild, earthy, and stony
profusion because it feasts at those so-called happy feastings on earth)
were hammered off it.[18] Then we'd see what its true nature is and be able
to determine whether it has many parts or just one and whether or in what
manner it is put together. But we've already given a decent account, I
think, of what its condition is and what parts it has when it is immersed
in human life.

We certainly have.

And haven't we cleared away the various other objections to our argument without having to invoke the rewards and reputations of justice, as
you said Homer and Hesiod did?[19] And haven't we found that justice itself   *b*
is the best thing for the soul itself, and that the soul—whether it has the
ring of Gyges or even it together with the cap of Hades[20]—should do just
things?

We have. That's absolutely true.

Then can there now be any objection, Glaucon, if in addition we return
to justice and the rest of virtue both the kind and quantity of wages that
they obtain for the soul from human beings and gods, whether in this life   *c*
or the next?

None whatever.

Then will you give me back what you borrowed from me during the
discussion?

What are you referring to in particular?

I granted your request that a just person should seem unjust and an
unjust one just, for you said that, even if it would be impossible for these
things to remain hidden from both gods and humans, still, this had to be
granted for the sake of argument, so that justice itself could be judged in
relation to injustice itself. Don't you remember that?   *d*

It would be wrong of me not to.

Well, then, since they've now been judged, I ask that the reputation
justice in fact has among gods and humans be returned to it and that we

18. See 519 ff.

19. See 357–367e.

20. The ring of Gyges is discussed at 359d–360a. The cap of Hades also made its
wearer invisible.

agree that it does indeed have such a reputation and is entitled to carry off the prizes it gains for someone by making him seem just. It is already clear that it gives good things to anyone who is just and that it doesn't deceive those who really possess it.

e   That's a fair request.

Then won't you first grant that it doesn't escape the notice of the gods at least as to which of the two is just and which isn't?

We will.

Then if neither of them escapes the gods' notice, one would be loved by the gods and the other hated, as we agreed at the beginning.[21]

That's right.

And won't we also agree that everything that comes to someone who is loved by gods, insofar as it comes from the gods themselves, is the best *613* possible, unless it is the inevitable punishment for some mistake he made in a former life?

Certainly.

Then we must suppose that the same is true of a just person who falls into poverty or disease or some other apparent evil, namely, that this will end well for him, either during his lifetime or afterwards, for the gods never neglect anyone who eagerly wishes to become just and who makes himself as much like a god as a human can by adopting a virtuous way of *b*   life.

It makes sense that such a person not be neglected by anyone who is like him.

And mustn't we suppose that the opposite is true of an unjust person? Definitely.

Then these are some of the prizes that a just person, but not an unjust one, receives from the gods.

That's certainly my opinion.

What about from human beings? What does a just person get from them? Or, if we're to tell the truth, isn't this what happens? Aren't clever but unjust people like runners who run well for the first part of the course but not for the second? They leap away sharply at first, but they become ridiculous by the end and go off uncrowned, with their ears drooping on their shoulders like those of exhausted dogs, while true runners, on the *c*   other hand, get to the end, collect the prizes, and are crowned. And isn't it also generally true of just people that, towards the end of each course of action, association, or life, they enjoy a good reputation and collect the prizes from other human beings?

Of course.

21. See 363 ff.

Then will you allow me to say all the things about them that you yourself said about unjust people? I'll say that it is just people who, when they're old enough, rule in their own cities (if they happen to want ruling office) *d* and that it is they who marry whomever they want and give their children in marriage to whomever they want. Indeed, all the things that you said about unjust people I now say about just ones.[22] As for unjust people, the majority of them, even if they escape detection when they're young, are caught by the end of the race and are ridiculed. And by the time they get old, they've become wretched, for they are insulted by foreigners and citizens, beaten with whips, and made to suffer those punishments, such as racking and burning, which you rightly described as crude.[23] Imagine *e* that I've said that they suffer all such things, and see whether you'll allow me to say it.

Of course I will. What you say is right.

Then these are the prizes, wages, and gifts that a just person receives from gods and humans while he is alive and that are added to the good things that justice itself provides.   *614*

Yes, and they're very fine and secure ones too.

Yet they're nothing in either number or size compared to those that await just and unjust people after death. And these things must also be heard, if both are to receive in full what they are owed by the argument.

Then tell us about them, for there aren't many things that would be more pleasant to hear.   *b*

It isn't, however, a tale of Alcinous that I'll tell you but that of a brave Pamphylian man called Er, the son of Armenias, who once died in a war.[24] When the rest of the dead were picked up ten days later, they were already putrefying, but when he was picked up, his corpse was still quite fresh. He was taken home, and preparations were made for his funeral. But on the twelfth day, when he was already laid on the funeral pyre, he revived and, having done so, told what he had seen in the world beyond. He said that, after his soul had left him, it travelled together with many others until

---

22. See especially 361e–362c.

23. See 361d.

24. Books 9–11 of the *Odyssey* were traditionally referred to as *Alkinou apologoi*, the tales of Alcinous. Included among them in Book 11 is the story of Odysseus' descent into Hades. Since the word translated by "brave" is *alkimou*, which is very similar to *Alkinou*, some sort of pun seems to be involved here. The following is one attractive possibility, but there are no doubt others as well. *Alkinou* might be taken as a compound of *alkē* (strength) + *nous* (understanding) and *alkimou* as a compound of *alkē* + *Mousa* (a Muse). Socrates would then be saying something like: It isn't a tale that shows strength of understanding that I'm going to tell but one that shows the strength of the Muse of storytelling. See 509d n. 25 for another pun involving *nous*.

c   they came to a marvellous place, where there were two adjacent openings in the earth, and opposite and above them two others in the heavens, and between them judges sat. These, having rendered their judgment, ordered the just to go upwards into the heavens through the door on the right, with signs of the judgment attached to their chests, and the unjust to travel downward through the opening on the left, with signs of all their deeds

d   on their backs. When Er himself came forward, they told him that he was to be a messenger to human beings about the things that were there, and that he was to listen to and look at everything in the place. He said that he saw souls departing after judgment through one of the openings in the heavens and one in the earth, while through the other two souls were arriving. From the door in the earth souls came up covered with dust and dirt and from the door in the heavens souls came down pure. And the

e   souls who were arriving all the time seemed to have been on long journeys, so that they went gladly to the meadow, like a crowd going to a festival, and camped there. Those who knew each other exchanged greetings, and those who come up from the earth asked those who came down from the heavens about the things there and were in turn questioned by them about the things below. And so they told their stories to one another, the former

615   weeping as they recalled all they had suffered and seen on their journey below the earth, which lasted a thousand years, while the latter, who had come from heaven, told about how well they had fared and about the inconceivably fine and beautiful sights they had seen. There was much to tell, Glaucon, and it took a long time, but the main point was this: For each in turn of the unjust things they had done and for each in turn of the people they had wronged, they paid the penalty ten times over, once in every century of their journey. Since a century is roughly the length of

b   a human life, this means that they paid a tenfold penalty for each injustice. If, for example, some of them had caused many deaths by betraying cities or armies and reducing them to slavery or by participating in other wrongdoing, they had to suffer ten times the pain they had caused to each individual. But if they had done good deeds and had become just and pious, they were rewarded according to the same scale. He said some other things about the stillborn and those who had lived for only a short

c   time, but they're not worth recounting. And he also spoke of even greater rewards or penalties for piety or impiety towards gods or parents and for murder with one's own hands.

    For example, he said he was there when someone asked another where the great Ardiaius was. (This Ardiaius was said to have been tyrant in some city in Pamphylia a thousand years before and to have killed his aged father and older brother and committed many other impious deeds as

d   well.) And he said that the one who was asked responded: "He hasn't arrived here yet and never will, for this too was one of the terrible sights we saw. When we came near the opening on our way out, after all our sufferings were over, we suddenly saw him together with some others, pretty well all of whom were tyrants (although there were also some private individuals among them who had committed great crimes). They thought that they were ready to go up, but the opening wouldn't let them through,   *e* for it roared whenever one of these incurably wicked people or anyone else who hadn't paid a sufficient penalty tried to go up. And there were savage men, all fiery to look at, who were standing by, and when they heard the roar, they grabbed some of these criminals and led them away, but they bound the feet, hands, and head of Ardiaius and the others, threw them down, and flayed them. Then they dragged them out of the way,   *616* lacerating them on thorn bushes, and telling every passer-by that they were to be thrown into Tartarus,[25] and explaining why they were being treated in this way." And he said that of their many fears the greatest each one of them had was that the roar would be heard as he came up and that everyone was immensely relieved when silence greeted him. Such, then, were the penalties and punishments and the rewards corresponding to them.   *b*

Each group spent seven days in the meadow, and on the eighth they had to get up and go on a journey. On the fourth day of that journey, they came to a place where they could look down from above on a straight column of light that stretched over the whole of heaven and earth,[26] more like a rainbow than anything else, but brighter and more pure. After another day, they came to the light itself, and there, in the middle of the light,[27] they saw the extremities of its bonds stretching from the heavens, for the light binds the heavens like the cables girding a trireme and holds   *c* its entire revolution together. From the extremities hangs the spindle of Necessity, by means of which all the revolutions are turned. Its stem and hook are of adamant, whereas in its whorl[28] adamant is mixed with other kinds of material. The nature of the whorl was this: Its shape was like that of an ordinary whorl, but, from what Er said, we must understand its   *d* structure as follows. It was as if one big whorl had been made hollow by being thoroughly scooped out, with another smaller whorl closely fitted into it, like nested boxes, and there was a third whorl inside the second,

---

25. Tartarus is the lowest part of Hades, the pit of hell.

26. *dia pantos tou ouranou kai gēs tetamenon* is usually translated as "stretched through the whole of heaven and earth." But "stretched over the whole of heaven and earth" is equally acceptable grammatically and gives a better overall sense. See 617b n. 29.

27. I.e. in the middle of the circle of light.

28. A whorl (*sphondulon*) is the weight that twirls a spindle.

and so on, making eight whorls altogether, lying inside one another, with their rims appearing as circles from above, while from the back they formed
e one continuous whorl around the spindle, which was driven through the center of the eighth. The first or outside whorl had the widest circular rim; that of the sixth was second in width; the fourth was third; the eighth was fourth; the seventh was fifth; the fifth was sixth; the third was seventh; and the second was eighth. The rim of the largest was spangled; that of the seventh was brightest; that of the eighth took its color from the seventh's shining on it; the second and fifth were about equal in brightness,
617 more yellow than the others; the third was the whitest in color; the fourth was rather red; and the sixth was second in whiteness. The whole spindle turned at the same speed, but, as it turned, the inner spheres gently revolved in a direction opposite to that of the whole. Of these inner spheres, the eighth was the fastest; second came the seventh, sixth, and
b fifth, all at the same speed; it seemed to them that the fourth was third in its speed of revolution; the fourth, third; and the second, fifth.[29] The spindle itself turned on the lap of Necessity. And up above on each of the rims of the circles stood a Siren, who accompanied its revolution, uttering a single sound, one single note. And the concord of the eight notes produced a single harmony. And there were three other beings sitting at equal distances from one another, each on a throne. These were the Fates,
c the daughters of Necessity: Lachesis, Clotho, and Atropos. They were dressed in white, with garlands on their heads, and they sang to the music of the Sirens. Lachesis sang of the past, Clotho of the present, and Atropos of the future. With her right hand, Clotho touched the outer circumference

---

29. Plato's description of the light and the spindle is difficult. He compares the light to *hypozomata*, the ropes that bind a trireme together. These ropes seem to have girded the trireme from stem to stern and to have entered it at both places. Within the trireme, they were connected to some sort of twisting device that allowed them to be tightened when the water caused them to stretch and become slack. The spindle of Necessity seems to be just such a twisting device. Hence, the extremities of the light's bonds must enter into the universe, just as the *hypozomata* enter the trireme, and the spindle must be attached to these extremities, so that its spinning tightens the light and holds the universe together. The light is thus like two rainbows around the universe (or the whorl of the spindle) whose ends enter the universe and are attached to the spindle. The upper half of the whorl of the spindle consists of concentric hemispheres that fit into one another, with their lips or rims fitting together in a single plane. The outer hemisphere is that of the fixed stars; the second is the orbit of Saturn; the third, of Jupiter; the fourth, of Mars; the fifth, of Mercury; the sixth, of Venus; the seventh, of the sun; and the eighth, of the moon. The earth is in the center. The hemispheres are transparent, and the widths of their rims are the distances of the heavenly bodies from one another. The most convincing discussion is J. S. Morrison, "Parmenides and Er." *The Journal of Hellenic Studies* (1955) 75: 59–68.

of the spindle and helped it turn, but left off doing so from time to time; Atropos did the same to the inner ones; and Lachesis helped both motions in turn, one with one hand and one with the other.   . *d*

When the souls arrived at the light, they had to go to Lachesis right away. There a Speaker arranged them in order, took from the lap of Lachesis a number of lots and a number of models of lives, mounted a high pulpit, and spoke to them: "Here is the message of Lachesis, the maiden daughter of Necessity: 'Ephemeral souls, this is the beginning of another cycle that will end in death. Your daimon or guardian spirit will not be assigned to you by lot; you will choose him. The one who has the first lot will be the first to choose a life to which he will then be bound by   *e* necessity. Virtue knows no master; each will possess it to a greater or less degree, depending on whether he values or disdains it. The responsibility lies with the one who makes the choice; the god has none.'" When he had said this, the Speaker threw the lots among all of them, and each—with the exception of Er, who wasn't allowed to choose—picked up the one that fell next to him. And the lot made it clear to the one who picked it up where in the order he would get to make his choice. After that, the models of lives were placed on the ground before them. There were far more of them than there were souls present, and they were of all kinds, *618* for the lives of animals were there, as well as all kinds of human lives. There were tyrannies among them, some of which lasted throughout life, while others ended halfway through in poverty, exile, and beggary. There were lives of famous men, some of whom were famous for the beauty of their appearance, others for their strength or athletic prowess, others still for their high birth and the virtue or excellence of their ancestors. And there were also lives of men who weren't famous for any of these things.   *b* And the same for lives of women. But the arrangement of the soul was not included in the model because the soul is inevitably altered by the different lives it chooses. But all the other things were there, mixed with each other and with wealth, poverty, sickness, health, and the states intermediate to them.

Now, it seems that it is here, Glaucon, that a human being faces the greatest danger of all. And because of this, each of us must neglect all other subjects and be most concerned to seek out and learn those that will   *c* enable him to distinguish the good life from the bad and always to make the best choice possible in every situation. He should think over all the things we have mentioned and how they jointly and severally determine what the virtuous life is like. That way he will know what the good and bad effects of beauty are when it is mixed with wealth, poverty, and a particular state of the soul. He will know the effects of high or low birth,   *d* private life or ruling office, physical strength or weakness, ease or difficulty in learning, and all the things that are either naturally part of the soul or are* acquired, and he will know what they achieve when mixed with one another. And from all this he will be able, by considering the nature of the soul, to reason out which life is better and which worse and to choose accordingly, calling a life worse if it leads the soul to become more unjust,

e   better if it leads the soul to become more just, and ignoring everything else: We have seen that this is the best way to choose, whether in life or death. Hence, we must go down to Hades holding with adamantine determination to the belief that this is so, lest we be dazzled there by

619 wealth and other such evils, rush into a tyranny or some other similar course of action, do irreparable evils, and suffer even worse ones. And we must always know how to choose the mean in such lives and how to avoid either of the extremes, as far as possible, both in this life and in all those

b   beyond it. This is the way that a human being becomes happiest.

Then our messenger from the other world reported that the Speaker spoke as follows: "There is a satisfactory life rather than a bad one available even for the one who comes last, provided that he chooses it rationally and lives it seriously. Therefore, let not the first be careless in his choice nor the last discouraged."

He said that when the Speaker had told them this, the one who came up first chose the greatest tyranny. In his folly and greed he chose it without adequate examination and didn't notice that, among other evils,

c   he was fated to eat his own children as a part of it. When he examined at leisure, the life he had chosen, however, he beat his breast and bemoaned his choice. And, ignoring the warning of the Speaker, he blamed chance, daimons, or guardian spirits, and everything else for these evils but himself. He was one of those who had come down from heaven, having lived his previous life under an orderly constitution, where he had participated in virtue through habit and without philosophy. Broadly speaking, indeed,

d   most of those who were caught out in this way were souls who had come down from heaven and who were untrained in suffering as a result. The majority of those who had come up from the earth, on the other hand, having suffered themselves and seen others suffer, were in no rush to make their choices. Because of this and because of the chance of the lottery, there was an interchange of goods and evils for most of the souls. However, if someone pursues philosophy in a sound manner when he comes to live here on earth and if the lottery doesn't make him one of the

e   last to choose, then, given what Er has reported about the next world, it looks as though not only will he be happy here, but his journey from here to there and back again won't be along the rough underground path, but along the smooth heavenly one.

Er said that the way in which the souls chose their lives was a sight

worth seeing, since it was pitiful, funny, and surprising to watch. For the *620*
most part, their choice depended upon the character of their former life.
For example, he said that he saw the soul that had once belonged to
Orpheus[30] choosing a swan's life, because he hated the female sex because
of his death at their hands, and so was unwilling to have a woman conceive
and give birth to him. Er saw the soul of Thamyris[31] choosing the life of
a nightingale, a swan choosing to change over to a human life, and other
musical animals doing the same thing. The twentieth soul chose the life
of a lion. This was the soul of Ajax, son of Telamon.[32] He avoided human   *b*
life because he remembered the judgment about the armor. The next soul
was that of Agamemnon, whose sufferings also had made him hate the
human race, so he changed to the life of an eagle. Atalanta[33] had been
assigned a place near the middle, and when she saw great honors being
given to a male athlete, she chose his life, unable to pass them by. After
her, he saw the soul of Epeius, the son of Panopeus, taking on the nature
of a craftswoman.[34] And very close to last, he saw the soul of the ridiculous   *c*
Thersites clothing itself as a monkey.[35] Now, it chanced that the soul of
Odysseus got to make its choice last of all, and since memory of its former
sufferings had relieved its love of honor, it went around for a long time,
looking for the life of a private individual who did his own work, and with
difficulty it found one lying off somewhere neglected by the others. He
chose it gladly and said that he'd have made the same choice even if he'd
been first. Still other souls changed from animals into human beings, or   *d*
from one kind of animal into another, with unjust people changing into
wild animals, and just people into tame ones, and all sorts of mixtures
occurred.

30. See 364e n. 10. According to one myth, Orpheus was killed and dismembered by
Thracian women or Maenads.

31. Thamyris was a legendary poet and singer, who boasted that he could defeat the
Muses in a song contest. For this they blinded him and took away his voice. He is
mentioned at *Iliad* 2.596–600.

32. Ajax is a great Homeric hero. He thought that he deserved to be awarded the
armor of the dead Achilles, but instead it went to Odysseus. Ajax was maddened by
this injustice and finally killed himself because of the terrible things he had done while
mad. See Sophocles, *Ajax*.

33. Atalanta was a mythical huntress, who would marry only a man who could beat
her at running. In most versions of the myth, losers were killed. Melanion received
three golden apples from Aphrodite, which he dropped one by one during his race with
Atalanta. She stopped to pick them up, and he won the race.

34. Epeius is mentioned at *Odyssey* 8.493 as the man who helped Athena make the
Trojan Horse.

35. Thersites is an ordinary soldier who criticizes Agamemnon at *Iliad* 2.211–277.
Odysseus beats him for his presumption and is widely approved for doing so.

After all the souls had chosen their lives, they went forward to Lachesis in the same order in which they had made their choices, and she assigned to each the daimon it had chosen as guardian of its life and fulfiller of its
e   choice. This daimon first led the soul under the hand of Clotho as it turned the revolving spindle to confirm the fate that the lottery and its own choice had given it. After receiving her touch, he led the soul to the spinning of Atropos, to make what had been spun irreversible. Then, without turning around, they went from there under the throne of Necessity and, when all of them had passed through, they travelled to the Plain
621 of Forgetfulness in burning, choking, terrible heat, for it was empty of trees and earthly vegetation. And there, beside the River of Unheeding, whose water no vessel can hold, they camped, for night was coming on. All of them had to drink a certain measure of this water, but those who weren't saved by reason drank more than that, and as each of them drank, he forgot everything and went to sleep. But around midnight there was a
b   clap of thunder and an earthquake, and they were suddenly carried away from there, this way and that, up to their births, like shooting stars. Er himself was forbidden to drink from the water. All the same, he didn't know how he had come back to his body, except that waking up suddenly he saw himself lying on the pyre at dawn.

And so, Glaucon, his story wasn't lost but preserved, and it would save us, if we were persuaded by it, for we would then make a good crossing
c   of the River of Forgetfulness, and our souls wouldn't be defiled. But if we are persuaded by me, we'll believe that the soul is immortal and able to endure every evil and every good, and we'll always hold to the upward path, practicing justice with reason in every way. That way we'll be friends both to ourselves and to the gods while we remain here on earth and
d   afterwards—like victors in the games who go around collecting their prizes—we'll receive our rewards. Hence, both in this life and on the thousand-year journey we've described, we'll do well and be happy.

INDEX

ACCOUNT, ARGUMENT, DISCUSSION (*logos*):
328d [conversation], 331d, 334a, d,
335a, 336b, e, 337e, 338d, 339d, 340d,
e, 341a, b, c [sense], 342b [sense],
343a, 344d, 345b, 348 a [replies], d
[mentioning], 349a, 351a, b [position],
352b [words], d, 353d [said], e, 354b,
357a, 358c, 359b, 360d, 361b, d, 362d,
e, 363c [stories], e, 364b, c, 365d, 366e
[conversations], 367b [theoretical argu-
ment], e [theoretical argument], 368b
[words], c, 369a [theory], c [theory],
376d, e, 376e [stories, story], 377e
[story], 378a [stories], e [stories], 380a,
381a, 382a [word], b [words], c [words],
e [word], 383a [words], 388e, 389a, d
[theory], 390a [words], 392a [story], c
[stories], 394d, e, 395b, 396a [word], e
[story], 398b [stories], d [words], 399d,
400a [words], c, d [words], 403c, 408d
[question], 411d, 413b, 414d [words],
421a, 425b [written], 431a [expression],
435d, 436b, 437d [word], 439a [word],
440a [proves], b, d, 442a [stories], c
[reason], 445c, 449c, 450a, b, c, 451b,
c, 452d, 453a, c, d, 457c, e, 465e,
472a, e [theoretical model], 473a [the-
ory], e [statement], 474a, 475a [word,
argument], c, 476a, b, 484a, 485a,
487b, c [words], e, 490d, 492d [words],
e [rule], 493d, 494e [reason], 497c
[theory], 498a, d, 499a, d, 500b [ar-
guing], c, 501e [theory], 503a, 507a, b
[words], 509d, 510c, d [claims], 511b,
518c, 522a [stories], 525d, 527a, 528a,
c, 529d, 531e, 532a, 533c, 534a [ratios,
arguments], b, c, d [theory], 538c, d,
539a, b, d 543c, 544a, b, 545b, c, 548b,
c, 549b, 550a, 554d, 560b–561b

[words], 563a [word], 564c [theory],
565e [story], 571b [reason], d, 576b,
578c, 581a, 582a–e, 584a, 586d, 588b
[words], d, 589d, 591a, 592a [theory],
596e, 597a, 599b, 601a [word], 603d,
607b, c, 608a, 610a, c, 611a, b, 612a, c,
614a, 617d [message]. *See also* REASON
(*logos*)

AESCHYLUS: 361b, 362a, 380a, 383a, b,
550c, 563b

ANGER. *See* SPIRIT

APPETITE, DESIRE (*epithumia*): 328d, 329c,
359c, 390c, 429d, 430b, e, 431b, c, d,
437b, d, e, 438a, 439d, 440a, b, 485d,
493b, 533b, 548b, 554a, b, d, 555a,
558d, 559b, c, e, 560a, d, 561a, c,
571a, b, 572b, c, e, 573a, b, d, e, 575d,
578a, 579e, 580d, e, 581a, 586d, 587b

APPETITIVE PART OF THE SOUL (*epithumēti-
kon*): 439d, e, 440e, 441a, 442a, 475b,
516d, 550b, 553c, 571e, 580e, 606d.
See also APPETITE, SPIRITED PART, RA-
TIONAL PART

ARCHILOCHUS: 365c

ARGUMENT. *See* ACCOUNT

ARISTOCRACY, ARISTOCRATIC PERSON:
338d, 445d, 544e, 545c, 547c, 587d.
See also DEMOCRACY, OLIGARCHY, PHI-
LOSOPHY, TYRANNY

ASCLEPIUS: 405c–408c, 599c

ASTRONOMY: 527c, 528d–531a, 531b

BAD, FORM OF THE: 476a

BEAUTIFUL. *See* fine

BECOMING (*genesis*): 519a, 525b, c, 526e,
533b [growing], 534a, 546c [births]

BEING (*ousia*): 329e [wealthy], 330b
[wealth], d [wealth], 359a [essence],
361b [substantial wealth], 372b [re-

586d, 591c, 616d, 619b. *See* INTELLI-
GIBLE

VIRTUE (*aretē*): 335b, c, d, 342a, 348c, e,
349a, 350d, 351a, 353b, c, d, e, 354b,
c, 363d, 364b, 365a, c, 378e, 381c,
402e, 403d, 407a, c, 409d [natural vir-
tue], 428a, 432b, 433e, 441d, 444d, e,
445b, c, 457a, 484e, 492a, e, 493a,
498e, 500d, 504d, 518d, e, 536a, 545b,
547c, 549b, 550e, 551a, 554e, 556a,
576c, 580b, 585c, 586a, 588a, 598e,
599d, 600d, e, 601d, 608b, c, 612c,
613b, 617e, 618a, c, 619c

VISIBLE: 507b, c, d, 508a, c, d, e, 509b, d,
510a, d, 511c, 516b, 517a, b, c, 519a,
b, 524c, 525d, 529b, c, 530b, 532b, d.
See also INTELLIGIBLE

WISE: *See* RATIONAL, REASON
WOMEN: 373c, 388a, 395e, 396a, 431c,
449a–471e, 540c, 549c, 557c, 563b,
605e, 618b
WRETCHED (*athlios*): 344a, 354a, 360d,
380b, 392b, 544a, 545a, 575c, 576c, d,
e, 577b, c, 578b, 579c, d, 580c, 589e,
606d, 613d. *See also* HAPPY (the opposite of wretched)